PORNOGRAPHY

Contemporary Issues

Series Editors: Robert M. Baird
Stuart E. Rosenbaum

PORNOGRAPHY

PRIVATE RIGHT OR PUBLIC MENACE?

Edited by
ROBERT M. BAIRD &
STUART E. ROSENBAUM

Prometheus Books
59 John Glenn Drive
Amherst, New York 14228-2197

Published 1998 by Prometheus Books

02 01 00 99 98   5 4 3 2 1

Library of Congress Cataloging-in-Publication Data

Pornography : private right or public menace? / edited by Robert M. Baird & Stuart E. Rosenbaum. — Rev. ed.
        p.   cm. — (Contemporary issues)
    Includes bibliographical references.
    ISBN 1–57392–207–2 (alk. paper)
    1. Pornography—Social aspects. 2. Pornography—Social aspects—United States. I. Baird, Robert M., 1937–   . II. Rosenbaum, Stuart E. III. Series: Contemporary issues (Amherst, N.Y.)
HQ471.P6462   1998
363.4'7—dc21   98–5614
                                                                        CIP

Printed in Canada on acid-free paper

Contents

Introduction

PART ONE: THE COMMUNICATIONS DECENCY ACT

1. The Legislative History of Senator Exon's
   Communications Decency Act:
   Regulating Barbarians on the Information Superhighway
   Robert Cannon   21

2. Supreme Court Case: *Reno* v. *American Civil Liberties Union*   30

3. Commentary: The Communications Decency Act
   Sen. Jim Exon   56

4. Statement on the Supreme Court's Decision Declaring
   Unconstitutional the Communications Decency Act
   Sen. Pat Leahy   59

5. You Figure It Out
   William F. Buckley Jr.   63

6. Zoned Out
   Jeffrey Rosen   66

7. Give Me Liberty, but Don't Give Me Filth
   An Interview with Robert Bork by Michael Cromartie   71
8. Slouching Towards Gomorrah
   Robert H. Bork   75
9. Pornography Drives Technology: Why *Not* to Censor the Internet
   Peter Johnson   80

PART TWO: FEMINIST PERSPECTIVES

10. Erotic and Pornography: A Clear and Present Difference
    Gloria Steinem   89
11. Against the Male Flood: Censorship, Pornography, and Equality
    Andrea Dworkin   94
12. Pornography and Degradation
    Judith M. Hill   100
13. Pornography and the Alienation of Male Sexuality
    Harry Brod   114
14. Pornography, Oppression, and Freedom: A Closer Look
    Helen E. Longino   122
15. Defamation and the Endorsement of Degradation
    Alan Soble   134

PART THREE: LIBERTARIAN PERSPECTIVES

16. Feminist Moralism, "Pornography," and Censorship
    Barbara Dority   149
17. Pornography as Representation: Aesthetic Considerations
    Theodore A. Gracyk   155
18. The Case Against Censorship of Pornography
    William A. Linsley   176
19. Redefining Obscenity
    Rita C. Manning   191
20. Liberty and Pornography
    Ronald Dworkin   202

PART FOUR: RELIGIOUS PERSPECTIVES

21. The Mental Poison
     Tim LaHaye   215

22. The Impact of Pornography on Marriage
     Thomas Parker   221

23. Pornography and the Religious Imagination
     Mary Jo Weaver   229

PART FIVE: THE CAUSAL ISSUE

24. America's Slide into the Sewer
     George F. Will   255

25. Elicitation of Violence: The Evidence
     F. M. Christensen   259

Selected Bibliography   283

Contributors   285

Introduction

What is Pornography?
   What are its effects on individuals and society?
   What can be done about it?
   What should be done about it?
   These questions are as important now as they were when this collection first appeared in 1991. The social context in which we now ask these questions, however, is significantly different. Perhaps the most dramatic distinction as concerns the questions of this volume is the increasing prominence of the Internet as a medium of communication, entertainment, and research. The Internet is a new form of connectedness in society. No longer are telephones, magazines, newspapers, and TVs the most promising avenues into citizens' homes. These have been supplanted by computers. Computers offer a more comprehensive medium of connection with the social, political, entertainment, and commercial enterprises of society than any prior sources of access to individuals' homes and resources.
   Like those prior sources, computers offer purveyors of pornography new possibilities of access to consumers. The World Wide Web is accessible to a home computer through any Internet service provider. The resources now available to ordinary consumers in the privacy of their homes are

unparalleled in the history of humanity. A few "clicks of a mouse" allows access to almost any source imaginable, including a range of explicit materials that would appeal to any sexual taste. Frequently, such Web sites require payment to the entity maintaining the site by credit card number. *Playboy,* for example, maintains such a site and requires subscribers to give their credit card number to access the more explicit sexual resources of the site. Other sites require only an adult identification number, which is available for a fee from Adult Check, a Web site dedicated to providing adult identification numbers so that sites providing sexually explicit materials can require the number for access. In this way, the sexually explicit sites can ensure that access to more explicit materials is restricted to those over eighteen years of age. Nonetheless, sites requiring credit card or identification numbers are among the minority. A few "clicks of a mouse" enable almost anyone to access materials that would be objectionable to all those who have traditionally objected to the availability of sexually explicit materials.

The World Wide Web, the Internet, is a highly controversial source of sexually explicit materials. The issues about restricting it, about holding providers legally responsible for making sexually explicit materials available to minors, about free speech, about citizen autonomy, and about paternalism are as acute for this new medium as they have been for every previous medium. This new medium—computers, the Internet, the World Wide Web —has become a new focal point for those who campaign against pornography. In February 1995, Nebraska Sen. James Exon introduced the Communications Decency Act in an effort to regulate what was available on the Internet. Senator Exon's CDA passed by a large majority of both houses of Congress and was signed without controversy by President Clinton. On June 27, 1997, the Supreme Court upheld a district court ruling that the legislation abridged freedom of speech as protected by the First Amendment to the United States Constitution. The first of the five parts of this collection is now an account detailing this legislation and the controversy that did, and still does, surround it. The rest of the collection remains undisturbed in content.

In the earlier edition of this volume, Part One focused on the reports about the issue of pornography of two prestigious national commissions: the Presidential Commission, which delivered its report in 1970, and the Attorney General's Commission, which delivered its report in 1986. The conflicting findings and recommendations of these two commissions are a measure of our national ambivalence about this issue. The Presidential Commission recommended not to regulate pornography. The Attorney General's Commission, on the other hand, recommended "as a matter of special urgency" prosecuting producers and distributors of materials portraying sexual violence, and members of the Commission also were unanimous about the desirability of prosecuting providers of materials they saw as "degrading."

The issues which motivated the two earlier national commissions remain substantially unchanged. Their current context, however, has made them more urgent. No issue more poignantly elicits ambivalence within ourselves and within our culture than that of pornography. On one hand, we think we must not compromise individual freedom of expression and choice about what materials to see, hear, or read; indeed, we are committed to this idea as a matter of constitutional principle. On the other hand, we think our film, recording, publishing, and Internet service provider industries produce materials harmful to some individuals or to society as a whole.

The goals of the Presidential Commission, the Attorney General's Commission, and of Senator Exon's Communications Decency Act were to seek resolution of these competing tendencies within American society. Cynics might be inclined simply to "write off" the commission reports as to-be-expected products of their respective political contexts, the "permissive" report a product of the late '60s and the "restrictive" report a product of the Reagan-inspired social agenda of the '80s. A further cynical response to the Exon CDA might see it as a piece of legislation too politically volatile to contest, thus accounting for its passage by a huge majority and for its uncontested signing by the President. The cynicism of these responses would be unfortunate in failing to acknowledge the genuine ambivalence of American attitudes toward pornography. The reports must be taken seriously precisely because they mirror this ambivalence.

Complicating questions about pornography is our reverence for the centrality of sexuality in a fully satisfying human life; we recognize individuals' sexuality as of profound importance to their happiness. Our recognition of this fact may move us to a tolerance of individual efforts to realize sexual personality that is greater than our customary acceptance of others' efforts to achieve economic or political goals. We are a society founded on respect for individual autonomy, and we encourage appropriate self-expression in matters of sexuality as well as in matters of economics or politics.

In spite of our general respect for individual sexual autonomy, some would seek to regulate production and distribution of sexually explicit materials in all media. These desires raise the issue of defining pornography, an issue complicated by the need to distinguish it from "mere" erotica and "moral realism." What people think pornographic and possibly harmful varies widely according to their judgments about the role sexuality ideally plays in human life, their sensitivity to the diversity of sexual expression, and their appreciation of sexuality in literary and artistic contexts. One perspective thinks all sexually explicit representations, pictures in *Playboy* for example, are pornographic and harmful. A more discriminating view sees sexually explicit representations as pornographic only if they are also "demeaning" or "degrading" to an individual or group (usually women). A still more discriminating view sees sexually explicit representations as objectionable only if they involve portrayals of violence toward an individual or group (usually women).

Complicating the question of how these different classes of sexually explicit materials should be treated is the fact that serious and important works of art not infrequently make use of such sexually explicit portrayals. The attitude of the work toward what is portrayed, its intention or purpose, is of crucial importance in deciding how to regard its sexually explicit representations. As it would be rash and ill-informed to take Tolstoy's *Anna Karenina* as an endorsement of suicide or Twain's *Huckleberry Finn* as an endorsement of slavery, it would be equally rash and ill-informed to take the film *$9\frac{1}{2}$ Weeks* as an endorsement of profligate or indiscriminate sexual behavior. Judgments about sexually explicit materials must always take into account the larger context of the work as a whole.

When Skywalker Records distributed 2 Live Crew's album *As Nasty As They Wanna Be*, they hoped for commercial success. They did not anticipate a pornography investigation by Florida's Broward County sheriff, but when Sheriff Nick Navarro's deputies warned record stores that selling the album might result in arrest on obscenity charges, Skywalker Records filed a federal complaint asking U.S. District Court Judge Jose Gonzalez for relief from unconstitutional prior restraint. Judge Gonzalez ruled against Skywalker Records in finding the album legally obscene. As the judge put it, "[the album] is an appeal to dirty thoughts and the loins, not to the intellect and the mind. . . . The recording depicts sexual conduct in graphic detail. The specificity of the descriptions makes the audio message analogous to a camera with a zoom lens, focusing on the sights and sounds of various . . . sexual acts. It cannot be reasonably argued that the violence, perversion, abuse of women, graphic depictions of all forms of sexual conduct, and microscopic descriptions of human genitalia contained on this recording are comedic art."[1]

Most Americans, like Judge Gonzalez, value artistic creativity and freedom of expression. Like Judge Gonzalez, however, when they see individual freedom of expression as harmful and as lacking intellectual, social, or artistic merit, many Americans are not bashful about "calling it as they see it," and voicing their objection. They believe freedom to speak, to express, and to consume are properly left to individual choice, but when exercise of that freedom yields harm and no overriding reason appears to legitimate the harm, then they think regulation and restriction of individuals' choices are warranted.

This rationale for censorship is much like the rationale for removing toys found to threaten the health or lives of children from the market. Toy companies may freely exercise their creativity to produce attractive and fascinating toys, but discovering that a product threatens children's safety legitimately results in efforts to remove it from the market. Likewise, when a drug company markets a product in the effort to profit from helping people and the product is subsequently found to yield harmful effects, then we generally think action to remove it from the market is warranted.

As noted above, people have different ideas of pornography, of what kinds of sexually explicit materials are objectionable, harmful, and lacking compensating intellectual, social, or artistic merit. When people do see sexually explicit representations as harmful they seek, by legal action or moral suasion, to remove them from the arena of public commerce. The belief that sexually explicit materials are harmful, however, is quite controversial. Showing a film, playing a musical lyric, or displaying a photograph are difficult to think of as harmful. How could viewing a photograph of unclad, passionately entwined lovers be harmful to the viewer? How could hearing lyrics of a group rapping about being macho and using women as sexual toys be harmful to the listener? If these things are harmful, surely they must appear so in a way very different from the way toys can be harmful to children or drugs can be harmful to their users. Understanding how films, photographs, and lyrics might be harmful to those exposed to them is crucial to understanding the position of those who would prohibit the distribution and consumption of sexually explicit materials.

Two potential harms naturally suggest themselves. The first is the harm of causing injuries to others of the same sort toys and drugs can cause, injuries to health or life. Just as a toy may be found harmful only after experience indicates more accurately than antecedent intentions and expectations how it affects children, likewise experience may indicate that viewing or hearing specific kinds of films, photographs, or lyrics can similarly lead to injuries to health or life. When opponents of pornography cite the testimony of convicted sex offenders about their regular use of sexually explicit materials, they think of themselves as adducing evidence that the offenders' use of those materials caused them to commit their particular crimes. Concern to avert this kind of injury, insofar as it might issue from viewing and hearing films, photographs, or lyrics, motivates empirical research into the causal effects of such materials on their consumers. If people are caused by their experience with some kinds of films, music, or photographs to harm others, then limiting the availability of those kinds of materials is as warranted as restricting the availability of toys or drugs found to be harmful to their users.

Another potential harm some see attending the availability of sexually explicit materials is harm to the values of those who experience it. Insofar as exposed individuals' values might be adversely affected, the larger society of which they are parts would also be adversely affected. A society in which significant numbers of people behave with sufficient disregard for the well being of others is a diminished society, one inadequate to cultivate in its members proper regard for the worth of others. The idea of this sort of harm, harm to individual and societal values, is more elusive and more controversial than the idea of the first sort of harm, injury to health or life. Nevertheless, it has been a powerful motive for feminists and religious leaders who have strong value commitments.

Although these different kinds of harm may seem quite distinct, some feminists and religious leaders have thought that harm to individual or social values might in some indirect way effect significant threats to citizens' health and lives. The "coarsening" of a culture, as George Will puts it in one of the essays that follow, may have behavioral consequences. If the idea of a causal connection among sexually explicit materials, consequent values, and resultant behavior becomes convincing, then less tolerance of pornographic materials, perhaps restrictions on their distribution and production, would be as warranted as current restrictions on pharmaceutical companies' distribution and production of drugs.

Having discovered that pharmaceutical companies, perhaps motivated by their desire to show a profit, occasionally market inadequately tested products, Congress established a federal agency, the FDA, to oversee and regulate their marketing activities. If evidence becomes equally compelling that companies marketing films, recordings, books, and magazines are occasionally, because of concern to make a profit, careless of consumers' health and lives, then perhaps another federal agency, analogous to the FDA and charged with overseeing and regulating film companies and publishers, would come to seem equally necessary.

The main objection to such an oversight agency is that it would be constitutionally unacceptable. The Bill of Rights, incorporating the First Amendment to the United States Constitution, expresses unequivocally our national commitment to freedom of speech and expression. Any law establishing an oversight agency like the FDA, charging it to regulate or restrict freedom of speech or expression on behalf of any particular set of values, no matter how pervasive those values appear in American society, would inevitably be found unconstitutional. The idea of constraints on expression to preserve or endorse particular value commitments is, finally, as un-American as ideas get.

As has been frequently remarked, however, this uniquely American commitment to freedom of speech and expression is not absolute. The

Supreme Court has held that several kinds of speech and expression are not protected by the First Amendment, among them inciting to violence, soliciting crimes, perjury, slander, libel, false advertising, and obscenity.[2] In spite of this official acknowledgment that some forms of speech and expression are not constitutionally protected, few efforts to restrict publication and distribution of sexually explicit materials have been made and fewer have been successful. In the case of 2 Live Crew's album, *As Nasty They Wanna Be*, Judge Gonzalez did find the album legally obscene, but the net effect on Skywalker Records was positive. While the obscenity finding made the album harder for Broward County residents to acquire, the attendant national publicity brought the album wider notoriety and increased profits for the producer and distributor. Although the sheriff's office successfully defended its actions in court, the producer and distributor were decisively more successful than the sheriff even though they lost the court case. This economic "halo effect" that accrues to producers and distributors in such obscenity proceedings is a reason many people and groups are reluctant to pursue their convictions in the legal arena.

Another reason for their reluctance is the difficulty even of winning such cases in court in view of the rigorous and vague legal standards that must be met. Current standards endorsed by the Supreme Court are as follows:

> The basic guidelines for the trier of fact must be: (a) whether "the average person, applying contemporary community standards" would find that the work, taken as a whole, appeals to the prurient interest . . . ; (b) whether the work depicts or describes, in a patently offensive way, sexual conduct specifically defined by the applicable state law; and (c) whether the work, taken as a whole, lacks serious literary, artistic, political, or scientific value.[3]

The vagueness evident throughout this statement is daunting even to those offended only by the most graphic of sexually explicit publications. The difficulty of proving in court that a publication violates this standard is obvious.

These two problems, the difficulty of winning in court and the likelihood that a court proceeding will increase publicity for, and distribution of, the materials challenged, lead many opponents to avoid legal proceedings.

Suppose, however, that researchers produced convincing evidence that materials alleged to be pornographic or obscene were responsible for causing real harm to health and life. Imagine also that the evidence produced was as convincing as that adduced to establish the harmfulness of certain toys or drugs. Given the current "state of the art" of pornography research and the absence of any clear-cut causal tendency of materials thought pornographic, this supposition may seem unrealistic. Research about materials thought pornographic may not resolve important causal questions, but real progress is not impossible.

If solid research supported the idea that pornographic materials caused significant threats to health and life, "piecemeal" attacks on those threats such as those of Sheriff Navarro and his deputies would seem even more clearly inadequate and counterproductive. Recourse to a federal agency, on the model of the FDA and charged with monitoring and regulating production and distribution of objectionable materials, might be the only effective way to address the threat to citizens' health and lives.

Such an agency would be welcomed by many religious leaders and by prominent feminists who think that some kinds of publications, films, and recordings are clearly harmful. The religious leaders typically revere traditional family values, and they see those values threatened by ready availability of sexually explicit materials. The feminists standardly see some kinds of sexually explicit materials as demeaning and harmful to women and as contrary to their own commitment to sexual equality.

Feminists, under the leadership of Andrea Dworkin and Catherine MacKinnon, have already made efforts in the direction of the kind of regulation of publications a federal agency would impose. They authored and saw enacted an antipornography ordinance in Indianapolis, Indiana. The ordinance prohibited any "production, sale, exhibition, or distribution" of materials depicting "the graphic sexually explicit subordination of women, whether in pictures or words" and it made no exception for materials of literary or artistic value.[4] The inevitable constitutional challenge resulted in a judgment that the ordinance was unconstitutional because it violated the First Amendment's prohibition against restrictions on freedom of speech.

The feminists' concerns in pushing for enactment of the Indianapolis ordinance were not lacking in merit. They sought to secure public support for treatment of women as equals worthy of respect rather than as mere means to men's sexual gratification; indeed, that the ordinance was enacted itself suggests wide sympathy for their position. But the Court's response to the ordinance suggests that feminists' efforts to legislate their own values in the matter of sexually explicit publications conflicts with a more fundamental American commitment to freedom of speech and expression. Apart from some solid evidence that real harm—a significantly increased chance of rape or physical/sexual abuse, for example—attends the use of some kinds of sexually explicit materials, the fundamental commitment to freedom of speech and expression will undoubtedly prevail.

What feminists and religious leaders need is evidence that concrete harm attends the use of sexually explicit materials. To date, that evidence is unavailable, and what research there is is controversial. If adequate evidence were available, court findings might change. The court might even permit congressional enactment of an oversight agency to screen materials suspected of being harmful. But short of such hard evidence, legal developments that would be satisfying to feminists and religious leaders seem unlikely.

We intend the essays of this volume to be informative across the main spectrum of controversy about the issue of pornography. Part One focuses on Senator Exon's Communications Decency Act and commentary relevant to it. Part Two focuses on the range of issues relevant to feminist concern about pornography. Part Three expresses the concerns of those strongly opposed to regulating sexually explicit materials because of their commitment to freedom of speech and expression. Part Four exhibits diverse religious perspectives on the issue of pornography. Part Five focuses on the causal issue, the last essay giving a careful account of relevant empirical research.

Each essay makes a unique contribution to the national conversation about this issue, and we hope readers will take each seriously. The more appreciation interested parties have for the diverse important perspectives relevant to this issue the wiser will be their responses to it.

NOTES

1. Mark Curriden, "But Is It Art," *Barrister* 17, no. 4 (Winter 1990–91): 13–14.

2. Helen Longino, "Pornography, Oppression, and Freedom: A Closer Look," in *Take Back the Night*, ed. Laura Lederer (New York: William Morrow & Co., 1980), p. 50. (This essay is included in the present volume.)

3. *Miller* v. *California*, 1973, quoted in Alan E. Sears, "The Legal Case for Restricting Pornography," in *Pornography: Research Advances and Policy Considerations*, ed. Dolf Zillman and Jennings Bryant (Hillsdale, N.J.: Lawrence Erlbaum Associates, 1989), p. 333.

4. Ronald Dworkin, "Liberty and Pornography," *The New York Review of Books* 38, no. 14 (August 15, 1991): 12–13. (This essay is included in the present volume.)

Part One

The Communications Decency Act

1

The Legislative History of Senator Exon's Communications Decency Act: Regulating Barbarians on the Information Highway

Robert Cannon

I. INTRODUCTION

On February 1, 1995, Senator James Exon (D-Neb.) attempted to do what had never been done before—regulate speech on the Internet. Introducing the Communications Decency Amendment (CDA), Senator Exon declared a danger to society: Barbarian pornographers are at the gate and they are using the Internet to gain access to the youth of America. Senator Exon proclaimed:

> The information superhighway should not become a red light district. This legislation will keep that from happening and extend the standards of decency which have protected telephone users to new telecommunications devices.
>
> Once passed, our children and families will be better protected from those who would electronically cruise the digital world to engage children in inappropriate communications and introductions. The Decency Act will also clearly protect citizens from electronic stalking and protect the sanctuary of the home from uninvited indecencies.

From the *Federal Communications Law Journal* 49, no. 1 (November 1996): 72. Reprinted by permission. Please consult original article for notes and references.

Robert Cannon is president of the Internet Telecommunications Project (<http://www.cais.net/cannon>, cannon@dc.net).

In a year of deregulation, Senator Exon called for more regulation. In the year when Speaker of the House Newt Gingrich placed the House of Representatives on the Internet, praising it as a landmark for democracy, Senator Exon warned America that the Internet was filled with dark places from which we needed government protection. In a year where Internet users were proclaiming the infinite utility of the World Wide Web, Senator Exon, who has apparently no Internet experience, declared a danger.

A. The Problem: The Availability of Pornography

Senator Exon was motivated out of a concern for the proliferation of pornography and indecency on the Internet and the easy access to that material by the youth of America. Not everyone shared his belief that there existed a substantial threat where one can go "click, click, click," and have access to pornography.

The greatest salvo in the debate over the availability of pornography on the Internet was Marty Rimm's study *Marketing Pornography on the Information Superhighway: A Survey of 917,410 Images, Descriptions, Short Stories, and Animations Downloaded 8.5 Million Times by Consumers in Over 2000 Cities in Forty Countries, Provinces, and Territories* (*Rimm Study*), published in the Georgetown University Law Review. Rimm purported to have conducted a thorough survey of the availability of pornography on the information superhighway. He concluded that pornography was rampant and freely available. In one of his most notorious statements, he concluded that 83.5 percent of the images available on the Usenet are pornographic.

The study became a front page "exclusive" in *Time* magazine. The ink was barely dry on the story before Senator Grassley waved a copy in front of the Senate in support of his antipornography legislation. The study became the source of endless articles and editorials. The opposition was sent scurrying, searching for ways to defend against this weapon of the censorship proponents. On-line discussion groups dedicated endless bandwidth to deliberating the merits of the study. And parents started curtailing surfing privileges of their children. When the skirmish died down, the study had been largely discredited and *Time* magazine published a follow-up article which was all but a retraction and apology for being duped into publishing the study. Nevertheless, the warning cry that the Internet was the dark home of pornographers after the children of America had been spread across the American psyche.

The problems of the *Rimm Study* were numerous. The *Rimm Study* was apparently not subject to peer review. Professors Donna L. Hoffman and

Thomas P. Novak criticized the study, concluding that Rimm's work was methodologically flawed. The ethics of Mr. Rimm's research procedures were questioned. He was accused of plagiarism. Finally, it was discovered that he was working both sides of this issue; Mr. Rimm was also the author of *The Pornographer's Handbook: How to Exploit Women, Dupe Men, & Make Lots of Money.* In the end, even Carnegie Mellon, his graduate school, distanced itself from the *Rimm Study.* As a final salvo in the *Rimm Study* skirmish, the United States Senate decided that it no longer needed to hear what Mr. Rimm had to say about pornography and pulled him from the witness list of the July 26, 1995, hearing concerning pornography on the Internet.

Rimm proved an easy target for the censorship opponents. But criticism of the *Rimm Study* did not discount the reality of pornography on the Internet. While at the local corner store there are at least some barriers which keep thirteen-year-old boys from buying *Playboy,* there are virtually no barriers keeping those boys from surfing through the pages of the *Playboy* World Wide Web site.

The debate over the *Rimm Study* was representative of the power of the Internet in the new democracy. In cyberspace, everyone can hear you scream. Information flows rapidly and freely. "Netizens" are ready to examine every aspect of every event. Marty Rimm made a mistake in publishing the *Rimm Study;* he also made a mistake in thinking that he could keep his past and his methods hidden. In the information age the level of debate has been raised; more information is available and it is available faster. Democracy, which thrives on discussion, disagreement, and debate, prospered because the ability to debate and the ability to have access to information relevant to the issues was heightened. The debate over the *Rimm Study* is representative of how this new form of democratic activism can prevent distortion from controlling public policy.

II. THE COMMUNICATIONS DECENCY ACT

A. The Act as Passed

Senator Exon, believing that God was on his side, set forth to battle the pornographers by introducing the most important piece of legislation that the Senator ever believed that he had worked on. "The fundamental purpose of the Communications Decency Act is to provide much needed protection for children." He proposed to create this protection by amending section 223 of Title 47, United States Code, entitled "Obscene or harassing telephone calls in the District of Columbia or in interstate or foreign communications."

The CDA, as passed, extends the antiharassment, indecency, and antiobscenity restrictions currently placed on telephone calls to "telecommunications devices" and "interactive computer services." Pursuant to the CDA, it is illegal to knowingly send to or display in a manner available to

> a person under 18 years of age, any comment, request, suggestion, proposal, image, or other communication that, in context, depicts or describes, in terms patently offensive as measured by contemporary community standards, sexual or excretory activities or organs, regardless of whether the user of such service placed the call or initiated the communication.

Violators are liable for "each intentional act of posting" and not each occasion of downloading or accessing. It is the intent of Congress that the CDA target content providers, not access providers or users.

In addition, owners of telecommunications facilities are liable where they knowingly permit their facilities to be used in a manner that violates the CDA. The penalty for violation was changed from $10,000 to fines pursuant to Title 18 of the United States Code and from a maximum of six months imprisonment to a maximum of two years.

1. The Defenses

The CDA added four defenses to section 223. . . .

In its original version, the CDA did not incorporate all of these defenses. This resulted in strong objections from the interactive computer service industry. The industry stated that they were subject to an impossible task: monitoring and censoring of millions of bits of information flowing across computers each day. As a result of the criticism received, Senator Exon incorporated the following defenses.

First, section 223(e)(1) provides a defense where an individual solely provides access to material not under the individual's control. The "access provider" defense extends to services and software which download and cache data from other computers as long as that content is not created on the service provider. According to Senator Exon, this defense

> explicitly exempts a person who provides access to or connection with a network like Internet that is not under that person's control. Providing access or connection is meant to include transmission, downloading, storage, navigational tools, and related capabilities which are incidental to the transmission of communications. An online service that is providing such services is not aware of the contents of the communications and should not be responsible for its contents. Of course this exemption does

not apply where the service provider is owned or controlled by or is in conspiracy with a maker of communications that is determined to be in violation of this statute.

This defense narrows the reach of the CDA. The conferees explicitly stated
that it is the purpose of the CDA "to target the criminal penalties of new sections 223(a) and (d) at *content providers* who violate this section and persons who conspire with such content providers, rather than entities that
simply offer general access to the Internet and other on-line content." This
defense is to be liberally applied.

The second defense is the "good faith" defense. It is a defense to prosecution if an individual takes, in good faith, "reasonable, effective, and appropriate" actions to prevent offensive material from being accessed by minors.
Offensive material which is transmitted despite an individual's good faith
efforts would not result in liability for the individual.

As a corollary to the good faith defense, individuals who make good
faith efforts to implement a defense under the CDA shall be protected from
other criminal or civil liability. This defense was in response to what Senator Exon felt was an absurd situation. If an Internet Service Provider (ISP)
exerted no editorial control over the transmissions on its computers, it was
free from liability according to the few cases that had been decided. If, however, an ISP exerts editorial control but is nevertheless unable to prevent all
harmful transmissions from passing over its computers, then the ISP could
be liable for the resulting harm.

Stratton Oakmont, Inc. v. *Prodigy* was the war cry of this absurdity.
According to the facts of *Stratton,* Prodigy had represented itself as a family
on-line service. The evidence revealed that Prodigy exercised editorial control by promulgating content guidelines which requested that users refrain
from certain conduct by using "a software screening program which automatically prescreens all bulletin board postings for offensive language," by
employing individuals whose duties include enforcement of the content
guidelines, and by use of an "emergency delete function" by which the individuals employed could censor the content of the service.

Stratton was a brokerage house in New York. An individual posted a
comment on Prodigy which Stratton claimed was libelous to its reputation.
Stratton sued Prodigy as a publisher of that information, demanding $200
million in damages. The New York court held that Prodigy was in fact liable
as a publisher. The court's holding was premised on the finding that Prodigy
represented, and in fact, that it exercised editorial control over its service.
The fact that Prodigy monitored its service only for obscenity and indecency
and not defamation was of no consequence. Since Prodigy entered the role

of censor, Prodigy became liable in the eyes of the New York court for everything on its service.

Congressmen on both sides of the debate found *Stratton* objectionable. Representatives of the on-line industry argued that laws like *Stratton* create a "Hobson's choice" between creating "child safe" areas that expose the ISP to liability as an editor, monitor, or publisher, and doing nothing in order to protect the ISP from liability. In order to encourage ISPs to monitor their services and act in the role of censor without fear, Senator Exon provided a defense against such civil or criminal liability. In the Conference Report, the conferees specifically stated that they were overturning *Stratton*.

2. Preemption and Jurisdiction

The CDA preempts state law as it applies to commercial entities and activities, nonprofit libraries, and institutions of higher learning. On the federal level, the CDA provides for virtually no FCC involvement. Originally, enforcement of the CDA was to be under the jurisdiction of the FCC. The Conference Committee placed it under the jurisdiction of the Department of Justice (DOJ). In addition, the Conference Committee removed language instructing the FCC to report every two years on the effectiveness of the CDA. Finally, the Conference Committee retained language from a competing House amendment stating that it is the policy of the federal government "to preserve the vibrant and competitive free market that presently exists for the Internet and other interactive computer services, unfettered by Federal or State regulation."

B. The Legislative History

At first, support for the CDA was uncertain. Then Senator Exon unveiled his infamous "Blue Book." At the request of Senator Exon, a friend downloaded from the Internet a collection of pornography. This was gathered in a blue folder and made accessible at Senator Exon's desk on the Senate floor so that everyone could observe the "filth" that was accessible to every boy and girl in this country. The Blue Book would be repeatedly cited throughout the debate in support of the CDA. Its existence is theorized to have helped reluctant senators vote for the CDA. No senator wanted to make what could be construed as a pro-pornography vote.

1. The Exon-Coats Revision

In order to ensure passage of his amendment, Senator Exon responded to the criticism and opposition which he received. On June 9, 1995, Senator Exon introduced a revised version of the CDA that included revisions to the original defenses. Senator Exon was attempting to appease several groups simultaneously. However, DOJ reaffirmed its opposition to the amendment and organizations on the conservative right indicated displeasure with new defenses that obstructed, in their opinion, the prosecution of pornographers.

2. The Loyal Opposition

The CDA faced strong opposition in the Senate from Senator Leahy. Senator Leahy introduced a competing amendment which proposed that the federal government take no additional efforts to regulate the Internet, and, instead, conduct a Department of Justice study to determine what additional forms of legislation would be required over and above current antiobscenity and pornography law, to successfully regulate on-line communications.

The Leahy Amendment was, in Senator Exon's opinion, an attempt to punt by conducting a federal study achieving nothing. Senator Leahy responded that it was in fact Senator Exon who was proposing the punt, that individuals phobic of on-line pornography wanted to pass the buck of responsibility of protecting our children on to the FCC. Senator Leahy argued that it was a punt to pass legislation out of fear without considering whether that legislation would be constitutional or even successful.

Attacks within the Senate came not only from those who believed that regulation [was] premature and imprudent, but also arose from those who believed that the CDA was too liberal, permitting loopholes through which pornographers could slither. The conservative opposition introduced alternative legislation which would censor the Internet without defenses.

The reception which the House of Representatives gave to the CDA was frigid. The Speaker of the House, Newt Gingrich . . . rejected Senator Exon's attempt to sterilize electronic space. On June 20, 1995, Speaker Gingrich pronounced that the CDA

> is clearly a violation of free speech and it's a violation of the right of adults to communicate with each other. I don't agree with it and I don't think it is a serious way to discuss a serious issue, which is, how do you maintain the right of free speech for adults while also protecting children in a medium which is available to both?

He went on to say that the reason why it had passed the Senate was that it was "seen as a good press release back home so people voted for it."

When the House voted on its version of the telecommunications bill, the House gave what appeared to be a resounding rejection of the CDA and any attempt to meddle with the Internet. The younger House, having more experience with the Internet, wanted nothing of the CDA and sought to distance itself from the appearance of a regulatory-hungry federal government ready to trample the prized freedoms found in cyberspace. In opposition to the CDA, Representatives Cox and Wyden introduced the Family Empowerment Amendment, which proclaimed an Internet free of government interference. This amendment was attached to the House's telecommunications bill in a virtually unanimous 420 to 4 vote.

The opposition proclaimed that the Cox/Wyden Amendment would block the CDA in conference. In truth, the Cox/Wyden Amendment was far from a victory. The Cox/Wyden Amendment specifically and curiously stated that "[n]othing in this section shall be construed to impair the enforcement of section 223 of" Title 47, the very statute that the CDA sought to amend. As a result, the House and Senate amendments were described as fitting together "like a hand in a glove."

The opposition proclaimed that the Cox/Wyden Amendment forbade FCC regulation of the Internet; it did not. The opposition claimed that it preempted state regulation of the Internet; it did not. The only thing that the amendment in fact did was to overrule *Stratton* by protecting from liability on-line services that make a good faith effort to restrict access to offensive material. This one affirmative act was, in fact, consistent with the provisions of the CDA. The Cox/Wyden Amendment was described as a bill without a verb. In response to a growing on-line opposition movement, congressmen were able to declare their allegiance to the First Amendment and cyberspace without actually committing themselves to legislation of significance. The victory was hollow.

In the midst of the hoopla over the imaginary victory, something was snuck through the back door of the House version of the telecommunications bill. Representative Bliley, on the day of the vote on the telecommunications bill, introduced the "Manager's Amendment." Item 41 of the Manager's Amendment, known also as the Hyde Amendment, extended the federal obscenity laws to cover interactive computer services.

The Manager's Amendment as a whole received little press. Representative Bryant stated that the amendment was created in darkness without input from the public or from Congress. He argued that the amendment appeared out of nowhere and the House was forced to vote on it without having the opportunity to review its terms. He and others argued that the Manager's Amendment, which altered the telecommunications bill from the form that was voted on and passed from the Commerce and Judiciary Committees, was a last-minute creation in order to appease the interests of big business. Throughout the debate, however (concerning the Manager's Amendment on the day of the House vote on the telecommunications bill), the Hyde Amendment, censoring the Internet, was not mentioned or discussed.

The Administration, through Larry Irving, Assistant Secretary for Communications and Information, U.S. Department of Commerce, voiced its opposition to the CDA. The Department of Justice issued statements denouncing the amendment and declaring that it, in fact, weakened their ability to prosecute on-line obscenity. Reed Hundt, chairman of the FCC, also spoke up in his opposition to the amendment.

Cyberspace itself rose up in strong opposition to the CDA. Although public opposition to legislation normally may not get significant coverage in legal analysis or the courtroom, opposition to the CDA is fascinating in the way in which it was the epitome of one of its own strongest arguments. The opposition heralded the Internet as a boon for democratic process and responsive representation. With the increased availability of information, ease of organization, and improved ability to contact one's congressional representatives, the opposition saw the Internet as something to be cherished; any attempt to infringe on its unique empowerment of free speech and democratic debate was to be warded off with vigilance. The opposition was the very proof of its own argument. A portion of the community was able to rise up, become quickly and highly educated, and convey its views to the governing body. The governing body, in turn, was able to quickly become aware of the positions of its constituents and respond. Democratic process was heightened. The essence of our democratic society—the free exchange of ideas and the belief that out of the cacophony of views we can reach reasonable and enlightened principles to guide our society—was improved. In his attempt to curtail some voices on the Internet, Senator Exon caused other voices to mature.

Instead of reveling in this revitalization of democracy, Senator Exon saw the on-line movement as a threat. He criticized the on-line movement, characterizing it as a bunch of First Amendment belly-achers. Senator Exon complained that the opposition had more concern for protecting pornographers than cooperating with his office.

3. Victory in the Senate and the House

On June 14, 1995, Senator Exon saw his attempt to protect the minds of the youth of America meet with victory. The CDA was successfully added to the Senate version of the telecommunications bill of 1995. On June 15, 1995, the Senate Telecommunications Competition and Deregulation Act, S. 652, passed the Senate. The House would soon thereafter pass its version of the telecommunications bill along with both the Cox/Wyden Amendment and the Manager's Amendment. . . .

2

Supreme Court Case:
Reno v. *American Civil Liberties Union*

SUPREME COURT OF THE UNITED STATES

No. 96–511

JANET RENO, ATTORNEY GENERAL OF THE UNITED STATES, et al.,
APPELLANTS *v.* AMERICAN CIVIL LIBERTIES UNION et al.

on appeal from the United States District Court for the
Eastern District of Pennsylvania

[June 26, 1997]

Justice Stevens delivered the opinion of the Court.

At issue is the constitutionality of two statutory provisions enacted to protect minors from "indecent" and "patently offensive" communications on the Internet. Notwithstanding the legitimacy and importance of the congressional goal of protecting children from harmful materials, we agree with the three-judge District Court that the statute abridges "the freedom of speech" protected by the First Amendment.

I

The District Court made extensive findings of fact, most of which were based on a detailed stipulation prepared by the parties. The findings describe the character and the dimensions of the Internet, the availability of sexually explicit material in that medium, and the problems confronting age verification for recipients of Internet communications. Because those findings provide the underpinnings for the legal issues, we begin with a summary of the undisputed facts.

The Internet

The Internet is an international network of interconnected computers. It is the outgrowth of what began in 1969 as a military program called "ARPANET," which was designed to enable computers operated by the military, defense contractors, and universities conducting defense-related research to communicate with one another by redundant channels even if some portions of the network were damaged in a war. While the ARPANET no longer exists, it provided an example for the development of a number of civilian networks that, eventually linking with each other, now enable tens of millions of people to communicate with one another and to access vast amounts of information from around the world. The Internet is "a unique and wholly new medium of worldwide human communication."

The Internet has experienced "extraordinary growth." The number of "host" computers—those that store information and relay communications—increased from about 300 in 1981 to approximately 9,400,000 by the time of the trial in 1996. Roughly 60 percent of these hosts are located in the United States. About 40 million people used the Internet at the time of trial, a number that is expected to mushroom to 200 million by 1999.

Individuals can obtain access to the Internet from many different sources, generally hosts themselves or entities with a host affiliation. Most colleges and universities provide access for their students and faculty; many corporations provide their employees with access through an office network; many communities and local libraries provide free access; and an increasing number of storefront "computer coffee shops" provide access for a small hourly fee. Several major national "online services" such as America Online, CompuServe, the Microsoft Network, and Prodigy offer access to their own extensive proprietary networks as well as a link to the much larger resources of the Internet. These commercial online services had almost 12 million individual subscribers at the time of trial.

Anyone with access to the Internet may take advantage of a wide variety of communication and information retrieval methods. These methods are constantly evolving and difficult to categorize precisely. But, as presently constituted, those most relevant to this case are electronic mail ("e-mail"), automatic mailing list services ("mail exploders," sometimes referred to as "listservs"), "newsgroups," "chat rooms," and the "World Wide Web." All of these methods can be used to transmit text; most can transmit sound, pictures, and moving video images. Taken together, these tools constitute a unique medium—known to its users as "cyberspace"—located in no particular geographical location but available to anyone, anywhere in the world, with access to the Internet.

E-mail enables an individual to send an electronic message—generally akin to a note or letter—to another individual or to a group of addressees. The message is generally stored electronically, sometimes waiting for the recipient to check her "mailbox" and sometimes making its receipt known through some type of prompt. A mail exploder is a sort of e-mail group. Subscribers can send messages to a common e-mail address, which then forwards the message to the group's other subscribers. Newsgroups also serve groups of regular participants, but these postings may be read by others as well. There are thousands of such groups, each serving to foster an exchange of information or opinion on a particular topic running the gamut from, say, the music of Wagner to Balkan politics to AIDS prevention to the Chicago Bulls. About 100,000 new messages are posted every day. In most newsgroups, postings are automatically purged at regular intervals. In addition to posting a message that can be read later, two or more individuals wishing to communicate more immediately can enter a chat room to engage in real-time dialogue—in other words, by typing messages to one another that appear almost immediately on the others' computer screens. The District Court found that at any given time "tens of thousands of users are engaging in conversations on a huge range of subjects." It is "no exaggeration to conclude that the content on the Internet is as diverse as human thought."

The best known category of communication over the Internet is the World Wide Web, which allows users to search for and retrieve information stored in remote computers, as well as, in some cases, to communicate back to designated sites. In concrete terms, the Web consists of a vast number of documents stored in different computers all over the world. Some of these documents are simply files containing information. However, more elaborate documents, commonly known as Web "pages," are also prevalent. Each has its own address—"rather like a telephone number." Web pages frequently contain information and sometimes allow the viewer to communicate with the page's (or "site's") author. They generally also contain "links" to other documents created by that site's author or to other (generally) related sites. Typically, the links are either blue or underlined text—sometimes images.

Navigating the Web is relatively straightforward. A user may either type the address of a known page or enter one or more keywords into a commercial "search engine" in an effort to locate sites on a subject of interest. A particular Web page may contain the information sought by the "surfer," or, through its links, it may be an avenue to other documents located anywhere on the Internet. Users generally explore a given Web page, or move to another, by clicking a computer "mouse" on one of the page's icons or links. Access to most Web pages is freely available, but some allow access only to those who have purchased the right from a commercial provider. The Web is thus comparable, from the readers' viewpoint, to both a vast library including millions of readily available and indexed publications and a sprawling mall offering goods and services.

From the publishers' point of view, it constitutes a vast platform from which to address and hear from a world-wide audience of millions of readers, viewers, researchers, and buyers. Any person or organization with a computer connected to the Internet can "publish" information. Publishers include government agencies, educational institutions, commercial entities, advocacy groups, and individuals. Publishers may either make their material available to the entire pool of Internet users, or confine access to a selected group, such as those willing to pay for the privilege. "No single organization controls any membership in the Web, nor is there any centralized point from which individual Web sites or services can be blocked from the Web."

Sexually Explicit Material

Sexually explicit material on the Internet includes text, pictures, and chat and "extends from the modestly titillating to the hardest-core." These files are created, named, and posted in the same manner as material that is not sexually explicit, and may be accessed either deliberately or unintentionally during the course of an imprecise search. "Once a provider posts its content on the Internet, it cannot prevent that content from entering any community." Thus, for example, "when the UCR/California Museum of Photography posts to its Web site nudes by Edward Weston and Robert Mapplethorpe to announce that its new exhibit will travel to Baltimore and New York City, those images are available not only in Los Angeles, Baltimore, and New York City, but also in Cincinnati, Mobile, or Beijing—wherever Internet users live. Similarly, the safer sex instructions that Critical Path posts to its Web site, written in street language so that the teenage receiver can understand them, are available not just in Philadelphia, but also in Provo and Prague."

Some of the communications over the Internet that originate in foreign countries are also sexually explicit.

Though such material is widely available, users seldom encounter such content accidentally. "A document's title or a description of the document will usually appear before the document itself . . . and in many cases the user will receive detailed information about a site's content before he or she need take the step to access the document. Almost all sexually explicit images are preceded by warnings as to the content." For that reason, the "odds are slim" that a user would enter a sexually explicit site by accident. Unlike communications received by radio or television, "the receipt of information on the Internet requires a series of affirmative steps more deliberate and directed than merely turning a dial. A child requires some sophistication and some ability to read to retrieve material and thereby to use the Internet unattended.

Systems have been developed to help parents control the material that may be available on a home computer with Internet access. A system may either limit a computer's access to an approved list of sources that have been identified as containing no adult material, it may block designated inappropriate sites, or it may attempt to block messages containing identifiable objectionable features. "Although parental control software currently can screen for certain suggestive words or for known sexually explicit sites, it cannot now screen for sexually explicit images." Nevertheless, the evidence indicates that "a reasonably effective method by which parents can prevent their children from accessing sexually explicit and other material which parents may believe is inappropriate for their children will soon be available."

Age Verification

The problem of age verification differs for different uses of the Internet. The District Court categorically determined that there "is no effective way to determine the identity or the age of a user who is accessing material through e-mail, mail exploders, newsgroups, or chat rooms." The Government offered no evidence that there was a reliable way to screen recipients and participants in such fora for age. Moreover, even if it were technologically feasible to block minors' access to newsgroups and chat rooms containing discussions of art, politics, or other subjects that potentially elicit "indecent" or "patently offensive" contributions, it would not be possible to block their access to that material and "still allow them access to the remaining content, even if the overwhelming majority of that content was not indecent.

Technology exists by which an operator of a Web site may condition access on the verification of requested information such as a credit card number or an adult password. Credit card verification is only feasible, however, either in connection with a commercial transaction in which the card is used, or by payment to a verification agency. Using credit card possession as a surrogate for proof of age would impose costs on noncommercial Web sites that would require many of them to shut down. For that reason, at the time of the trial, credit card verification was "effectively unavailable to a substantial number of Internet content providers." Moreover, the imposition of such a requirement "would completely bar adults who do not have a credit card and lack the resources to obtain one from accessing any blocked material."

Commercial pornographic sites that charge their users for access have assigned them passwords as a method of age verification. The record does not contain any evidence concerning the reliability of these technologies. Even if passwords are effective for commercial purveyors of indecent material, the District Court found that an adult password requirement would impose significant burdens on noncommercial sites, both because they would discourage users from accessing their sites and because the cost of creating and maintaining such screening systems would be "beyond their reach."

In sum, the District Court found:

> Even if credit card verification or adult password verification were implemented, the Government presented no testimony as to how such systems could ensure that the user of the password or credit card is in fact over 18. The burdens imposed by credit card verification and adult password verification systems make them effectively unavailable to a substantial number of Internet content providers.

II

The Telecommunications Act of 1996 was an unusually important legislative enactment. As stated on the first of its 103 pages, its primary purpose was to reduce regulation and encourage "the rapid deployment of new telecommunications technologies." The major components of the statute have nothing to do with the Internet; they were designed to promote competition in the local telephone service market, the multichannel video market, and the market for over-the-air broadcasting. The Act includes seven Titles, six of which are the product of extensive committee hearings and the subject of discussion in Reports prepared by Committees of the Senate and the House of Representatives. By contrast, Title V—known as the "Communications Decency Act of 1996" (CDA)—contains provisions that were either added in executive committee after the hearings were concluded or as amendments offered during floor debate on the legislation. An amendment offered in the Senate was the source of the two statutory provisions challenged in this case. They are informally described as the "indecent transmission" provision and the "patently offensive display" provision.

The first, §223(a), prohibits the knowing transmission of obscene or indecent messages to any recipient under 18 years of age. It provides in pertinent part:

(a) Whoever—
(1) in interstate or foreign communications— . . .
(B) by means of a telecommunications device knowingly—
(i) makes, creates, or solicits, and
(ii) initiates the transmission of,
any comment, request, suggestion, proposal, image, or other communication which is obscene or indecent, knowing that the recipient of the communication is under 18 years of age, regardless of whether the maker of such communication placed the call or initiated the communication; . . .
(2) knowingly permits any telecommunications facility under his control to be used for any activity prohibited by paragraph (1) with the intent that it be used for such activity,
shall be fined under Title 18, or imprisoned not more than two years, or both.

The second provision, §223(d), prohibits the knowing sending or displaying of patently offensive messages in a manner that is available to a person under 18 years of age. It provides:

(d) Whoever—
(1) in interstate or foreign communications knowingly—
(A) uses an interactive computer service to send to a specific person or persons under 18 years of age, or
(B) uses any interactive computer service to display in a manner available to a person under 18 years of age,
any comment, request, suggestion, proposal, image, or other communication that, in context, depicts or describes, in terms patently offensive as measured by contemporary community standards, sexual or excretory activities or organs, regardless of whether the user of such service placed the call or initiated the communication; or
(2) knowingly permits any telecommunications facility under such person's control to be used for an activity prohibited by paragraph (1) with the intent that it be used for such activity,
shall be fined under Title 18, or imprisoned not more than two years, or both.

The breadth of these prohibitions is qualified by two affirmative defenses. One covers those who take "good faith, reasonable, effective, and appropriate actions" to restrict access by minors to the prohibited communications. The other covers those who restrict access to covered material by requiring certain designated forms of age proof, such as a verified credit card or an adult identification number or code.

III

On February 8, 1996, immediately after the President signed the statute, 20 plaintiffs filed suit against the Attorney General of the United States and the Department of Justice challenging the constitutionality of §§223(a)(1) and 223(d). A week later, based on his conclusion that the term "indecent" was too vague to provide the basis for a criminal prosecution, District Judge Buckwalter entered a temporary restraining order against enforcement of §223(a)(1)(B)(ii) insofar as it applies to indecent communications. A second suit was then filed by 27 additional plaintiffs, the two cases were consolidated, and a three-judge District Court was convened pursuant to §561 of the Act. After an evidentiary hearing, that Court entered a preliminary injunction against enforcement of both of the challenged provisions. Each of the three judges wrote a separate opinion, but their judgment was unanimous.

Chief Judge Sloviter doubted the strength of the Government's interest in regulating "the vast range of online material covered or potentially covered by the CDA," but acknowledged that the interest was "compelling" with respect to some of that material. She concluded, nonetheless, that the statute "sweeps more broadly than necessary and thereby chills the expression of adults" and that the terms "patently offensive" and "indecent" were "inherently vague." She also determined that the affirmative defenses were not "technologically or economically feasible for most providers," specifically considering and rejecting an argument that providers could avoid liability by "tagging" their material in a manner that would allow potential readers to screen out unwanted transmissions. Chief Judge Sloviter also rejected the Government's suggestion that the scope of the statute could be narrowed by construing it to apply only to commercial pornographers.

Judge Buckwalter concluded that the word "indecent" in §223(a)(1)(B) and the terms "patently offensive" and "in context" in §223(d)(1) were so vague that criminal enforcement of either section would violate the "fundamental constitutional principle" of "simple fairness," and the specific protections of the First and Fifth Amendments. He found no statutory basis for the Government's argument that the challenged provisions would be applied only to "pornographic" materials, noting that, unlike obscenity, "indecency has *not* been defined to exclude works of serious literary, artistic, political, or scientific value." Moreover, the Government's claim that the work must be considered patently offensive "in context" was itself vague because the relevant context might "refer to, among other things, the nature of the communication as a whole, the time of day it was conveyed, the medium used, the identity of the speaker, or whether or not it is accompanied by appropriate warnings." He believed that the unique nature of the Internet aggravated the vagueness of the statute.

Judge Dalzell's review of "the special attributes of Internet communication" disclosed by the evidence convinced him that the First Amendment denies Congress the power to regulate the content of protected speech on the Internet. His opinion explained at length why he believed the Act would abridge significant protected speech, particularly by noncommercial speakers, while "[p]erversely, commercial pornographers would remain relatively unaffected." He construed our cases as requiring a "medium-specific" approach to the analysis of the regulation of mass communication, and concluded that the Internet—as "the most participatory form of mass speech yet developed,"—is entitled to "the highest protection from governmental intrusion."

The judgment of the District Court enjoins the Government from enforcing the prohibitions in §223(a)(1)(B) insofar as they relate to "indecent" communications, but expressly preserves the Government's right to investigate and prosecute the obscenity or child pornography activities prohibited therein. The injunction against enforcement of §§223(d)(1) and (2) is unqualified because those provisions contain no separate reference to obscenity or child pornography.

. . . In its appeal, the Government argues that the District Court erred in holding that the CDA violated both the First Amendment because it is overbroad and the Fifth Amendment because it is vague. While we discuss the vagueness of the CDA because of its relevance to the First Amendment overbreadth inquiry, we conclude that the judgment should be affirmed without reaching the Fifth Amendment issue. We begin our analysis by reviewing the principal authorities on which the Government relies. Then, after describing the overbreadth of the CDA, we consider the Government's specific contentions, including its submission that we save portions of the statute either by severance or by fashioning judicial limitations on the scope of its coverage.

IV

In arguing for reversal, the Government contends that the CDA is plainly constitutional under three of our prior decisions: (1) *Ginsberg* v. *New York* (1968); (2) *FCC* v. *Pacifica Foundation* (1978); and (3) *Renton* v. *Playtime Theatres, Inc.* (1986). A close look at these cases, however, raises—rather than relieves—doubts concerning the constitutionality of the CDA.

In *Ginsberg*, we upheld the constitutionality of a New York statute that prohibited selling to minors under 17 years of age material that was considered obscene as to them even if not obscene as to adults. We rejected the defendant's broad submission that "the scope of the constitutional freedom of expression secured to a citizen to read or see material concerned with sex cannot be made to depend on whether the citizen is an adult or a minor." In rejecting that contention, we relied not only on the State's independent interest in the well-being of its youth, but also on our consistent recognition of the principle that "the parents' claim to authority in their own household to direct the rearing of their children is basic in the structure of our society." In four important respects, the statute upheld in Ginsberg was narrower than the CDA. First, we noted in Ginsberg that "the prohibition against sales to minors does not bar parents who so desire from purchasing the magazines for their children." Under the CDA, by contrast, neither the parents' consent—nor even their participation—in the communication would avoid the application of the statute. Second, the New York statute applied only to commercial transactions, whereas the CDA contains no such limitation. Third, the New York statute applied its definition of material that is harmful to minors with the requirement that it be "utterly without redeeming social importance for minors." The CDA fails to provide us with any definition of the term "indecent" as used in §223(a)(1) and, importantly, omits any requirement that the "patently offensive" material covered by §223(d) lack serious literary, artistic, political, or scientific value. Fourth, the New York statute defined a minor as a person under the age of 17, whereas the CDA, in applying to all those under 18 years, includes an additional year of those nearest majority.

In *Pacifica*, we upheld a declaratory order of the Federal Communications Commission, holding that the broadcast of a recording of a 12-minute monologue entitled "Filthy Words" that had previously been delivered to a live audience "could have been the subject of administrative sanctions." The Commission had found that the repetitive use of certain words referring to excretory or sexual activities or organs "in an afternoon broadcast when children are in the audience was patently offensive" and concluded that the monologue was indecent "as broadcast." The respondent did not quarrel with the finding that the afternoon broadcast was patently offensive, but contended that it was not "indecent" within the meaning of the relevant statutes because it contained no prurient appeal. After rejecting respondent's statutory arguments, we confronted its two constitutional arguments: (1) that the Commission's construction of its authority to ban indecent speech was so broad that its order had to be set aside even if the broadcast at issue was unprotected; and (2) that since the recording was not obscene, the First Amendment forbade any abridgement of the right to broadcast it on the radio.

In the portion of the lead opinion not joined by Justices Powell and Blackmun, the plurality stated that the First Amendment does not prohibit all governmental regulation that depends on the content of speech. Accordingly, the availability of constitutional protection for a vulgar and offensive monologue that was not obscene depended on the context of the broadcast. Relying on the premise that "of all forms of communication" broadcasting had received the most limited First Amendment protection, the Court concluded that the ease with which children may obtain access to broadcasts, "coupled with the concerns recognized in Ginsberg," justified special treatment of indecent broadcasting.

As with the New York statute at issue in Ginsberg, there are significant differences between the order upheld in *Pacifica* and the CDA. First, the order in *Pacifica*, issued by an agency that had been regulating radio stations for decades, targeted a specific broadcast that represented a rather dramatic departure from traditional program content in order to designate when— rather than whether—it would be permissible to air such a program in that particular medium. The CDA's broad categorical prohibitions are not limited to particular times and are not dependent on any evaluation by an agency familiar with the unique characteristics of the Internet. Second, unlike the CDA, the Commission's declaratory order was not punitive; we expressly refused to decide whether the indecent broadcast "would justify a criminal prosecution." Finally, the Commission's order applied to a medium which as a matter of history had "received the most limited First Amendment protection," in large part because warnings could not adequately protect the listener from unexpected program content. The Internet, however, has no comparable history. Moreover, the District Court found that the risk of encountering indecent material by accident is remote because a series of affirmative steps is required to access specific material.

In *Renton,* we upheld a zoning ordinance that kept adult movie theatres out of residential neighborhoods. The ordinance was aimed, not at the content of the films shown in the theaters, but rather at the "secondary effects"—such as crime and deteriorating property values—that these theaters fostered: " 'It is th[e] secondary effect which these zoning ordinances attempt to avoid, not the dissemination of "offensive" speech.' " According to the Government, the CDA is constitutional because it constitutes a sort of "cyberzoning" on the Internet. But the CDA applies broadly to the entire universe of cyberspace. And the purpose of the CDA is to protect children from the primary effects of "indecent" and "patently offensive" speech, rather than any "secondary" effect of such speech. Thus, the CDA is a content-based blanket restriction on speech, and, as such, cannot be "properly analyzed as a form of time, place, and manner regulation."

These precedents, then, surely do not require us to uphold the CDA and are fully consistent with the application of the most stringent review of its provisions.

V

In *Southeastern Promotions, Ltd.* v. *Conrad,* (1975), we observed that "[e]ach medium of expression . . . may present its own problems." Thus, some of our cases have recognized special justifications for regulation of the broadcast media that are not applicable to other speakers. . . . In these cases, the Court relied on the history of extensive government regulation of the broadcast medium. . . .

Those factors are not present in cyberspace. Neither before nor after the enactment of the CDA have the vast democratic fora of the Internet been subject to the type of government supervision and regulation that has attended the broadcast industry. Moreover, the Internet is not as "invasive" as radio or television. The District Court specifically found that "[c]ommunications over the Internet do not 'invade' an individual's home or appear on one's computer screen unbidden. Users seldom encounter content 'by accident.' " It also found that "[a]lmost all sexually explicit images are preceded by warnings as to the content," and cited testimony that " 'odds are slim' that a user would come across a sexually explicit sight by accident." . . .

Finally, unlike the conditions that prevailed when Congress first authorized regulation of the broadcast spectrum, the Internet can hardly be considered a "scarce" expressive commodity. It provides relatively unlimited, low-cost capacity for communication of all kinds. The Government estimates that "[a]s many as 40 million people use the Internet today, and that figure is expected to grow to 200 million by 1999." This dynamic, multifaceted category of communication includes not only traditional print and news services, but also audio, video, and still images, as well as interactive, real-time dialogue. Through the use of chat rooms, any person with a phone line can become a town crier with a voice that resonates farther than it could from any soapbox. Through the use of Web pages, mail exploders, and newsgroups, the same individual can become a pamphleteer. As the District Court found, "the content on the Internet is as diverse as human thought." We agree with its conclusion that our cases provide no basis for qualifying the level of First Amendment scrutiny that should be applied to this medium.

VI

Regardless of whether the CDA is so vague that it violates the Fifth Amendment, the many ambiguities concerning the scope of its coverage render it problematic for purposes of the First Amendment. For instance, each of the two parts of the CDA uses a different linguistic form. The first uses the word "indecent," while the second speaks of material that "in context, depicts or describes, in terms patently offensive as measured by contemporary community standards, sexual or excretory activities or organs." Given the absence of a definition of either term, this difference in language will provoke uncertainty among speakers about how the two standards relate to each other and just what they mean. Could a speaker confidently assume that a serious discussion about birth control practices, homosexuality, the First Amendment issues raised by the Appendix to our *Pacifica* opinion, or the consequences of prison rape would not violate the CDA? This uncertainty undermines the likelihood that the CDA has been carefully tailored to the congressional goal of protecting minors from potentially harmful materials.

The vagueness of the CDA is a matter of special concern for two reasons. First, the CDA is a content-based regulation of speech. The vagueness of such a regulation raises special First Amendment concerns because of its obvious chilling effect on free speech. Second, the CDA is a criminal statute. In addition to the opprobrium and stigma of a criminal conviction, the CDA threatens violators with penalties including up to two years in prison for each act of violation. The severity of criminal sanctions may well cause speakers to remain silent rather than communicate even arguably unlawful words, ideas, and images. . . .

The Government argues that the statute is no more vague than the obscenity standard this Court established in *Miller* v. *California.* But that is not so. In *Miller,* this Court reviewed a criminal conviction against a commercial vendor who mailed brochures containing pictures of sexually explicit activities to individuals who had not requested such materials. Having struggled for some time to establish a definition of obscenity, we set forth in *Miller* the test for obscenity that controls to this day:

(a) whether the average person, applying contemporary community standards would find that the work, taken as a whole, appeals to the prurient interest; (b) whether the work depicts or describes, in a patently offensive way, sexual conduct specifically defined by the applicable state law; and (c) whether the work, taken as a whole, lacks serious literary, artistic, political, or scientific value.

Because the CDA's "patently offensive" standard (and, we assume *arguendo,* its synonymous "indecent" standard) is one part of the three-prong Miller test, the Government reasons, it cannot be unconstitutionally vague.

The Government's assertion is incorrect as a matter of fact. The second prong of the *Miller* test—the purportedly analogous standard—contains a critical requirement that is omitted from the CDA: that the proscribed material be "specifically defined by the applicable state law." This requirement reduces the vagueness inherent in the open-ended term "patently offensive" as used in the CDA. Moreover, the *Miller* definition is limited to "sexual conduct," whereas the CDA extends also to include (1) "excretory activities" as well as (2) "organs" of both a sexual and excretory nature.

The Government's reasoning is also flawed. Just because a definition including three limitations is not vague, it does not follow that one of those limitations, standing by itself, is not vague. Each of *Miller*'s additional two prongs—(1) that, taken as a whole, the material appeal to the "prurient" interest, and (2) that it "lac[k] serious literary, artistic, political, or scientific value"—critically limits the uncertain sweep of the obscenity definition.

The second requirement is particularly important because, unlike the "patently offensive" and "prurient interest" criteria, it is not judged by contemporary community standards. This "societal value" requirement, absent in the CDA, allows appellate courts to impose some limitations and regularity on the definition by setting, as a matter of law, a national floor for socially redeeming value. The Government's contention that courts will be able to give such legal limitations to the CDA's standards is belied by *Miller*'s own rationale for having juries determine whether material is "patently offensive" according to community standards: that such questions are essentially ones of *fact.*

In contrast to *Miller* and our other previous cases, the CDA thus presents a greater threat of censoring speech that, in fact, falls outside the statute's scope. Given the vague contours of the coverage of the statute, it unquestionably silences some speakers whose messages would be entitled to constitutional protection. That danger provides further reason for insisting that the statute not be overly broad. The CDA's burden on protected speech cannot be justified if it could be avoided by a more carefully drafted statute.

VII

We are persuaded that the CDA lacks the precision that the First Amendment requires when a statute regulates the content of speech. In order to deny minors access to potentially harmful speech, the CDA effectively suppresses a large amount of speech that adults have a constitutional right to receive and to address to one another. That burden on adult speech is unacceptable if less restrictive alternatives would be at least as effective in achieving the legitimate purpose that the statute was enacted to serve.

In evaluating the free speech rights of adults, we have made it perfectly clear that "[s]exual expression which is indecent but not obscene is protected by the First Amendment. . . . ("[W]here obscenity is not involved, we have consistently held that the fact that protected speech may be offensive to some does not justify its suppression.") Indeed, *Pacifica* itself admonished that "the fact that society may find speech offensive is not a sufficient reason for suppressing it."

It is true that we have repeatedly recognized the governmental interest in protecting children from harmful materials. But that interest does not justify an unnecessarily broad suppression of speech addressed to adults. As we have explained, the Government may not "reduc[e] the adult population . . . to . . . only what is fit for children." . . . "[R]egardless of the strength of the government's interest" in protecting children, "[t]he level of discourse reaching a mailbox simply cannot be limited to that which would be suitable for a sandbox." . . .

In arguing that the CDA does not so diminish adult communication, the Government relies on the incorrect factual premise that prohibiting a transmission whenever it is known that one of its recipients is a minor would not interfere with adult-to-adult communication. The findings of the District Court make clear that this premise is untenable. Given the size of the potential audience for most messages, in the absence of a viable age verification process, the sender must be charged with knowing that one or more minors will likely view it. Knowledge that, for instance, one or more members of a 100-person chat group will be minor—and therefore that it would be a crime to send the group an indecent message—would surely burden communication among adults.

The District Court found that at the time of trial existing technology did not include any effective method for a sender to prevent minors from obtaining access to its communications on the Internet without also denying access to adults. The Court found no effective way to determine the age of a user who is accessing material through e-mail, mail exploders, newsgroups, or chat rooms. As a practical matter, the Court also found that it would be prohibitively expensive for noncommercial—as well as some commercial—speakers who have Web sites to verify that their users are adults. These limitations must inevitably curtail a significant amount of adult communication on the Internet. By contrast, the District Court found that "[d]espite its limitations, currently available *user-based* software suggests that a reasonably effective method by which *parents* can prevent their children from accessing sexually explicit and other material which *parents* may believe is inappropriate for their children will soon be widely available."

The breadth of the CDA's coverage is wholly unprecedented. Unlike the regulations upheld in *Ginsberg* and *Pacifica*, the scope of the CDA is not limited to commercial speech or commercial entities. Its open-ended prohibitions embrace all nonprofit entities and individuals posting indecent messages or displaying them on their own computers in the presence of minors. The general, undefined terms "indecent" and "patently offensive" cover large amounts of nonpornographic material with serious educational or other value. Moreover, the "community standards" criterion as applied to the Internet means that any communication available to a nation-wide audience will be judged by the standards of the community most likely to be offended by the message. The regulated subject matter includes any of the seven "dirty words" used in the *Pacifica* monologue, the use of which the Government's expert acknowledged could constitute a felony. It may also extend to discussions about prison rape or safe sexual practices, artistic images that include nude subjects, and arguably the card catalogue of the Carnegie Library.

For the purposes of our decision, we need neither accept nor reject the Government's submission that the First Amendment does not forbid a blanket prohibition on all "indecent" and "patently offensive" messages communicated to a 17-year-old—no matter how much value the message may contain and regardless of parental approval. It is at least clear that the strength of the Government's interest in protecting minors is not equally strong throughout the coverage of this broad statute. Under the CDA, a parent allowing her 17-year-old to use the family computer to obtain information on the Internet that she, in her parental judgment, deems appropriate could face a lengthy prison term. Similarly, a parent who sent his 17-year-old college freshman information on birth control via e-mail could be incarcerated even though neither he, his child, nor anyone in their home community, found the material "indecent" or "patently offensive," if the college town's community thought otherwise.

The breadth of this content-based restriction of speech imposes an especially heavy burden on the Government to explain why a less restrictive provision would not be as effective as the CDA. It has not done so. The arguments in this Court have referred to possible alternatives such as requiring that indecent material be "tagged" in a way that facilitates parental control of material coming into their homes, making exceptions for messages with artistic or educational value, providing some tolerance for parental choice, and regulating some portions of the Internet—such as commercial web sites—differently than others, such as chat rooms. Particularly in the light of the absence of any detailed findings by the Congress, or even hearings addressing the special problems of the CDA, we are persuaded that the CDA is not narrowly tailored if that requirement has any meaning at all.

VIII

In an attempt to curtail the CDA's facial overbreadth, the Government advances three additional arguments for sustaining the Act's affirmative pro-hibitions: (1) that the CDA is constitutional because it leaves open ample "alternative channels" of communication; (2) that the plain meaning of the Act's "knowledge" and "specific person" requirement significantly restricts its permissible applications; and (3) that the Act's prohibitions are "almost always" limited to material lacking redeeming social value.

The Government first contends that, even though the CDA effectively censors discourse on many of the Internet's modalities—such as chat groups, newsgroups, and mail exploders—it is nonetheless constitutional because it provides a "reasonable opportunity" for speakers to engage in the restricted speech on the World Wide Web. This argument is unpersuasive because the CDA regulates speech on the basis of its content. A "time, place, and manner" analysis is therefore inapplicable. . . . It is thus immaterial whether such speech would be feasible on the Web (which, as the Govern-ment's own expert acknowledged, would cost up to $10,000 if the speaker's interests were not accommodated by an existing Web site, not including costs for database management and age verification). The Government's position is equivalent to arguing that a statute could ban leaflets on certain subjects as long as individuals are free to publish books. In invalidating a number of laws that banned leafletting on the streets *regardless of* their con-tent—we explained that "one is not to have the exercise of his liberty of expression in appropriate places abridged on the plea that it may be exer-cised in some other place."

The Government also asserts that the "knowledge" requirement of both §§223(a) and (d), especially when coupled with the "specific child" element found in §223(d), saves the CDA from overbreadth. Because both sections prohibit the dissemination of indecent messages only to persons known to be under 18, the Government argues, it does not require transmitters to "refrain from communicating indecent material to adults; they need only refrain from disseminating such materials to persons they know to be under 18." This argument ignores the fact that most Internet fora—including chat rooms, newsgroups, mail exploders, and the Web—are open to all comers. The Government's assertion that the knowledge requirement somehow protects the communications of adults is therefore untenable. Even the strongest reading of the "specific person" requirement of §223(d) cannot save the statute. It would confer broad powers of censorship, in the form of a "heckler's veto," upon any opponent of indecent speech who might simply log on and inform the would-be discoursers that his 17-year-old child—a "specific person . . . under 18 years of age,"—would be present.

Finally, we find no textual support for the Government's submission that material having scientific, educational, or other redeeming social value will necessarily fall outside the CDA's "patently offensive" and "indecent" prohibitions.

IX

The Government's three remaining arguments focus on the defenses provided in §223(e)(5). First, relying on the "good faith, reasonable, effective, and appropriate actions" provision, the Government suggests that "tagging" provides a defense that saves the constitutionality of the Act. The suggestion assumes that transmitters may encode their indecent communications in a way that would indicate their contents, thus permitting recipients to block their reception with appropriate software. It is the requirement that the good faith action must be "effective" that makes this defense illusory. The Government recognizes that its proposed screening software does not currently exist. Even if it did, there is no way to know whether a potential recipient will actually block the encoded material. Without the impossible knowledge that every guardian in America is screening for the "tag," the transmitter could not reasonably rely on its action to be "effective."

For its second and third arguments concerning defenses—which we can consider together—the Government relies on the latter half of §223(e)(5), which applies when the transmitter has restricted access by requiring use of a verified credit card or adult identification. Such verification is not only technologically available but actually is used by commercial providers of sexually explicit material. These providers, therefore, would be protected by the defense. Under the findings of the District Court, however, it is not economically feasible for most noncommercial speakers to employ such verification. Accordingly, this defense would not significantly narrow the statute's burden on noncommercial speech. Even with respect to the commercial pornographers that would be protected by the defense, the Government failed to adduce any evidence that these verification techniques actually preclude minors from posing as adults. Given that the risk of criminal sanctions "hovers over each content provider, like the proverbial sword of Damocles," the District Court correctly refused to rely on unproven future technology to save the statute. The Government thus failed to prove that the proffered defense would significantly reduce the heavy burden on adult speech produced by the prohibition on offensive displays.

We agree with the District Court's conclusion that the CDA places an unacceptably heavy burden on protected speech, and that the defenses do not constitute the sort of "narrow tailoring" that will save an otherwise patently invalid unconstitutional provision. In *Sable,* we remarked that the speech restriction at issue there amounted to " 'burn[ing] the house to roast the pig.' " The CDA, casting a far darker shadow over free speech, threatens to torch a large segment of the Internet community. . . .

XI

In this Court, though not in the District Court, the Government asserts that— in addition to its interest in protecting children—its "[e]qually significant" interest in fostering the growth of the Internet provides an independent basis for upholding the constitutionality of the CDA. The Government apparently assumes that the unregulated availability of "indecent" and "patently offensive" material on the Internet is driving countless citizens away from the medium because of the risk of exposing themselves or their children to harmful material.

We find this argument singularly unpersuasive. The dramatic expansion of this new marketplace of ideas contradicts the factual basis of this contention. The record demonstrates that the growth of the Internet has been and continues to be phenomenal. As a matter of constitutional tradition, in the absence of evidence to the contrary, we presume that governmental regulation of the content of speech is more likely to interfere with the free exchange of ideas than to encourage it. The interest in encouraging freedom of expression in a democratic society outweighs any theoretical but unproven benefit of censorship.

For the foregoing reasons, the judgment of the district court is affirmed. *It is so ordered.*

JUSTICE O'CONNOR, with whom The Chief Justice joins, concurring in the judgment in part and dissenting in part.

I write separately to explain why I view the Communications Decency Act of 1996 (CDA) as little more than an attempt by Congress to create "adult zones" on the Internet. Our precedent indicates that the creation of such zones can be constitutionally sound. Despite the soundness of its purpose, however, portions of the CDA are unconstitutional because they stray from the blueprint our prior cases have developed for constructing a "zoning law" that passes constitutional muster.

Appellees bring a facial challenge to three provisions of the CDA. The first, which the Court describes as the "indecency transmission" provision, makes it a crime to knowingly transmit an obscene or indecent message or image to a person the sender knows is under 18 years old. What the Court classifies as a single " 'patently offensive display' " provision is in reality two separate provisions. The first of these makes it a crime to knowingly send a patently offensive message or image to a specific person under the age of 18 ("specific person" provision). The second criminalizes the display of patently offensive messages or images "in a[ny] manner available" to minors ("display" provision). None of these provisions purports to keep indecent (or patently offensive) material away from adults, who have a First Amendment right to obtain this speech. ("Sexual expression which is indecent but not obscene is protected by the First Amendment.") Thus, the undeniable purpose of the CDA is to segregate indecent material on the Internet into certain areas that minors cannot access.

The creation of "adult zones" is by no means a novel concept. States have long denied minors access to certain establishments frequented by adults. States have also denied minors access to speech deemed to be "harmful to minors." The Court has previously sustained such zoning laws, but only if they respect the First Amendment rights of adults and minors. That is to say, a zoning law is valid if (i) it does not unduly restrict adult access to the material; and (ii) minors have no First Amendment right to read or view the banned material. As applied to the Internet as it exists in 1997, the "display" provision and some applications of the "indecency transmission" and "specific person" provisions fail to adhere to the first of these limiting principles by restricting adults' access to protected materials in certain circumstances. Unlike the Court, however, I would invalidate the provisions only in those circumstances.

I

Our cases make clear that a "zoning" law is valid only if adults are still able to obtain the regulated speech. If they cannot, the law does more than simply keep children away from speech they have no right to obtain—it interferes with the rights of adults to obtain constitutionally protected speech and effectively "reduce[s] the adult population . . . to reading only what is fit for children." The First Amendment does not tolerate such interference. . . . If the law does not unduly restrict adults' access to constitutionally protected speech. however, it may be valid. In *Ginsberg* v. *New York* (1968), for example, the Court sustained a New York law that barred store owners from selling pornographic magazines to minors in part because adults could still buy those magazines.

The Court in *Ginsberg* concluded that the New York law created a constitutionally adequate adult zone simply because, on its face, it denied access only to minors. The Court did not question—and therefore necessarily assumed—that an adult zone, once created, would succeed in preserving adults' access while denying minors' access to the regulated speech. Before today, there was no reason to question this assumption, for the Court has previously only considered laws that operated in the physical world, a world with two characteristics that make it possible to create "adult zones": geography and identity. A minor can see an adult dance show only if he enters an establishment that provides such entertainment. And should he attempt to do so, the minor will not be able to conceal completely his identity (or, consequently, his age). Thus, the twin characteristics of geography and identity enable the establishment's proprietor to prevent children from entering the establishment, but to let adults inside.

The electronic world is fundamentally different. Because it is no more than the interconnection of electronic pathways, cyberspace allows speakers and listeners to mask their identities. Cyberspace undeniably reflects some form of geography; chat rooms and Web sites, for example, exist at fixed "locations" on the Internet. Since users can transmit and receive messages on the Internet without revealing anything about their identities or ages however, it is not currently possible to exclude persons from accessing certain messages on the basis of their identity.

Cyberspace differs from the physical world in another basic way: Cyberspace is malleable. Thus, it is possible to construct barriers in cyberspace and use them to screen for identity, making cyberspace more like the physical world and, consequently, more amenable to zoning laws. This transformation of cyberspace is already underway (cyberspace "is moving . . . from a relatively unzoned place to a universe that is extraordinarily well zoned.") Internet speakers (users who post material on the Internet) have begun to zone cyberspace itself through the use of "gateway" technology. Such technology requires Internet users to enter information about themselves—perhaps an adult identification number or a credit card number—before they can access certain areas of cyberspace, much like a bouncer checks a person's driver's license before admitting him to a nightclub. Internet users who access information have not attempted to zone cyberspace itself, but have tried to limit their own power to access information in cyberspace, much as a parent controls what her children watch on television by installing a lock box. This user-based zoning is accomplished through the use of screening software (such as Cyber Patrol or SurfWatch) or browsers with screening capabilities, both of which search addresses and text for keywords that are associated with "adult" sites and, if the user wishes, blocks access to such sites. The Platform for Internet Content Selection (PICS) project is designed to facilitate user-based zoning by encouraging Internet speakers to rate the content of their speech using codes recognized by all screening programs.

Despite this progress, the transformation of cyberspace is not complete. Although gateway technology has been available on the World Wide Web for some time now, it is not available to *all* Web speakers, and is just now becoming technologically feasible for chat rooms and Usenet newsgroups. Gateway technology is not ubiquitous in cyberspace, and because without it "there is no means of age verification," cyberspace still remains largely unzoned—and unzoneable. User-based zoning is also in its infancy. For it to be effective, (i) an agreed-upon code (or "tag") would have to exist; (ii) screening software or browsers with screening capabilities would have to be able to recognize the "tag"; and (iii) those programs would have to be widely available—and widely used—by Internet users. At present, none of these conditions is true. Screening software "is not in wide use today" and "only a handful of browsers have screening capabilities." There is, moreover, no agreed-upon "tag" for those programs to recognize.

Although the prospects for the eventual zoning of the Internet appear promising, I agree with the Court that we must evaluate the constitutionality of the CDA as it applies to the Internet as it exists today. Given the present state of cyberspace, I agree with the Court that the "display" provision cannot pass muster. Until gateway technology is available throughout cyberspace, and it is not in 1997, a speaker cannot be reasonably assured that the speech he displays will reach only adults because it is impossible to confine speech to an "adult zone." Thus, the only way for a speaker to avoid liability under the CDA is to refrain completely from using indecent speech. But this forced silence impinges on the First Amendment right of adults to make and obtain this speech and, for all intents and purposes, "reduce[s] the adult population [on the Internet] to reading only what is fit for children." As a result, the "display" provision cannot withstand scrutiny.

The "indecency transmission" and "specific person" provisions present a closer issue, for they are not unconstitutional in all of their applications. As discussed above, the "indecency transmission" provision makes it a crime to transmit knowingly an indecent message to a person the sender knows is under 18 years of age. The "specific person" provision proscribes the same conduct, although it does not as explicitly require the sender to know that the intended recipient of his indecent message is a minor. Appellant urges the Court to construe the provision to impose such a knowledge requirement, and I would do so. . . .

So construed, both provisions are constitutional as applied to a conversation involving only an adult and one or more minors—e.g., when an adult speaker sends an e-mail knowing the addressee is a minor, or when an adult and minor converse by themselves or with other minors in a chat room. In this context, these provisions are no different from the law we sustained in *Ginsberg*. Restricting what the adult may say to the minors in no way restricts the adult's ability to communicate with other adults. He is not prevented from speaking indecently to other adults in a chat room (because there are no other adults participating in the conversation) and he remains free to send indecent e-mails to other adults. The relevant universe contains only one adult, and the adult in that universe has the power to refrain from using indecent speech and consequently to keep all such speech within the room in an "adult" zone.

The analogy to *Ginsberg* breaks down, however, when more than one adult is a party to the conversation. If a minor enters a chat room otherwise occupied by adults, the CDA effectively requires the adults in the room to stop using indecent speech. If they did not, they could be prosecuted under the "indecency transmission" and "specific person" provisions for any indecent statements they make to the group, since they would be transmitting an indecent message to specific persons, one of whom is a minor. The CDA is therefore akin to a law that makes it a crime for a bookstore owner to sell pornographic magazines to anyone once a minor enters his store. Even assuming such a law might be constitutional in the physical world as a reasonable alternative to excluding minors completely from the store, the absence of any means of excluding minors from chat rooms in cyberspace restricts the rights of adults to engage in indecent speech in those rooms. The "indecency transmission" and "specific person" provisions share this defect.

But these two provisions do not infringe on adults' speech in *all* situations. And as discussed below, I do not find that the provisions are overbroad in the sense that they restrict minors' access to a substantial amount of speech that minors have the right to read and view. Accordingly, the CDA can be applied constitutionally in some situations. Normally, this fact would require the Court to reject a direct facial challenge. ("A facial challenge to a legislative Act [succeeds only if] the challenger . . . establish[es] that no set of circumstances exists under which the Act would be valid.") Appellees' claim arises under the First Amendment, however, and they argue that the CDA is facially invalid because it is "substantially overbroad"—that is, it "sweeps too broadly . . . [and] penaliz[es] a substantial amount of speech that is constitutionally protected." I agree with the Court that the provisions are overbroad in that they cover any and all communications between adults and minors, regardless of how many adults might be part of the audience to the communication.

This conclusion does not end the matter, however. Where, as here, "the parties challenging the statute are those who desire to engage in protected speech that the overbroad statute purports to punish . . . [t]he statute may forthwith be declared invalid to the extent that it reaches too far, but otherwise left intact." There is no question that Congress intended to prohibit certain communications between one adult and one or more minors. See 47 U.S. C. A. §223(a)(1)(B) (May 1996 Supp.) (punishing "[w]hoever . . . initiates the transmission of [any indecent communication] knowingly that the recipient of the communication is under 18 years of age"); §223(d)(1)(A) (punishing "[w]hoever . . . send[s] to a specific person or persons under 18 years of age [a patently offensive message]"). There is also no question that Congress would have enacted a narrower version of these provisions had it known a broader version would be declared unconstitutional. ("If . . . the application [of any provision of the CDA] to any person or circumstance is held invalid, . . . the application of such provision to other persons or circumstances shall not be affected thereby"). I would therefore sustain the indecency transmission" and "specific person" provisions to the extent they apply to the transmission of Internet communications where the party initiating the communication knows that all of the recipients are minors.

II

Whether the CDA substantially interferes with the First Amendment rights of minors, and thereby runs afoul of the second characteristic of valid zoning laws, presents a closer question. In *Ginsberg,* the New York law we sustained prohibited the sale to minors of magazines that were "harmful to minors." Under that law, a magazine was "harmful to minors only if it was obscene as to minors. Noting that obscene speech is not protected by the First Amendment, *Roth* v. *United States* (1957), and that New York was constitutionally free to adjust the definition of obscenity for minors, the Court concluded that the law did not "invad[e] the area of freedom of expression constitutionally secured to minors." New York therefore did not infringe upon the First Amendment rights of minors.

The Court neither "accept[s] nor reject[s]" the argument that the CDA is facially overbroad because it substantially interferes with the First Amendment rights of minors. I would reject it. *Ginsberg* established that minors may constitutionally be denied access to material that is obscene as to minors. As *Ginsberg* explained, material is obscene as to minors if it (i) is "patently offensive to prevailing standards in the adult community as a whole with respect to what is suitable . . . for minors"; (ii) appeals to the prurient interest of minors; and (iii) is "utterly without redeeming social importance for minors." Because the CDA denies minors the right to obtain material that is "patently offensive"—even if it has some redeeming value for minors and even if it does not appeal to their prurient interests—Congress' rejection of the Ginsberg "harmful to minors" standard means that the CDA could ban some speech that is "indecent" (i.e., "patently offensive") but that is not obscene as to minors.

I do not deny this possibility, but to prevail in a facial challenge, it is not enough for a plaintiff to show "some" overbreadth. Our cases require a proof of "real" and "substantial" overbreadth, and appellees have not carried their burden in this case. In my view, the universe of speech constitutionally protected as to minors but banned by the CDA—i.e., the universe of material that is "patently offensive," but which nonetheless has some redeeming value for minors or does not appeal to their prurient interest—is a very small one. Appellees cite no examples of speech falling within this universe and do not attempt to explain why that universe is substantial "in relation to the statute's plainly legitimate sweep." That the CDA might deny minors the right to obtain material that has some "value" is largely beside the point. While discussions about prison rape or nude art may have some redeeming education value for *adults,* they do not necessarily have any such value for *minors,* and under *Ginsberg,* minors only have a First Amendment right to obtain patently offensive material that has "redeeming social importance *for minors"* (emphasis added). There is also no evidence in the record to support the contention that "many [e]-mail transmissions from an adult to a minor are conversations between family members," and no support for the legal proposition that such speech is absolutely immune from regulation. Accordingly, in my view, the CDA does not burden a substantial amount of minors' constitutionally protected speech.

Thus, the constitutionality of the CDA as a zoning law hinges on the extent to which it substantially interferes with the First Amendment rights of adults. Because the rights of adults are infringed only by the "display" provision and by the "indecency transmission" and "specific person" provisions as applied to communications involving more than one adult, I would invalidate the CDA only to that extent. Insofar as the "indecency transmission" and "specific person" provisions prohibit the use of indecent speech in communications between an adult and one or more minors, however, they can and should be sustained. The Court reaches a contrary conclusion, and from that holding that I respectfully dissent.

3

Commentary:
The Communications Decency Act[*]

Sen. Jim Exon

The Exon-Coats Communications Decency Act stands for the simple premise that it is wrong to provide pornography to children on computers just as it is wrong to do it on a street corner or anywhere else. The three-judge panel that ruled against our law ignored previous court rulings that have upheld that simple notion, as well as other well-established laws that protect children from indecent material over a telephone, on radio and television, or cable. The ruling clears the way for a final decision by the U.S. Supreme Court.

It is important to understand what the Decency Act is and what it is not. The Decency Act makes it a crime to knowingly use a telecommunications device or interactive computer to send an indecent material in a manner accessible to a child. The new law does not ban any constitutionally protected material from adults.

From the *Federal Communications Law Journal* 49, no. 1 (November 1996): 95–97. Reprinted by permission.

*This commentary was written after the three-judge Philadelphia District Court ruled that provisions of the Communications Decency Act abridged the "freedom of speech" protected by the First Amendment, but before the U.S. Supreme Court upheld that judgment.

If someone let a child browse freely through an adult bookstore or an X-rated video arcade, I suspect and hope that most people would call the police to arrest that person. Yet, these very offenses occur every day in America's electronic neighborhoods. A child can get on the information superhighway and freely ride to on-line "red light" districts that contain some of the most perverse and depraved pornographic material available.

The Philadelphia court found that there were no effective measures to determine the age of computer users. This technological argument is faulty because as a relatively new medium, the Internet and other interactive computer services are infinitely changeable and their architecture does and can accommodate child screening. The court overlooks that a number of Internet sites already block child access by requiring credit card or adult PIN numbers like those used for automatic teller machines to access certain sites. Even if such technology were not available, the statute does not require those who traffic in electronic pornography to do the impossible—only what is "reasonable, effective, and appropriate."

The second line of criticism was with the law's "indecency" standard. The Philadelphia court found the term "indecency" and its rendition in the statute to be vague. The court brushed aside years of U.S. Supreme Court rulings which not only found the indecency standard sufficiently clear, but which applied that very standard to radio, television, telephone, and cable use. Here, the court's disagreement does not seem to be with the Congress but with the U.S. Supreme Court which has repeatedly upheld the indecency standard.

The definition of indecency contained in the new law applies to material that is "in context, patently offensive, and depicts or describes sexual or excretory activities or organs." In other words, what goes behind the counter in the convenience store should be restricted to *adults only* on the Internet as well. The Philadelphia court overlooks that no court has applied the indecency standard to prohibit serious works of art, literature, or medical information. In this regard, the court feasted on a plate of red herrings.

Congress took great care to craft the law so that it zeroed in on protecting children from indecency, as the U.S. Supreme Court has repeatedly acknowledged as a compelling state interest. Congress modeled the statute after the existing dial-a-porn law which allows telephone sex services to ply their wares to adults but prohibits access by minors. The U.S. Supreme Court has already found that the dial-a-porn law does not violate the First Amendment. Adult material which is otherwise legal would still be available to adults. The Decency Act is clear and cannot be violated by accident. There must be a knowing violation and the material must be patently (that is obviously) offensive by contemporary community standards.

It is true that since our law was proposed, various software programs have been developed to block some pornographic material and I am pleased the computer industry finally agreed there is a problem. But it is also true that this software can't block everything. And shouldn't the person who knowingly gives pornography to a child be held responsible under the law? I say the answer is yes.

The Philadelphia court ignores that it is fundamentally wrong to knowingly give pornography to children or to display pornography in a public place. Some opponents of the Decency Act seem to rationalize that the framers of the Constitution plotted at great length to make certain that the profiteering pornographer, the pervert, and the pedophile would be free to practice their pursuits in the presence of children on a taxpayer-created and subsidized computer network.

If there is anything positive that came from this ruling in Philadelphia, it is that it was so radical and so sweeping in ignoring existing laws and previous court ruling that it will crumble under Supreme Court scrutiny. I am hopeful that the high court, relying on its own precedents, will find the Decency Act to be constitutional. As one editorial writer recently put it, it is a weak society indeed that cannot find some constitutional way to protect its kids.

4

Statement on the Supreme Court's Decision Declaring Unconstitutional the Communications Decency Act

Sen. Pat Leahy

Today, the Supreme Court unanimously struck down as unconstitutional the so-called Communications Decency Act. This law would have effectively banned "indecent" or "patently offensive" speech from the Internet, no matter its political, literary, artistic or scientific value and no matter that the speech is between consenting adults.

The Supreme Court posed the right question: "Could a speaker confidently assume that a serious discussion about birth control practices, homosexuality, . . . or the consequences of prison rape would not violate the CDA? This uncertainty undermines the likelihood that the CDA has been carefully tailored to the congressional goal of protecting minors from potentially harmful materials."

As a recent editorial in Vermont's *Times Argus* succinctly noted: "To obey this law, Internet users would have to avoid discussing matters routinely covered in books, magazines, and newspapers. Who would want to drive on that kind of information superhighway?"

The Supreme Court has made clear that we do not forfeit our First Amendment rights when we go on-line. This decision is a landmark in the history of the Internet and a firm foundation for its future growth. Altering

---

This chapter originally appeared as a June 26, 1997 press release.

the protections of the First Amendment for on-line communications would
have crippled this new mode of communication.

This ruling comes as a vindication for the fifteen members of the Senate who joined with me to vote against the CDA. Too many members feared the demagogic syllogism that if they voted against a censorship law purporting to protect children, they must be in favor of exposing children to inappropriate violent or pornographic material. This is a false syllogism.

I prosecuted child abusers as State's Attorney in Vermont and have worked my entire professional life to protect children from those who would prey on them. The sixteen of us who voted against the Communications Decency Act did not vote in favor of child pornography and none among us would defend child pornographers.

On the contrary, we all want to protect our children from indecent and inappropriate materials, whether that material is broadcast over the airwaves, carried over cable lines, or transmitted to our computer screens. But there are better ways to target offenders. We have a duty to ensure that the means we use to protect our children do not do more harm than good.

The Supreme Court's ruling today is no victory for child pornography:
It is a triumph for the First Amendment.

We can spend much time and energy in Congress trying to out-muscle each other to the most popular position on regulating the content of television programs or Internet offerings, and from all appearances, we probably will. We should take heed of the Supreme Court's decision today, however, and be wary of efforts to jump into regulating the content of any form of speech.

Congress did jump when confronted with the CDA. The Supreme Court takes pains in its decision to note at least three times in its opinion that this law was brought as an amendment on the floor of the Senate and passed as part of the Telecommunications Act, without the benefit of hearings, findings, or considered deliberation.

As the Supreme Court noted in its decision, I cautioned against such speedy action at the time. Not surprisingly, the end result was passage of an unconstitutional law.

Mixing government and politics with free speech issues often produces a corrosive concoction that erodes our constitutional freedoms. Even well-intentioned laws for the protection of children deserve close examination to ensure that we are not stepping over constitutional lines. The Supreme Court stated:

> we have repeatedly recognized the governmental interest in protecting
> children from harmful materials. . . . But that interest does not justify an

unnecessarily broad suppression of speech addressed to adults. As we have explained, the Government may not "reduc[e] the adult population . . . to . . . only what is fit for children."

We should not be substituting the government's judgment for that of parents about what is appropriate for their children to access on-line. The Supreme Court pointed out excellent examples of how the CDA would have operated to do just that, stating:

> Under the CDA, a parent allowing her seventeen-year-old to use the family computer to obtain information on the Internet that she, in her parental judgment, deems appropriate could face a lengthy prison term. . . . Similarly, a parent who sent his seventeen-year-old college freshman information on birth control via e-mail could be incarcerated even though neither he, his child, or anyone in their home community, found the material "indecent" or "patently offensive," if the college town's community thought otherwise.

I attended the Supreme Court argument on the so-called Communications Decency Act and was concerned when several of the Justices asked about the "severability" clause in the CDA: They wanted to know how much of the statute could be stricken as unconstitutional and how much could be left standing. The majority of the Supreme Court resisted the temptation to do the job of Congress and judicially rewrite the "indecency" and "patently offensive" provisions of the CDA to be constitutional. The Court stated, "This Court 'will not rewrite a . . . law to conform it to constitutional requirements.' "

It is our job to write constitutional laws that address the needs and concerns of Americans. On this issue, our work is not done. There is no lack of criminal laws on the books to protect children on-line, including laws criminalizing the on-line distribution of child pornography and obscene materials and prohibiting the on-line harassment, luring, and solicitation of children for illegal sexual activity. Protecting children, whether in cyberspace or physical space, depends on aggressively enforcing these existing laws and supervising children to ensure they do not venture where the environment is unsafe. This will do more—and more effectively—than passing feel-good, unconstitutional legislation.

But, as I said, our work is not done. The CDA became law because of the genuine concern of many Americans about the inappropriate material unquestionably accessible to computer-savvy children over the Internet. Parents, teachers, librarians, content providers, on-line service providers, and policy-makers need to come together to find effective ways to address this concern. I have long believed that we need to put the emphasis where it would be most effective: on parental and user empowerment tools to control the information that children may access on-line. I applaud the efforts already underway to bring concerned groups together to define steps we can take to make the on-line world a comfortable one for families.

One of the continuing challenges we will face in making the best use of our burgeoning information technologies is in adding value to all that they offer. Anyone who uses the Internet knows that there is a lot of junk out there. For example, students searching for background on the Holocaust may easily come across diatribes on the Internet claiming that the Holocaust never happened. In our classrooms, in our homes, in our libraries, we must teach our children to be discerning users of this powerful new tool.

We are blessed in the United States to enjoy the oldest and most effective constitutional protections of free speech anywhere. The struggle facing succeeding generations of Americans in preserving free speech liberties often is difficult, and it means standing firm in the face of sometimes fleeting but usually intense political pressures. The United States is in the vanguard of grappling with these issues, and the world is watching closely to see how we resolve them.

What we have to offer is the capability and the temperament to show the world how the Internet can be used to its fullest. We must not succumb to short-sighted political pressures by adopting a model of censorship.

The administration has acknowledged the importance of American leadership against efforts springing up around the globe to censor and control the content of the information accessible on the Internet in its white paper called "A Framework for Global Electronic Commerce." To support the "broadest possible free flow of information across international borders," the administration will seek to "promote the use of industry . . . self-regulation and rating systems, and technical solutions to empower parents and other users to resolve contentious access issues (e.g., children's access and violence)."

Vigilant defense of freedom of thought, opinion, and speech will be crucially important as the Internet graduates from infancy and on to adolescence and maturity. Giving full-force to the First Amendment on-line is a victory for the First Amendment, for American technology, and for democracy.

5

You Figure It Out

William F. Buckley Jr.

The most recent objection to the Communications Decency Act was filed on Monday by Microsoft, the American Library Association, and the Society for Professional Journalists. Their arguments are much the same as those of the American Civil Liberties Union filed about eight minutes after the bill was signed by President Clinton. And days after that, the District Court in Philadelphia estopped enforcement of the Act on the grounds that the word "decency" was insufficiently defined. Argument will proceed.

Here are points to consider in this rerun of the *People* v. *Obscenity,* in which Obscenity regularly wins.

1. The vote in the House was 414 to 16 in favor of the Act. In the Senate, 91 to 5. And of course, President Clinton signed it. That's 506 out of 527 human beings all of whom swore to uphold the Constitution of the United States. Yet learned and experienced men and women who oppose the Act merely laugh at any suggestion that they actually did believe the Act to be constitutional. Specifically, Ira Glasser, the Executive Director of the ACLU, and Susan Estrich, Professor of Law at the University of Southern California, who eight years ago managed the presidential campaign of Michael Dukakis. What's going on here?

2. By way of background, what sometimes is lumped in under obscenity is three categories of material. One is erotica: literature or art intended to arouse sexual desire (*American Heritage Dictionary*). A second is pornography: pictures, writing, or other material that is sexually explicit (*AHD*). A third is perversity. This is the stuff of the Marquis de Sade.

3. Perversity is every now and then stopped. A few weeks ago, the felony conviction of Robert and Carleen Thomas was upheld. Their gig was something called Amateur Action, a computer bulletin board that advertised itself as The Nastiest Place on Earth, and featured graphic images of children raped by their parents, and other stuff the fingers balk at even typing.

But the ACLU takes the position that the First Amendment protects any "speech." And indeed it does, but the great swindle of the century has been the transmutation of obscenity into "speech." The absolutists go a long way: burning the American flag is a form of speech, they tell you. This would be understandable if the person protesting American policy were blind and dumb and had available to him to express himself on Capitol Hill only a box of matches and a few American flags. This is not to say that the lines between erotica and pornography or pornography and perversion are clearly drawn, but neither is the line clearly drawn that demands "reasonable" compliance with various provisions of the law.

4. Perspectives change, and they have changed during the past fifty years in the direction of promiscuity. In the early sixties reasonable people differed on whether *Fanny Hill* was obscene (Answer: of course it's obscene, and it's a delight). During the sixties, Simone de Beauvoir was pleading the "right" to read the Marquis de Sade ("Must We Burn de Sade?"). So that the question became muddled: Ought works of obscenity and even perversion be permitted to exist (i.e., should they not be burned?); or, as was the case in France for 175 years, is the work of de Sade something that should be kept in the libraries for the edification of those whose business it is to probe the forlorn atolls of twisted minds?

5. Leaving us with the Internet. There are obscenity laws that apply to television broadcasting, though they are lax; and to radio; and, as a matter of fact, to telephone lines. The philosophical postulate here is that the air is public property and government has custodial responsibilities over that which belongs to the people, who can through their representatives define toxicity as more merely than particulates emitted by asbestos, or whatever. The Communications Decency Act is aimed at protecting children, and prosecutions under it are supposed to bear the burden of proving that the smut-merchants had every reason to believe that children would be tapping in on their product. The lawyers call this *scienter,* knowingly. But the ACLU is correct here that whatever one's hopes for Internet-style V-chips that would

block out noxious web sites, there can't be any assurance that the horny six-teen-year-old isn't going to succeed in tapping in on that stuff.

In which event you may have a law that is unenforceable, but does that make it unconstitutional?

6

Zoned Out

Jeffrey Rosen

Spring fever is in the air at the Supreme Court as the justices prepare to hear arguments about the constitutionality of the Communications Decency Act on March 19. To familiarize themselves with the technological obstacles to finding pornography in cyberspace, some law clerks have obtained lists of especially salacious addresses on the World Wide Web and diligently browsed at their leisure. Not since the justices gathered to watch dirty movies in the basement of the Court during the 1960s (Justice Harlan, almost blind, asked his clerks to narrate as the action unfolded) have clerkly duties been quite so arduous.

In cyberspace, too, the mood is giddy. "WHY WE'LL WIN" boasts the website of the Electronic Frontier Foundation; and, indeed, there is a widespread expectation that the justices, in *ACLU* v. *Reno,* will agree with the three district court judges in Philadelphia who struck down the Communications Decency Act last June. But the triumphalism is premature. In light of technological and legal changes over the past year, there is now a plausible argument for *upholding* the constitutionality of the CDA that a majority of the Court might find convincing. In capsule form, here it is.

The CDA has two parts. The first part says, in effect, that if you display "indecent" or "patently offensive" material on the Internet, "in a manner available to a person under 18 years of age," you are a criminal. The second part says that you have a defense to prosecution if you take "reasonable, effective, and appropriate actions" to restrict access to minors, by "requiring use of a verified credit card, debit account, adult access code, or adult personal identification number."

The best argument for upholding this electronic Comstockery can be summed up in a single world: zoning. Solicitor General Walter Dellinger, in his brief, and Lawrence Lessig of the University of Chicago, in a series of powerful articles, urge us to view the CDA as an Internet zoning ordinance that channels indecent material away from children while guaranteeing full access to adults. First Amendment law recognizes three categories of sexually explicit speech: obscenity, which can be banned; ordinary speech, which must be protected; and indecency, which can be restricted for children but not for adults. In its zoning cases, the Court has said that government can move porn shops to red light districts, where children can't easily find them, or require porn sellers to check identification before selling over the counter.

In cyberspace, of course, it's much harder to discriminate on the basis of age. Users are anonymous, and teenage boys don't have to wear stilts and a mustache to disguise the fact that they are teenage boys. Just as clustering porn shops near the docks is a permissible way of discouraging crime and sloth in residential neighborhoods, the argument goes, putting porn behind electronic doors is a permissible way of ensuring that the Internet is the kind of neighborhood that parents will let their children enter in the first place.

When the three judges in Philadelphia rejected the zoning argument last June, they assumed that individual speakers on the Internet would have to set up their own adult identification sites to avoid prosecution, a prospect they found "either technologically impossible or economically prohibitive." But, since last June, the technology has changed in response to the market. Services with names like "Adult Check" and "Porno Press" now provide adult identification numbers to individual Internet users for a one-time fee of $9.95, charged to a credit card; the number then serves as a "key" that provides easy access to all the Internet sites that put up the "gates" required by the CDA. This system is no longer "economically prohibitive" for the Internet sites that use it; on the contrary, "Adult Check" actually *pays* the sites a fee for each user they refer.

So the age verification system doesn't appear to be an insuperable burden for porn suppliers. Is it an unconstitutional burden for adult porn consumers? The answer isn't obvious. Obtaining an adult identification number requires some effort, a minimal fee, a credit card or money order, and the associated stigma of having the fee show up on your credit card bill. In the future, civil liberties organizations might set up their own adult verification sites to minimize the stigma—you could order your password from "ACLU check" rather than "Adult Check"—but consumers of porn would still have to identify themselves as consumers of porn. (Today, by contrast, free samples can be downloaded anonymously from the Web and from Usenet newsgroups.) Whether the embarrassment of this act of self-identification is comparable to the embarrassment of being observed by your neighbors sneaking out of an adult bookstore is hard to say. In an adult bookstore, at least, you can wear dark glasses and pay cash to protect your anonymity. If the Court decides, in the end, that the disincentives created by the adult identification system would greatly restrict the ability of adults to buy *Playboy,* it should probably strike down the CDA. But, because the Internet has vastly diminished the opportunity costs associated with buying porn (you no longer need to drive from Cincinnati to Kentucky, for example), the justices might reasonably conclude that the burdens of an adult I.D. are comparatively small.

The opponents of the CDA have another argument along the same lines. An adult identification system isn't the "least restrictive means" of keeping porn out of the hands of children, they argue, because there's a less restrictive, and more effective, technology available: the Platform for Internet Content Selection, or PICS. PICS is a rating and filtering technology, like the V-chip, that permits content providers, or third-party interest groups, to set up their own private rating systems for any "PICS-compatible" document that is posted online. Individual users can then choose the rating system that best reflects their own values, and any material that offends them will be blocked from their homes.

The ACLU praises PICS for allowing individual users to exercise perfect choice about what comes into their homes. Lawrence Lessig, by contrast, suggests that "PICS is the devil," from a free speech perspective, because it allows censorship at any point on the chain of distribution. Countries like China or Singapore, or American corporations afraid of lawsuits, can decide what kind of speech they want to make available to their workers, and impose draconian restrictions from above. In the long run, Lessig suggests, PICS will suppress more speech than an adult identification system would, because it will allow those who control access to individual terminals to filter out uncongenial ideas. But for the Supreme Court to accept this as a constitutional argument would require it to embrace a collectivist view of the First Amendment, which says that citizens should be exposed to a diversity of views, whether they want to be or not. If, on the other hand, you believe that the First Amendment is more concerned with preventing government from restricting the autonomy of individual speakers, then PICS seems less intrusive than checking IDs.

Up until now, I've been discussing the CDA as if its language about "indecent" or "patently offensive" material, "as measured by contemporary community standards" that "depicts or describes sexual or excretory activities or organs," refers only to the kind of sexually explicit speech that the Supreme Court has said can be restricted for children. The Clinton Justice Department has tried to support this view by announcing that it will enforce the statute only against commercial pornographers. But this is hardly the most natural reading of the statute. In striking down the CDA, two of the three judges in Philadelphia held that the phrases "indecent" and "patently offensive" are unconstitutionally vague and might inhibit speech that has nothing to do with pornography, such as discussion groups about gay rights or Joyce's *Ulysses.*

The vagueness argument, however, is hard to sustain in light of an unfortunate Supreme Court opinion handed down on June 28, 1996, several weeks after the Philadelphia decision. Justice Stephen Breyer, joined by three of his colleagues, held that the Cable Television Consumer Protection Act, which permits cable operators to ban programming that depicts "sexual or excretory activities or organs in a patently offensive manner," is vague but not "impermissably vague." The "patently offensive" language for defining indecency, Breyer held breezily, was "similar" (although not identical) to the Supreme Court's test for defining obscenity; and Breyer concluded that Congress intended to prohibit "pictures of oral sex, bestiality and rape, and not . . . scientific or educational programs (at least unless done with a highly unusual lack of concern for viewer reaction)."

The imprecision of Breyer's analysis threatens to confuse an already confused area of the law. But, in light of Breyer's holding that the government has a compelling interest in shielding children from "indecent" speech, it will be hard to argue that the identical language in the CDA is unconstitutionally vague.

Opponents can try to argue that the amorphous "indecency" standard is especially inappropriate for cyberspace, where everyone is a broadcaster, but not everyone has a lawyer. (In real space, there are just a few broadcasters, and all of them have lawyers.) Moreover, the category of "indecency" was cobbled together because of the uniquely intrusive qualities of television, and on the Internet it's easier to protect children with electronic gateways. But this ends up being an argument in favor of the CDA, not against it.

Justice Breyer's indulgent view of the Cable Television Act shows the hazards of constitutional pragmatism. He criticized his colleagues for lacking the "flexibility necessary to allow government to respond to very serious practical problems," such as protecting children from indecency. But he failed to consider the degree to which the distinctions between indecency, pornography, and obscenity are increasingly unstable in a global information age. Cable television and the Internet have called into question the distinction between pornography and obscenity by exposing the incoherence of geographically identifiable "community standards": Especially in cyberspace, it's unrealistic to expect individual speakers to be able to predict the standards of the thousands of communities that their words and pictures may enter without their consent. It wouldn't be inconsistent with recent trends in law and technology for the Court to uphold the Communications Decency Act. It would, however, be a mistake.

7

Give Me Liberty, but Don't Give Me Filth

An Interview with Robert Bork
by Michael Cromartie

Almost a decade after his bitterly contested nomination to the U.S. Supreme Court, Robert H. Bork remains one of America's most prominent legal theorists. His ordeal transformed him into a public figure and an outspoken observer of American political, legal, and cultural life. With the recent publication of his *Slouching Towards Gomorrah: Modern Liberalism and American Decline* (Regan Books/HarperCollins, 1996), Bork, who taught constitutional law at Yale Law School, attempts to chart our nation's transformation into a culture that rewards self-gratification and equality without merit. Describing himself as a "generic Protestant," he warns that "large chunks of the moral life of the United States have disappeared altogether, and more are in the process of extinction."

Christianity Today advisory editor Michael Cromartie visited with Bork in his Washington office at the American Enterprise Institute, where Bork is the John H. Olin Scholar in Legal Studies.

Your book describes the role the Supreme Court has played in promoting cultural decline in America. How has that happened?

This interview first appeared in *Christianity Today* (May 19, 1997): 28–29. Reprinted by permission of Michael Cromartie.

Consider *Cohen* v. *California* (1971), a case in which a young man wore a jacket into a courthouse that had obscenities written on the back that suggested performing an implausible sexual act with the Selective Service System. He was arrested, and the Supreme Court said he couldn't be convicted. One of the reasons given was "Who was to say what was obscene?" The majority opinion actually said, "One man's vulgarity is another man's lyric." If you want radical individualism and moral relativism, there you are.

You write that "Sooner or later censorship is going to have to be considered as popular culture continues plunging to ever more sickening lows." Are you advocating censorship?

Yes.

What fine distinctions do you make?

I don't make any fine distinctions; I'm just advocating censorship. It's odd that we've grown so sensitive about the topic of censorship that if somebody mentions it everybody begins to shake all over and say, "Oh my! That's an unthinkable thought." We had censorship in this country up until the last couple of decades. Almost all of our national existence we had censorship. When I was practicing law in Chicago as a young lawyer, the city of Chicago had a censorship board for movies. It didn't suppress any good art, it didn't eliminate any ideas; but it did keep a certain amount of filth out of the theaters.

How would this censorship actually work?

We don't have to guess how censorship would work; we've seen it work. It's just like any other law. You get the elected representatives to write a code about what is obscene and can be prohibited, and then an executive branch official applies the code to some instance. If the person involved thinks the code has been misapplied, or that the code itself is defective, he goes to the courts for relief. Unfortunately, the Supreme Court, in the service of radical individualism (I am talking about *Cohen* v. *California*), has set up three tests you have to get through to prosecute obscenity, and it's almost impossible to satisfy those three tests. The Court became very nervous about allowing any prohibition of offensive sexual acts in public, though as recently as 1942 the Court said unanimously that of course there was no constitutional problem with barring the lewd, the profane, or the obscene, because they weren't ideas.

Therefore they weren't protected by the free-speech clause?

That's right. The original meaning of the speech clause was the protection of ideas and the circulation of ideas, not the protection of self-gratification through pornography and other stuff. In fact, in the early cases, the pornographers, when they were prosecuted, didn't even raise the First Amendment, because nobody thought it was relevant. I think that's a big cultural shift the Court has worked on us.

What would the response be from an ACLU lawyer?

You are inhibiting my liberty and my right to express myself. And the answer to that is yes, that is precisely what we are after. We're talking almost entirely about obscenity in various forms. We're not talking about anything else.

The fact is, we have a hard time censoring parts of rap music that are so obviously detrimental to African-American culture.

It's detrimental to everybody's culture. Some of those rappers are white, and 75 percent of the best-selling rap records are sold to white suburban teenagers. Which tells you a couple of things, one of them being the collapse of moral courage. Where are their parents? Why haven't they said to them, "Get that staff out of here and don't ever listen to it again"? They don't.

Some have argued that moral and cultural decline or renewal are not really affected by the law or by politics. Do you agree?

Politics is not the same as culture. Even if we had a conservative President and a conservative Congress, that would not affect what is taking place in the universities, in Hollywood, the network news, and so forth. Politics has an indirect bearing on culture, because a president, for example, can use the bully pulpit of the presidency to influence attitudes. Whether he can influence them more than the universities and television is a highly dubious proposition.

On "life issues," you've had some evolution in your own thinking. You now see them as crucial core issues. How have your views changed?

I describe in the book that my view has changed because I had just never thought about abortion much. I lived in a culture where people took abortion for granted—a little inconvenient because it was illegal, but there was nothing immoral about it. It wasn't until much later that I came to realize that this was not just a lump of tissue but an individual human being, that I began to get nervous and my view began to change.

You explain that changing our views on abortion will also affect the way we look at many other things.

This, I think, is a society and culture that increasingly values the convenience of the individual above all else, which is another way of saying radical individualism or radical autonomy. Having children is often inconvenient. I cite the figures that the reasons women give for having an abortion show that over 90 percent of abortions are for convenience, not for any medical problem or for any other problem; 43 percent of them are repeat abortions, so it's mainly a birth-control device.

Now, of course, we're moving on to assisted suicide and euthanasia, which is presented as a way of allowing people to die with dignity and not in agony. But the fact is that most of them will have nothing to do with that. Even most of Kevorkian's patients are not terminally ill. (I guess you can't call them "patients"—Kevorkian's "subjects.") Most of the people who will be killed under assisted suicide will not necessarily be terminally ill; they will be people who are burdens on their families. As I say in the book, people tend to be inconvenient at both ends of their lives. We kill them in the womb, and then we kill them in the nursing home.

Can this culture in decline turn itself around?

I'm sure it can, but whether it will is a much harder question. The signs aren't good. I think if enough people who are aware of the kind of thing I describe in the book—that our culture is in decline in almost every area, from popular music to religion—and if they realized there was a common cause to this, they might begin to resist what is happening. When I say "resist," I don't mean trying to elect a president or anything as grand as that. They might try to resist it in their public schools, they might try to resist it in their church, they might try to resist it in the universities where they work. By and large, the people who are making this cultural attack are a minority, even in the universities. But they are activists, and they control the dialogue.

The other thing is that there may be signs of a religious renewal in this country. It's not quite clear that there is, but Promise Keepers clearly reflects a religious impulse. The evangelical movement is certainly growing stronger. And one can hope that the more orthodox people in Catholicism, Protestantism, and Judaism will stiffen their spines and do battle in those denominations.

8

Slouching Towards Gomorrah

Robert H. Bork

Technology is now bringing worse material than we have ever seen or imagined, and, as technology develops further, the material will become still worse. The Internet now provides users access to what Simon Winchester calls "an untrammeled, uncontrolled, wholly liberated ocean of information."[1] He thought it wonderful. Then one day he came upon a category called alt.sex, which has fifty-five groups including alt.sex.anal, alt.sex. intergen (intergenerational: the pedophile bulletin board), alt.sex.snuff (the killing of the victim) which includes subcategories for bestiality, torture, bloodletting, and sadistic injury.

The first category Winchester tried was alt.sex.stories, which contained a story about the kidnapping of two children. The castration of the six-year-old boy is "reported in loving detail" and occurs before he is shot. The seven-year-old girl is then repeatedly raped by nine men before having her nipples cut off and her throat slashed. There were two hundred such stories and the number was growing daily. "You want tales of fathers sodomizing their three-year-old daughters, or of mothers performing fellatio on their prepubescent sons, or of girls coupling with horses, or of the giving of enemas to child virgins? Then you need do no more than visit the newsgroup that is named 'alt.sex.stories' and all will reliably be there, 24 hours a day, for everyone with a computer and a telephone, anywhere on (or above) the face of the earth."[2] The stories are written by pseudonymous authors and are filtered through two or three computers so that the authors and the points of origin are not known. The material is not only disgusting, it is a dangerous incitement. There is, for example: "A long and graphic account of exactly how and at what hour you wait outside a girls' school, how best to bundle a seven-year-old into your van, whether to tell her at the start of her ordeal that she is going to be killed at the end of it . . . how best to tie her down, which aperture to approach first, and with what—such things can only tempt those who verge on such acts to take a greater interest in them."[3]

Users can download pornographic pictures as well as prose from the Internet. And there is a lot of both available. The demand, moreover, is for material that can't be easily found elsewhere—pedophilia, sadomasochism, eroticized urination, defecation, and vaginal and rectal fisting. Among the most popular are sex acts with a wide variety of animals, nude children, and incest. The adult bulletin board service describes videos for sale and also provides over 25,000 pictures. The material is too obscene to be quoted here, but it involves girls defecating, girls eating feces (in both cases far more obscene language is used), oral sex with animals. One video is described as "Rape, torture, pussy nailed to table." It is impossible in short compass to give an adequate idea of the depravity that is being sold, apparently profitably.

The Internet, Stephen Bates informs us, offers plans for making bombs, instructions for painless suicide, the anti-Semitic forgery *Protocols of the Elders of Zion* (compressed for faster downloading), and racist diatribes, along with sexual perversion. There are certain to be offline harms from this material. "Pedophiles will abuse children they first met online, kids will blow off fingers with [the] Net's bomb recipes, despondent teens will poison themselves using recipes from *alt.suicide.holiday.* Maybe all these tragedies would have occurred without the Net, but that's tough to prove."[4] It would be even tougher to prove that this material has any social value. Only the most radical individualism imaginable could countenance these uses of the Internet.

What Winchester says of the alt.sex.stories he read is true of these other categories of prose and images: "Surely such essays tell the thinker of forbidden thoughts that there exists somewhere out there a like-minded group of men for whom such things are really not so bad, the enjoyment of which, if no one is so ill-starred as to get caught, can be limitless. Surely it is naive folly—or, the other end of the spectrum, gross irresponsibility—to suppose otherwise."[5]

But the situation is likely to get still worse than this. The pornographic video industry is now doing billions of dollars' worth of business and volume is increasing rapidly.[6] Companies are acquiring inventories of videos for cable television, and a nationwide chain of pornographic video retail stores is in the works. This may, however, be only a transitional phase. George Gilder predicts that computers will soon replace television, allowing viewers to call up digital films and files of whatever they may desire from around the world. He discounts the idea that "liberated children [will] rush away from the network nurse, chasing Pied Piper pederasts, snuff-film sadists, and other trolls of cyberspace."[7] (The "network nurse," as a matter of fact, looks increasingly like a lady of the evening.) The computer will give everyone his own channel to do with as he wishes, and Gilder predicts a spectacular proliferation of programs on specialized cultural, scientific, and practical subjects.

That will certainly happen, but the presence of wholesome films and files does not rule out the presence of the corrupt and even diabolical. The Internet is proving that. The more private viewing becomes, the more likely it is that salacious and perverted tastes will be indulged. That proposition is demonstrated by the explosion of pornographic films and profits when videocassettes enabled customers to avoid the embarrassment of entering "adult" theaters. An even greater surge in the demand for perverted sex with violence will certainly occur when customers don't even have to check cassettes out of a store. Calling up films in their own homes, they will not have to face a clerk or let other customers see them browsing through X-rated films.

When digital films become available for viewing on home computers, we are likely to discover that Gilder's "trolls of cyberspace" are very real, very popular, and a very great menace. Imagine [the] Internet's alt.sex.stories on digital film available on home computers anywhere in the world. The dramatization, in living color with lurid special effects, of men castrating and then shooting a six-year-old boy, then gang raping and killing a seven-year-old girl is certain to trigger imitations by borderline perverts. Don't think such films won't be made; they will. Don't think that they will not be defended on First Amendment grounds; they will. And don't suppose it will not be said that the solution is simple: If you don't like it, don't watch it. That, too, will be argued.

A great many people are willing to deplore such material but unwilling to take or allow action to stop its distribution. When the Senate Commerce Committee approved a proposal to impose criminal penalties on anyone who transmits on Internet material that is "obscene, lewd, lascivious, filthy, or indecent," ferocious opposition immediately developed from a coalition of business and civil liberties organizations. The wording of the bill leaves much to be desired, but that is not the primary objection these groups have. They do not want restrictions, period, no matter how carefully drawn. The coalition includes, of course, the ACLU and the ubiquitous Time Warner, which John Leo has said is "associated one way or another with most of the high-profile, high-profit acts, black and white, that are pumping nihilism into the culture. . . . We are living through a cultural collapse, and major corporations are presiding over that collapse and grabbing everything they can on the way down."[8]

We are still on the way down and they are still grabbing. I do not suppose for a moment that Time Warner would produce films of the material to be found on the Internet's alt.sex. Nor would any major entertainment corporation. Not today or tomorrow, but as we grow accustomed to brutal and perverted sex, inhibitions will be lowered still further. Some businesses will make such films and some civil libertarians will deplore them, adding, of course, that they should not be banned. In the absence of restraints of some sort, however, everything that can be imagined, and some things that can't, yet, will eventually be produced and shown.

Reflecting on where we have come, Maggie Gallagher wrote: "Sex was remade in the image of Hugh Hefner; Eros demoted from a god to a buffoon. Over the last thirty years, America transformed itself into a pornographic culture.[9] Gallagher accepted Angela Carter's definition, stated in somewhat more basic Anglo-Saxon, that pornography is basically propaganda for fornication, and offered a definition of her own: "[A] pornographic culture is not one in which pornographic materials are published and distributed. A pornographic culture is one which accepts the ideas about sex on which pornography is based."[10]

That is quite right, as far as it goes, but our popular culture has gone far beyond propagandizing for fornication. That seems almost innocent nowadays. What America increasingly produces and distributes is now propaganda for every perversion and obscenity imaginable. If many of us accept the assumptions on which that is based, and apparently many do, then we are well on our way to an obscene culture. The upshot is that American popular culture is in a free fall, with the bottom not yet in sight. This is what the liberal view of human nature has brought us to. The idea that men are naturally rational, moral creatures without the need for strong external restraints has been exploded by experience. There is an eager and growing market for depravity, and profitable industries devoted to supplying it. Much of such resistance as there is comes from people living on the moral capital accumulated by prior generations. That capital may be expected to dwindle further—cultures do not unravel everywhere all at once. Unless there is vigorous counterattack, which must, I think, resort to legal as well as moral sanctions, the prospects are for a chaotic and unhappy society, followed, perhaps, by an authoritarian and unhappy society.

The question is whether we are really content to accept that.

NOTES

1. Simon Winchester, "An Electronic Sink of Depravity," *The Spectator,* February 4, 1995, p. 9.

2. Ibid., p. 10.

3. Ibid., p. 11.

4. Stephen Bates, "Alt.Many.Of.These.Newsgroups.Are.Repellent," *The Weekly Standard*, October 30, 1995, p. 27.

5. Winchester, p. 11.

6. John R. Wilke, "A Publicly Held Firm Turns X-Rated Videos Into a Hot Business," *Wall Street Journal*, July 11, 1994, p. 1.

7. George Gilder, "Breaking the Box," *National Review*, August 15, 1994, p. 37.

8. John Leo, "The Leading Cultural Polluter," *U.S. News & World Report*, March 27, 1995, p. 16.

9. Maggie Gallagher, *Enemies of Eros: How the Sexual Revolution Is Killing Family, Marriage, and Sex and What We Can Do About It* (Chicago: Bonus Books, 1989), p. 251.

10. Ibid., p. 252.

9

Pornography Drives Technology:
Why *Not* to Censor the Internet

Peter Johnson

INTRODUCTION

Constitutional issues aside, the basic problem with the Communications Decency Act is its assault on free expression. If enforced, it will stifle the free use of what Judge Dalzell, in *ACLU* v. *Reno,* called "the most participatory marketplace of mass speech that this country—and indeed the world—has yet seen."

Some have complained of the Communications Decency Act's overbreadth—that it would cast too wide a net and sweep up not only smut, but also nonprurient discussions of sex, health, AIDS, abortion, and other sex-related public issues. This essay, to the contrary, presents head-on the case for smut itself. My contention is that the Communications Decency Act will inhibit the free flow of the very sort of material that has traditionally been a new medium's most popular early use, that is, pornography.

Throughout the history of new media, from vernacular speech to movable type, to photography, to paperback books, to videotape, to cable and pay-TV, to "900" phone lines, to the French Minitel, to the Internet, to CD-ROMs and laser discs, pornography has shown technology the way.

From the *Federal Communications Law Journal* 49, no. 1 (November 1996): 217–26. Reprinted by permission. Please consult original article for notes and references.

"Great art is always flanked by its dark sisters, blasphemy and pornography." The same is true of the more mundane arts we call media. Where there is the Gutenberg Bible, there is also Rabelais; where the U.S. mails, dirty postcards; where the three-volume hardback novel, paperback pulp fiction; where HBO, *Midnight Blue*; where CompuServe, the *Plain Brown Wrapper* library.

Pornography, far from being an evil that the First Amendment must endure, is a positive good that encourages experimentation with new media. The First Amendment thus has not only intellectual, moral, political, and artistic value, but practical and economic value as well. It urges consenting adults, uninhibited by censorship, to look for novel ways to use the new media and novel ways to make money out of the new uses. Therefore, while it may be politically impossible and socially unwise to encourage computer pornography, legislators should at least leave it alone and let the medium follow where pornography leads.

I. HISTORY

Both English and Italian can trace their emergence as popular tongues partly to pornography. Before the fourteenth century, the gentry of England spoke as much French as English, while the Italian language was a hodgepodge of Latin-derived tongues varying from city-state to city-state. Geoffrey Chaucer's *Canterbury Tales* (1387) and Giovanni Boccaccio's *Decameron* (1349–51), larded with the sexy and the scatological, passed in manuscript from hand to hand and read aloud to a largely illiterate populace, helped create national languages in both countries. By writing long and popular works in London English and in Florentine, Chaucer and Boccaccio transformed local vernaculars into national speech. Pornography helped.

The printing press appeared a half-century after Chaucer's death in 1400 and soon spread throughout Europe. Early printing, though voluminous, was largely devoted to the Bible, to other theological, legal, and scientific works, to texts for scholars like the Greek and Latin classics, to popular sheet music, and to local religious and political broadsides. Martin Luther's ninety-five theses, for instance, nailed to the church door in Wittenberg on October 31, 1517, leafleted Germany in two weeks and Europe in two months, thanks to the printing press.

But two less noble works did more to popularize print and bring literacy to the masses than the scholarly works. These were Pietro Aretino's *Postures* (1524) and Francois Rabelais' *Gargantua and Pantagruel* (1530–40). Of the two, the *Postures* was the more pornographic in the strict sense, a series of engravings of sexual positions, each with a ribald sonnet. Rabelais' work, on the other hand, instantly entered the canon, where it has remained ever since. His tales of the two courtly giants, Gargantua and his son Pantagruel, the vinous monk Friar John and the reprobate scholar Panurge, are classics of satire and adventure, spoofing every vestige of the Middle Ages from feudal war to scholasticism to law to religion, with hearty doses of sex and scatology. Playful governesses introduce Gargantua to sex; Gargantua's horse pisses an army away; a woman scares the devil away by exposing her vagina; Panurge scatters musk on a fine lady who scorned him, exciting the dogs of Paris to rapine and rut. Both Aretino's and Rabelais' works were censured, but since censure at the time made no distinction between political, religious, and social heresies, one cannot be sure they were banned for smut. What is sure is that both were popular, Aretino remaining *the* underground porn classic for centuries, Rabelais traveling a somewhat higher road. Rabelais' boast in *Gargantua and Pantagruel* that "more copies of it have been sold by the printers in two months than there will be of the Bible in nine years" was first, probably true, and second, prescient advice to new media: Sex sells.

Three hundred years after Rabelais, photography became a new medium for porn to exploit. Begun as a staid art, requiring long exposures and great stillness, including a headclamp to immobilize the seated subject, photography first lent itself to portraits and landscapes. It was not long, however, before the Civil War taught photography two new uses. The first and more famous was the battlefield photography of Mathew Brady. The second, the more infamous, was pornography. Soldiers demanded more than letters from home, they demanded erotica. So great was the traffic to the front, not only of dirty books, but soon of erotic daguerreotypes and photographs, that Congress passed the first U.S. law proscribing obscenity via the mails. Congress, as usual, was late. By the time the bill passed, it was 1865, the war was over, and the boys were home with their pictures in their pockets.

Before the electronic era, the greatest example of pornography showing technology the way was the paperback book. Though paperbacks were in use as early as the French Revolution and continued to circulate throughout the nineteenth century as an alternative to hardback publishing, paperbacks were more an expansion of pamphleteering than a medium in their own right. The later part of the nineteenth century saw the growth of the "dime" novel, a brassy subculture to the mainstream three-volume hardcover that monopolized legitimate fiction. Printed on cheap paper, and hence called "pulp" fiction, early paperbacks included westerns, mysteries, tall tales, foreign-language stories for the growing immigrant market, and, of course, pornography. Increased literacy kept paperbacks thriving, though somewhat scorned, until World War II. Then, suddenly, the paperback's cheapness became its strength: Wartime shortages demanded that books be printed cheaply; books shipped wholesale to readers overseas had to be lightweight. Paperbacks filled both bills. A government-financed publishing project, the Armed Services Editions, adopted "pulp" technology wholesale, and, after the war, the paperback became the legitimate heir to publishing's crown. Here, then, is a true example of pornography actually developing a new technology that, first, the government (no less) and then the legitimate market adopted whole.

By the mid-1980s a new communications revolution was in full swing, of which the Telecommunications Act of 1996 is late acknowledgment. The key term in this revolution is convergence. Telephone, television, computer, and recording technologies are converging upon one another and commingling in so many ways that it will soon be nonsense to speak of media as if they were distinct. More television arrives by wire than by air; more phone calls come through air than through wire; phone lines and computers converge to create cyberspace. Nonetheless, at the edges of the growing web of networks, some strings still dangle that identify the sources of all this convergence. Tug one and up pops porn.

Cable TV started simply, as an antenna attached to a cable that would retransmit broadcast signals to remote areas. The cable revolution began by creating programming specifically for cable and charging money for it. First came individual channels like HBO and Showtime, then entire cable networks. One of the first uses of pay-cable was pornography: People would pay to watch X- and R-rated films at home. When cable systems began competing to wire up entire communities, one of the things communities demanded was leased- or public-access channels, to keep the cable operator from entirely dominating local programming. What they wanted was worthy alternative programming produced by local civic and educational groups. What they got was porn. *Midnight Blue,* produced by *Screw* magazine, is one of leased access' longest running shows. So are the offerings of ecdysiast Robin Byrd and Lou Maletta of the Gay Cable Network.

Videotape first emerged as a cheap and efficient alternative to film (later kinescope) for TV production. Its development for home use owes its birth to Sony and Betamax but its maturity to porn. Predicting that the greatest use of home VCRs would be time-shifting, that is, recording TV shows off the air for later viewing, Sony designed Betamax tape with a one hour playing time. When the market for videotape proved not to be time shifting, but prerecorded movies instead, longer-playing tape was demanded, and VHS arose to meet the demand. Though Beta eventually went to a four-hour format, it was too late. Within years, two-, four-, and six-hour VHS tape became the industry standard.

What were people watching on these early videotapes? The early home video rental stores, the outlets that drove Betamax from the market, were almost exclusively pornographic, drawing on the same clientele as early nickelodeons. The same was true of home video sales. It was not until the mid-1980s that first, local videorental stores, and next, national chains like Blockbuster entered the field with videos for the mass-market. By then, porn had shown the way. Thus, the victory of VHS over Betamax, and the triumph of video rental and purchase over time-shifting, is a rare example of pornography specifically adopting a product and a method of retailing that drove its competitor from the market.

Other participants in the communications revolution that have been helped by pornography include "900" phone numbers, CD-ROMs, and laser discs. In fact, the French Minitel, which many see as the prototype of the computer-mediated telephone system, owes whatever success it has attained largely to its use for exchanging sexual messages.

Some commentators suggest that porn gravitates to new media because new media are more free from restraint than existing ones, whose content authorities have learned to regulate. Though this may be partly true, it does not explain the exuberance with which porn revels in new media. Print, after all, is cheap to produce and free of regulation; if all porn sought were freedom from restraint, it would stick to books and pictures. Clearly, something bigger is at work. Porn, like its subject matter, is always eager to experiment. It is also free from ideological and sociological baggage. Its design is, simply, to get to market as quickly and easily as possible. When new media offer new markets, porn spies them quickly and rushes to fill them, like an amoeba extruding a new pseudopod where its skin is thinnest.

II. THE VALUE OF PORNOGRAPHY

Pornography has several values beyond serving as a test-driver for new media. As suggested above in the Betamax-VHS battle, porn, with little cash to spare and its nose to the ground, is often first to sniff out the practical uses of new media, leading the way for profitable investment by the mainstream.

Furthermore, porn draws curiosity seekers, who stay to see what else the new media can do. There is a convenient dovetailing in the audience for computers and pornography: Young, white males dominate both markets. Gadget-playing, girl-crazy young men will stay longer at a terminal that supplies both girls and gadgets. Finally, several studies have suggested that, far from creating sexist, violent feelings in young men, pornography has a calming, cathartic effect, easing adolescent cares with a dose of mild erotica.

Other values of pornography have been suggested. For one thing, the very fear that pornography arouses in parents may redound to society's advantage. In order to keep indecent messages from reaching their computer-literate children, parents themselves must become computer-literate and learn to use blocking and screening devices. If Congress is allowed to assume the parental role, parents will have less incentive to learn what their children already know. Furthermore, far from fearing what computer sex may be teaching, parents can use the computer as an opportunity to discuss sex in a meaningful way with their children.

Finally, sex on the computer is far better for children than another kind of sex that is drawing Congressional fire, that is, sex on television. While sex and violence on television shoulder the blame for sex and violence in society, several studies have suggested that something else about television is the real culprit. That is, the passive, solitary nature of television-watching is an anti-social activity, which steals children's time away from more active, engaging kinds of play. Thus, when children erupt in violence after watching television, it is not because they have been watching too much sex or violence but because they have been watching too much television. Computers, by contrast, are interactive and socializing, feeding the very skills that TV starves. Therefore, anything, including the risque, that entices children from the TV to the computer is a good thing.

III. HOW MUCH COMPUTER PORN IS THERE?

For a while it looked as if a 1994–95 Carnegie-Mellon study would answer this question. The CMU study purported to record eighteen months of Internet users' viewing of computer porn. Among the study's findings were that 83.5 percent of the images stored on the Usenet newsgroups are pornographic, that a third of the newsgroups most visited by college students are sexually explicit, that the five largest adult bulletin-board systems have revenues over one million dollars per year, that their customers are nation- and world-wide, that pornography is readily available to minors, and that the predominant images on computer nets are pedophilic, hebephilic, and paraphilic, including bondage, sadomasochism, urination, defecation, and bestiality.

So long awaited and explosive was the CMU study that it was featured on the cover of *Time* and read whole into the Congressional Record. Unfortunately, much of it proved untrue. Within a week of the study's publication, the Internet, the very medium purportedly studied, breathed a fire-storm of flame messages, discrediting both the study and its author Marty Rimm. Among the problems with the study were that it conflated findings from adults-only bulletin boards, which require credit cards and proof of age, with those from public networks, which do not; that it failed to report that pornography represents only one-half of 1 percent of Internet images; and that it counted, not actual downloadings, but only opportunities to download. The problems with Rimm himself went deeper: he was only an undergraduate at Carnegie-Mellon; his own university calls his project improperly supervised; as a high school student he authored a study inflating the incidence of gambling among New Jersey teenagers; and members of his Carnegie-Mellon research team have disclaimed involvement. Confronted with the controversy, the Senate disinvited Rimm, their star witness, from its summer 1995 hearings on the Communications Decency Act.

Therefore it is impossible to answer the question, "How much computer porn is there?" The answer seems to be: less than the CMU study indicates, but enough to unnerve Congress. The two leading compendia of computer porn list a generous double handful of adult bulletin boards, all of which offer materials similar to what is available in print and many of which simply scan pictures from available books and magazines. The CMU study confirmed, not the amount of computer porn, but the amount of public nervousness about it. Its value lies in pointing out how susceptible a skittish public is to bogus statistics and how welcome a thorough, unbiased study would be. Unfortunately, the CMU study is so discredited that even if it contains some accuracy, nobody can separate it from the chaff.

CONCLUSION

Since, therefore, nobody has proven either the extent or the harm of cyber-porn, the safest choice is to leave it alone. The Telecommunications Act of 1996 and the Communications Decency Act, in particular, represent an attack on cyberporn which, constitutional or not, will have a chilling effect on some of the new medium's most adventurous pioneers. One of the advantages of reading the history of pornography is to show how instrumental it has been in flexing the muscles of new media, from vernacular speech to print to photography to videotape. Far from viewing cyberpornographers as pariahs, society would do well to view them as mountain men and women in the mold of Jedediah Smith, who discovered and opened the passes of the Rockies for entire families to follow west. These early rogues were scruffy and smelly, perhaps not fit for polite society, but they did good service. Though uncivilized, they showed the roads for civilization to follow. We need not let the cyber-pioneers into every home, but society will benefit hugely by letting them roam free.

Part Two
Feminist Perspectives

10

Erotica and Pornography:
A Clear and Present Difference

Gloria Steinem

Human beings are the only animals that experience the same sex drive at times when we can and cannot conceive.

Just as we developed uniquely human capacities for language, planning, memory, and invention along our evolutionary path, we also developed sexuality as a form of expression; a way of communicating that is separable from our need for sex as a way of perpetuating ourselves. For humans alone, sexuality can be and often is primarily a way of bonding, of giving and receiving pleasure, bridging differentness, discovering sameness, and communicating emotion.

We developed this and other human gifts through our ability to change our environment, adapt physically, and, in the long run, affect our own evolution. But as an emotional result of this spiraling path away from other animals, we seem to alternate between periods of exploring our unique abilities to forge new boundaries, and feelings of loneliness in the unknown that we ourselves have created; a fear that sometimes sends us back to the comfort of the animal world by encouraging us to exaggerate our sameness with it.

The separation of "play" from "work," for instance, is a problem only in the human world. So is the difference between art and nature, or an intellectual accomplishment and a physical one. As a result, we celebrate play, art, and invention as leaps into the unknown; but any imbalance can send us back to nostalgia for our primate past and the conviction that the basics of work, nature, and physical labor are somehow more worthwhile or even more moral.

In the same way, we have explored our sexuality as separable from conception: a pleasurable, empathetic bridge to strangers of the same species. We have even invented contraception—a skill that has probably existed in some form since our ancestors figured out the process of birth—in order to extend this uniquely human difference. Yet we also have times of atavistic suspicion that sex is not complete—or even legal or intended-by-god—if it cannot end in conception.

No wonder the concepts of "erotica" and "pornography" can be so crucially different, and yet so confused. Both assume that sexuality can be separated from conception, and therefore can be used to carry a personal message. That's a major reason why, even in our current culture, both may be called equally "shocking" or legally "obscene," a word whose Latin derivative means "dirty, containing filth." This gross condemnation of all sexuality that isn't harnessed to childbirth and marriage has been increased by the current backlash against women's progress. Out of fear that the whole patriarchal structure might be upset if women really had the autonomous power to decide our reproductive futures (that is, if we controlled the most basic means of production—the production of human beings), right-wing groups are not only denouncing pro-choice abortion literature as "pornographic," but are trying to stop the sending of all contraceptive information through the mails by invoking obscenity laws. In fact, Phyllis Schlafly recently denounced the entire Women's Movement as "obscene."

Not surprisingly, this religious, visceral backlash has a secular, intellectual counterpart that relies heavily on applying the "natural" behavior of the animal world to humans. That application is questionable in itself, but these Lionel Tiger-ish studies make their political purpose even more clear in the particular animals they select and the habits they choose to emphasize. For example, some male primates (marmosets, titi monkeys, night monkeys) carry and/or generally "mother" their infants. Tiger types prefer to discuss chimps and baboons, whose behavior is very "male chauvinist." The message is that females should accept their "destiny" of being sexually dependent and devote themselves to bearing and rearing their young.

Defending against such reaction in turn leads to another temptation: merely to reverse the terms, and declare that all nonprocreative sex is

good. In fact, however, this human activity can be as constructive or destructive, moral or immoral, as any other. Sex as communication can
send messages as different as life and death; even the origins of "erotica"
and "pornography" reflect that fact. After all, "erotica" is rooted in "eros"
or passionate love, and thus in the idea of positive choice, free will, the
yearning for a particular person. (Interestingly, the definition of erotica
leaves open the question of gender.) "Pornography" begins with a root
"porno," meaning "prostitution" or "female captives," thus letting us know
that the subject is not mutual love, or love at all, but domination and
violence against women. (Though, of course, homosexual pornography
may imitate this violence by putting a man in the "feminine" role of victim.) It ends with a root "graphos," meaning "writing about" or "description of," which puts still more distance between subject and object, and
replaces a spontaneous yearning for closeness with objectification and
voyeurism. The difference is clear in the words. It becomes even more
so by example.

Look at any photo or film of people making love; really making love.
The images may be diverse, but there is usually a sensuality and touch
and warmth, an acceptance of bodies and nerve endings. There is always
a spontaneous sense of people who are there because they want to be,
out of shared pleasure.

Now look at any depiction of sex in which there is clear force, or
an unequal power that spells coercion. It may be very blatant, with weap-
ons of torture or bondage, wounds and bruises, some clear humiliation,
or an adult's sexual power being used over a child. It may be much more
subtle: a physical attitude of conqueror and victim, the use of race or
class difference to imply the same thing, perhaps a very unequal nudity,
with one person exposed and vulnerable while the other is clothed. In
either case, there is no sense of equal choice or equal power.

The first is erotic: a mutually pleasurable, sexual expression between
people who have enough power to be there by positive choice. It may
or may not strike a sense-memory in the viewer, or be creative enough
to make the unknown seem real; but it doesn't require us to identify with
a conqueror or a victim. It is truly sensuous, and may give us a contagion
of pleasure.

The second is pornographic: its message is violence, dominance, and
conquest. It is sex being used to reinforce some inequality, or to create
one, or to tell us that pain and humiliation (ours or someone else's) are
really the same as pleasure. If we are to feel anything, we must identify
with conqueror or victim. That means we can only experience pleasure
through the adoption of some degree of sadism or masochism. It also

means that we may feel diminished by the role of conqueror, or enraged, humiliated, and vengeful by sharing identity with the victim.

Perhaps one could simply say that erotica is about sexuality, but pornography is about power and sex-as-weapon—in the same way we have come to understand that rape is about violence, and not really about sexuality at all.

Yes, it's true that there are women who have been forced by violent families and dominating men to confuse love with pain; so much so that they have become masochists. (A fact that in no way excuses those who administer such pain.) But the truth is that, for most women—and for men with enough humanity to imagine themselves in the predicament of women—pornography could serve as aversion-conditioning toward sex.

Of course, there will always be personal differences about what is and is not erotic, and there may be cultural differences for a long time to come. Many women feel that sex makes them vulnerable and therefore may continue to need more sense of personal connection and safety than men do before allowing any erotic feelings. Men, on the other hand, may continue to feel less vulnerable, and therefore more open to such potential danger as sex with strangers. Women now frequently find competence and expertise erotic in men, but that may pass as we develop those qualities in ourselves. As some men replace the need for submission from child-like women with the pleasure of cooperation from equals, they may find a partner's competence to be erotic, too.

Such group changes plus individual differences will continue to be reflected in sexual love between people of the same gender, as well as between women and men. The point is not to dictate sameness, but to discover ourselves and each other through a sexuality that is an exploring, pleasurable, empathetic part of our lives; a human sexuality that is unchained both from unwanted pregnancies and from violence.

But that is a hope, not a reality. At the moment, fear of change is increasing both the indiscriminate repression of all nonprocreative sex in the religious and "conservative" male-dominated world, and the pornographic vengeance against women's sexuality in the secular world of "liberal" or "radical" men. It's almost futuristic to debate what is and is not truly erotic, when many women are again being forced into compulsory motherhood, and the number of pornographic murders, tortures, and women-hating images are on the increase in both popular culture and real life.

Together, both of the above forms of repression perpetuate that familiar division: wife or whore; "good" woman who is constantly vulnerable to pregnancy or "bad" woman who is unprotected from violence.

Both roles would be upset if we were to control our own sexuality. And that's exactly what we must do.

In spite of all our atavistic suspicions and training for the "natural" role of motherhood, we took up the complicated battle for reproductive freedom. Our bodies had borne the health burden of endless births and poor abortions, and we had a greater motive than men for separating sexuality and conception.

Now we have to take up the equally complex burden of explaining that all nonprocreative sex is not alike. We have a motive: our right to a uniquely human sexuality, and sometimes even to survival. As it is, our bodies have too rarely been enough our own to develop erotica in our own lives, much less in art and literature. And our bodies have too often been the objects of pornography and the woman-hating, violent practice that it preaches. Consider also our spirits that break a little each time we see ourselves in chains or full labial display for the conquering male viewer, bruised or on our knees, screaming a real or pretended pain to delight the sadist, pretending to enjoy what we don't enjoy, to be blind to the images of our sisters that really haunt us—humiliated often enough ourselves by the truly obscene idea that sex and the domination of women must be combined.

Sexuality is human, free, separate—and so are we.

But until we untangle the lethal confusion of sex with violence, there will be more pornography and less erotica. There will be little murders in our beds—and very little love.

11

Against the Male Flood: Censorship, Pornography, and Equality

Andrea Dworkin

. . . In the amendment to the Human Rights Ordinance of the City of Minneapolis written by Catharine A. MacKinnon and myself, pornography is defined as the graphic, sexually explicit subordination of women whether in pictures or in words that also includes one or more of the following: women are presented dehumanized as sexual objects, things, or commodities; or women are presented as sexual objects who enjoy pain or humiliation; or women are presented as sexual objects who experience sexual pleasure in being raped; or women are presented as sexual objects tied up or cut up or mutilated or bruised or physically hurt; or women are presented in postures of sexual submission; or women's body parts are exhibited, such that women are reduced to those parts; or women are presented being penetrated by objects or animals; or women are presented in scenarios of degradation, injury, abasement, torture, shown as filthy or inferior, bleeding, bruised, or hurt in a context that makes these conditions sexual.

This statutory definition is an objectively accurate definition of what pornography is, based on an analysis of the material produced by the

$8-billion-a-year industry, and also on extensive study of the whole range of pornography extant from other eras and other cultures. Given the fact that women's oppression has an ahistorical character—a sameness across time and cultures expressed in rape, battery, incest, and prostitution— it is no surprise that pornography, a central phenomenon in that oppression, has precisely that quality of sameness. It does not significantly change in what it is, what it does, what is in it, or how it works, whether it is, for instance, classical or feudal or modern, Western or Asian; whether the method of manufacture is words, photographs, or video. What has changed is the public availability of pornography and the numbers of live women used in it because of new technologies: not its nature. Many people note what seems to them a qualitative change in pornography—that it has gotten more violent, even grotesquely violent, over the last two decades. The change is only in what is publicly visible: not in the range or preponderance of violent pornography (e.g., the place of rape in pornography stays constant and central, no matter where, when, or how the pornography is produced); not in the character, quality, or content of what the pornographers actually produce; not in the harm caused; not in the valuation of women in it, or the metaphysical definition of what women are; not in the sexual abuse promoted, including rape, battery, and incest; not in the centrality of its role in subordinating women. Until recently, pornography operated in private, where most abuse of women takes place.

The oppression of women occurs through sexual subordination. It is the use of sex as the medium of oppression that makes the subordination of women so distinct from racism or prejudice against a group based on religion or national origin. Social inequality is created in many different ways. In my view, the radical responsibility is to isolate the material means of creating the inequality so that material remedies can be found for it.

This is particularly difficult with respect to women's inequality because that inequality is achieved through sex. Sex as desired by the class that dominates women is held by that class to be elemental, urgent, necessary, even if or even though it appears to *require* the repudiation of any claim women might have to full human standing. In the subordination of women, inequality itself is sexualized: made into the experience of sexual pleasure, essential to sexual desire. Pornography is the material means of sexualizing inequality; and that is why pornography is a central practice in the subordination of women.

Subordination itself is a broad, deep, systematic dynamic discernible in any persecution based on race or sex. Social subordination has four main parts. First, there is *hierarchy,* a group on top and a group on the bottom. For women, this hierarchy is experienced both socially and sexually, publicly and privately. Women are physically integrated into the society in which we are held to be inferior, and our low status is both put in place and maintained by the sexual usage of us by men; and so women's experience of hierarchy is incredibly intimate and wounding.

Second, subordination is *objectification*. Objectification occurs when a human being, through social means, is made less than human, turned into a thing or commodity, bought and sold. When objectification occurs, a person is de-personalized, so that no individuality or integrity is available socially or in what is an extremely circumscribed privacy (because those who dominate determine its boundaries). Objectification is an injury right at the heart of discrimination: those who can be used as if they are not fully human are no longer fully human in social terms; their humanity is hurt by being diminished.

Third, subordination is *submission*. A person is at the bottom of a hierarchy because of a condition of birth; a person on the bottom is dehumanized, an object or commodity; inevitably, the situation of that person requires obedience and compliance. That diminished person is expected to be submissive; there is no longer any right to self-determination, because there is no basis in equality for any such right to exist. In a condition of inferiority and objectification, submission is usually essential for survival. Oppressed groups are known for their abilities to anticipate the orders and desires of those who have power over them, to comply with an obsequiousness that is then used by the dominant group to justify its own dominance: the master, not able to imagine a human like himself in such degrading servility, thinks the servility is proof that the hierarchy is natural and that objectification simply amounts to seeing these lesser creatures for what they are. The submission forced on inferior, objectified groups precisely by hierarchy and objectification is taken to be the proof of inherent inferiority and subhuman capacities.

Fourth, subordination is *violence*. The violence is systematic, endemic enough to be unremarkable and normative, usually taken as an implicit right of the one committing the violence. In my view, hierarchy, objectification, and submission are the preconditions for systematic social violence against any group targeted because of a condition of birth. If violence against a group is both socially pervasive and socially normal, then hierarchy, objectification, and submission are already solidly in place.

The role of violence in subordinating women has one special characteristic congruent with sex as the instrumentality of subordination: the violence is supposed to be sex for the woman too—what women want and like as part of our sexual nature; it is supposed to give women pleasure (as in rape); it is supposed to mean love to a woman from her point of view (as in battery). The violence against women is seen to be done not just in accord with something compliant in women, but in response to something active in and basic to women's nature.

Pornography uses each component of social subordination. Its particular medium is sex. Hierarchy, objectification, submission, and violence all become alive with sexual energy and sexual meaning. A hierarchy, for instance, can have a static quality; but pornography, by sexualizing it, makes it dynamic, almost carnivorous, so that men keep imposing it for the sake of their own sexual pleasure—for the sexual pleasure it gives them to impose it. In pornography, each element of subordination is conveyed through the sexually explicit usage of women: pornography in fact is what women are and what women are for and how women are used in a society premised on the inferiority of women. It is a metaphysics of women's subjugation: our existence delineated in a definition of our nature; our status in society predetermined by the uses to which we are put. The woman's body is what is materially subordinated. Sex is the material means through which the subordination is accomplished. Pornography is the institution of male dominance that sexualizes hierarchy, objectification, submission, and violence. As such, pornography creates inequality, not as artifact but as a system of social reality; it creates the necessity for and the actual behaviors that constitute sex inequality.

Subordination can be so deep that those who are hurt by it are utterly silent. Subordination can create a silence quieter than death. The women flattened out on the page are deathly still, except for *hurt me. Hurt me* is not women's speech. It is the speech imposed on women by pimps to cover the awful, condemning silence. The Three Marias of Portugal went to jail for writing this: "Let no one tell me that silence gives consent, because whoever is silent dissents."[1] The women say the pimp's words: the language is another element of the rape; the language is part of the humiliation; the language is part of the forced sex. Real silence might signify dissent, for those reared to understand its sad discourse. The pimps cannot tolerate literal silence—it is too eloquent as testimony —so they force the words out of the woman's mouth. The women say pimp's words: which is worse than silence. The silence of the women not in the picture, outside the pages, hurt but silent, used but silent, is staggering in how deep and wide it goes. It is a silence over centuries: an exile into speechlessness. One is shut up by the inferiority and the abuse. One is shut up by the threat and the injury. In her memoir of the Stalin period, *Hope Against Hope,* Nadezhda Mandelstam wrote that screaming "is a man's way of leaving a trace, of telling people how he lived and died. By his screams he asserts his right to live, sends a message to the outside world demanding help and calling for resistance. If nothing else is left, one must scream. Silence is the real crime against humanity."[2] Screaming is a man's way of leaving a trace. The scream of a man is never misunderstood as a scream of pleasure by passers-by or politicians or historians, nor by the tormentor. A man's scream is a call for resistance. A man's scream asserts his right to live, sends a message; he leaves a trace. A woman's scream is the sound of her female will and her female pleasure in doing what the pornographers say she is for. Her scream is a sound of celebration to those who overhear. Women's way of leaving a trace is the silence, centuries' worth: the entirely inhuman silence that surely one day will be noticed, someone will say that something is wrong, some sound is missing, some voice is lost; the entirely inhuman silence that will be a clue to human hope denied, a shard of evidence that a crime has occurred, the crime that created the silence; the entirely inhuman silence that is a cold, cold condemnation of what those who speak have done to those who do not.

But there is more than the *hurt me* forced out of us, and the silence in which it lies. The pornographers actually use our bodies as their language. We are their speech. Our bodies are the building blocks of their sentences. What they do to us, called speech, is not unlike what Kafka's Harrow machine—"The needles are set in like the teeth of a harrow and the whole thing works something like a harrow, although its action is limited to one place and contrived with much more artistic skill"[3]—did to the condemned in "In the Penal Colony":

> Our sentence does not sound severe. Whatever commandment the prisoner has disobeyed is written upon his body by the Harrow. This prisoner, for instance"—the officer indicated the man—"will have written on his body: HONOR THY SUPERIORS!"[4]
>
> . . . The Harrow is beginning to write; when it finishes the first draft of the inscription on the man's back, the layer of cotton wool begins to roll and slowly turns the body over, to give the Harrow fresh space for writing. . . . So it keeps on writing deeper and deeper . . .[5]

Asked if the prisoner knows his sentence, the officer replies: " 'There would be no point in telling him. He'll learn it on his body.' "[6]

This is the so-called speech of the pornographers, protected now by law.

Protecting what they "say" means protecting what they do to us, how they do it. It means protecting their sadism on our bodies, because that is how they write: not like a writer at all; like a torturer. Protecting what they "say" means protecting sexual exploitation, because they cannot "say" anything without diminishing, hurting, or destroying us. Their rights of speech express their rights over us. Their rights of speech require our inferiority: and that we be powerless in relation to them. Their rights of speech mean that *hurt me* is accepted as the real speech of women, not speech forced on us as part of the sex forced on us but originating with us because we are what the pornographers "say" we are.

If what we want to say is not *hurt me,* we have the real social power only to use silence as eloquent dissent. Silence is what women have instead of speech. Silence is our dissent during rape unless the rapist, like the pornographer, prefers *hurt me,* in which case we have no dissent. Silence is our moving, persuasive dissent during battery unless the batterer, like the pornographer, prefers *hurt me.* Silence is a fine dissent during incest and for all the long years after.

Silence is not speech. We have silence, not speech. We fight rape, battery, incest, and prostitution with it. We lose. But someday someone will notice: that people called women were buried in a long silence that meant dissent and that the pornographers—with needles set in like the teeth of a harrow—chattered on.

NOTES

1. Maria Isabel Barreno, Maria Teresa Horta, and Maria Velho da Costa, *The Three Marias: New Portuguese Letters,* trans. Helen R. Lane (New York: Bantam Books, 1976), p. 291.

2. Nadezhda Mandelstam, *Hope Against Hope,* trans. Max Hayward (New York: Atheneum, 1978), pp. 42–43.

3. Franz Kafka, "In the Penal Colony," pp. 191–227, *The Penal Colony,* trans. Willa and Edwin Muir (New York: Schocken Books, 1965), p. 194.

4. Kafka, "In the Penal Colony," p. 197.

5. Kafka, "In the Penal Colony," p. 203.

6. Kafka, "In the Penal Colony," p. 197.

12

Pornography and Degradation

Judith M. Hill

The issue of pornography has often been approached from a utilitarian point of view, with the discussion focusing on what the consequences of pornography might be. There is a great deal of literature concerning whether or not the availability of pornographic material is responsible for violence against women, or for promoting a depersonalized attitude toward sexual relationships. There is not a great deal of agreement on these empirical questions (Berger, 1977).

Recently, there have been several attempts to introduce city or county ordinances banning the sale of pornography, in Minneapolis, Indianapolis, Los Angeles, and Suffolk, New York. The proponents of these ordinances have argued that pornography violates the civil rights of women, apparently a nonutilitarian argument. However, their argument turns on the premise that *the effect* of pornography is to deny equal opportunities to women. Thus far, the courts have rejected this line of reasoning, and the constitutionality of the proposed statutes, largely because they are not convinced that the consequences of pornography are such as to warrant restrictions of First Amendment rights.

I am interested in presenting an argument that does not appeal to the consequences of pornography, a strictly nonutilitarian argument that rests on the hypothesis that pornography degrades women. I believe that

From *Hypatia* 2, no. 2 (Summer 1987):39–54 Copyright © 1987 by Judith M. Hill. Reprinted by permission of the author.

pornography *does* degrade women. However, the concept of degradation is a slippery one, which, like other concepts of oppression, has not been examined as carefully as it must be if we are going to discuss oppression illuminatingly. In the first part of this article, therefore, I will offer an analysis of the concept of degradation. In the second part, I will show why and how pornography degrades women.

I

I propose that we begin with the assumption that degradation involves, literally, a de-grading. This proposition is, I realize, both vague and ambiguous. It is ambiguous because "de-grade" may suggest either (1) to *down*-grade, to lower the worth of, to de-value, or (2) to *assign* a lower grade to, to give a lower evaluation, to characterize as of lesser worth. In other words, de-gradation may be thought to entail either a real loss of worth, or an imputed loss of worth. In either case, the proposal is vague, because it gives no indication of the *kind* of value that must be lost, or imputed to be lost, in order for degradation to take place.

The following examples suggest a direction we might take in firming up this proposal.

In William Styron's novel, *Sophie's Choice,* Sophie mentions that although the Nazis routinely shaved the heads of all inmates at Auschwitz, those inmates who occupied positions of favor were permitted to wear headscarves in order to hide their "degrading baldness."

In Emma Goldman's autobiography, recounting a period of time spent in prison, she describes as "degrading" the prisoners being forced to march in lockstep while carrying buckets of excrement from their cells to the river.

In both these cases, the writers are describing environments in which severe physical abuse was a commonplace. The horrors of the Nazi death camps are well-known. The plight of working class women in prisons in the late nineteenth and early twentieth centuries was also appalling: forced labor under sweatshop conditions, with inadequate food, crowded living quarters, and no medical facilities. Given the context of physical abuse in both cases, it is significant that what Goldman and Styron's Sophie focus on as degrading is not any physical abuse or deprivation at all, but on practices the importance of which (to both practitioner and victim) is largely symbolic. In both cases, it is a kind of public display of low status which is described as degrading.

Extrapolating from Styron and Goldman, I would suggest that the de-grading involved in degradation is a lowering of *moral* status. A person is not degraded merely by losing status as president of the company or as most valuable player or as woman of the year. Degradation is not to be confused with decline or defeat. It is not a matter of losing power or prestige or privilege, but of losing something considerably more central to one's personhood. To give this account a Kantian interpretation: degradation involves being treated as though one were a means only, as though one were not an end in herself, as though one were something less than a person.

However, degradation is not *simply* a matter of being treated as something less than a person. If this were true, then shaved heads and forced marches would be the least of the degradations inflicted upon Sophie and Goldman, for in much of the physical and mental abuse they suffered they were treated as less than persons. It is not a sufficient condition of degradation that a person be treated as something less than a person.

I am inclined to say that it is a necessary condition of degradation that a person *be perceived*—by herself or by others—as being treated as something less than a person. Degradation occurs with the creation of a public impression that a person is being treated as something less than a person. Thus, baldness was degrading within the context of Auschwitz because it marked one as a member of the class that was being treated as subhuman. Forced marches for prisoners doing housekeeping chores were degrading because their sole purpose was to exhibit—for the benefit of the prisoners and the guards, at least—the complete submissiveness and obedience of the prisoners and the complete control of the guards; forced marches served as a demonstration that the prisoners could be treated in whatever manner, however inhuman, that the guards desired.

In short, degradation is a public phenomenon. If there is no perception of a person being treated as though she were a means only, then she is not degraded, although she may be exploited or cheated or abused. For example, consider the difference between an employer who underpays employees while expressing contempt for them, and an employer who underpays employees while cultivating an image of benevolent concern. The former degrades her employees; the latter "merely" cheats them. Or, consider the difference between a man who publicly treats his wife as a servant, and a man who treats his wife as a means only while expressing love and affection for her. Again, the former degrades his wife; the latter "merely" takes advantage of her.

Although degradation requires a public perception of someone being treated as a means only, this perception need not be widely shared: it is often enough that the victim perceives it, i.e., that it be public in principle only. On the other hand, it may be true that the degradation is more severe if the perception is more widespread. To be actually observed in public being treated as less than a person is more degrading than being subjected to the same treatment in private.

This suggests, to return to a question raised above, that degradation involves a de-grading in the sense of imputing a lesser value to, rather than in the sense of lessening the value of. *Covert* treatment of a person as a means only—a matter of exploitation or abuse rather than of degradation, if my analysis is correct—implies *no* conviction on the agent's part that his action is morally justifiable, that the other deserves to be treated as a means only. Such actions do not, therefore, impute a lesser moral worth to the victim. However, an agent who lets his victims know that he is intentionally treating her as means only, exhibits a certain contempt for her, demonstrates a certain conviction that his action is justifiable, that she deserves to be treated as less than a person. Finally, an agent who treats his victim as something less than a person in public places, for the whole world to observe, demonstrates a conviction that her worthlessness is so extreme that all the world can be counted upon to regard him as justified in treating her accordingly. In short, the more public the display of contempt, the stronger is the imputation of moral worthlessness.

It may sometimes be thought that degradation de-grades not only in the sense of imputing lesser moral worth to a person, but also in the sense of actively lessening the moral worth of a person. In particular, I suspect that people who degrade others often vaguely think of this as a kind of challenge or as a test. One meets the challenge, passes the test, by insisting (presumably at whatever cost) on being treated with respect. One fails the test by acquiescing; and the penalty for failure is the loss of one's right to be treated with respect. Thus, degradation carries with it its own justification: people who allow themselves to be treated as less than persons deserve to be treated as less than persons.

This is a mistake. A person does not have to earn the right to be treated as an end in himself, to be treated with fairness and consideration; and a person does not forfeit these rights by failing to insist that they be respected. These are rights a person has simply in virtue of being a person, in virtue of having the potential (in theory, at least) for certain kinds of behavior. Consequently, degradation is always morally wrong. It does not become less wrong because the degraded person acquiesces.

On the other hand, Thomas Hill (1973) has argued, correctly I think, that although one does not forfeit moral rights by acquiescing to degradation, such acquiescence is not always morally neutral. Hill's argument proceeds in terms of a moral duty of self-respect. There are, he allows, circumstances under which even a self-respecting person could not reasonably be expected to object to degrading treatment—(e.g., when she does not understand that her rights are being violated, or that she has a right to object, or when it might be dangerous or in some way disastrous for her to object; and certainly no moral blame attaches to a failure to insist on being treated with respect under such circumstances. However, when a person is aware that her rights are being violated, and the cost of objecting to such treatment would not be excessive, then a person fails in her moral duty to herself if she fails to insist on her rights.

Although I agree with the spirit of Hill's argument, I would be more comfortable making the point in terms of moral courage than in terms of a duty of self-respect. Moral courage, like physical courage, is a trait one develops by exercising it. When a person acts in a cowardly manner, in a situation in which courage is called for, she takes a step in the formation of her own character. Obviously, no single act of moral cowardice will make one a moral coward. However, it becomes more and more difficult to insist on one's rights each time one fails to do so. If a person habitually acquiesces to degrading treatment while understanding that she has a right to object, and under circumstances in which there is no reason to expect severe reprisals for objecting, she cultivates moral cowardice, a weak character.

Thus, degradation does not merely impute a lesser value to the degraded person. A person who acquiesces habitually and unnecessarily to degradation becomes a lesser person, in the sense that she will have a lesser capacity to act in a moral manner.

It does not by any means follow that such a person deserves to be treated as less than a person. As I have said, a person does not have to earn the right to be treated as an end in herself. It *does* follow that degradation should be taken very seriously. A person who tolerates degrading treatment because it would be embarrassing to object, or because it would result in some financial loss, is risking her moral character. To summarize: a person is degraded when she is publicly, or at least overtly, treated as a means only, as something less than a person. Degradation involves a de-grading at least in the sense that it entails a (false) imputation of a lower moral status than persons, as such, are ordinarily accorded; and sometimes also in the sense that it involves a diminution of the moral courage of the person degraded.

II

Now we may turn to the question of whether or not pornography degrades women.

Obviously, the answer to this question will depend in part on what we identify as pornography. The Indianapolis and Minneapolis city ordinances, which were framed primarily by Andrea Dworkin and Catherine MacKinnon, defined pornography as "the graphic sexually explicit subordination of women, whether in pictures or in words." The proposed ordinances listed six conditions, at least one of which would have to be present in order to qualify a work as pornographic. Among these conditions were: (1) presenting women as sexual objects "who enjoy pain and humiliation"; (2) presenting women as "experiencing pleasure in being raped"; (3) presenting women as objects for "domination, conquest, violation, exploitation, possession or use." (Shipp 1984)

It should be noted that Andrea Dworkin is of the opinion that, in fact, virtually all of what passes for "adult entertainment" falls into one or more of these categories. She points out that, etymologically, pornography is "the depiction of vile whores"; and that after extensive research on the content and nature of contemporary "adult entertainment," she has concluded that it is *still* best described as the depiction of vile whores. "The fact that pornography is widely believed to be 'sexual representation' or 'depictions of sex' emphasizes only that the valuation of women as low whores is widespread and that the sexuality of women is perceived as low and whorish in itself" (Dworkin 1981, 201). In short, although Dworkin's proposed ordinances do not mandate censorship of sexually explicit, or obscene, material, *as such*, it is probably fair to say that she expects them to have the effect of eliminating most of what is commonly regarded as pornography.

Perhaps for this reason, some critics of the Minneapolis and Indianapolis ordinances have drawn the conclusion that these ordinances threaten all sexually explicit material. Civil libertarian Nat Hentoff (1984), for example, decried the ordinances as endangering "such works as . . . *Dr. Zhivago*, . . . *Lolita*, and of course, bountiful sections of the Old Testament." As I understand the proposed ordinances, they would *not* ban such works; and it is not *my* intention in this paper to object to such works as these. Therefore, in order to avoid this sort of misunderstanding, I will elaborate a bit on the Dworkin/MacKinnon definition of pornography, narrowing in on a genre I shall call Victim Pornography.

Victim Pornography is the graphic depiction of situations in which women are degraded by sexual activity, *viz.*, (a) situations in which a woman is treated by a man (or by another woman) as a means of obtaining sexual pleasure, while he shows no consideration for her pleasure or desires or well-being, and (b) situations in which a woman is not only subjected to such treatment, but suggests it to the man in the first place. Furthermore, Victim Pornography presents such activity as entertaining. There is no suggestion that women should not be treated as less than persons; and often there is no hint that a woman might dislike such treatment.[1]

I believe that Victim Pornography does comprise at least a very large part of what passes today for adult entertainment. Dworkin is right in maintaining that much of what is commonly regarded as pornography is a celebration of violence and exploitation. However, I want to emphasize that the issue I am addressing is *not* the morality of what is commonly regarded as pornography: I am not concerned here with material that is sexually explicit, or obscene, as such. The focus of my discussion is neither *Lady Chatterley's Lover* nor *Playboy's* "Ten Coeds At Home," but Victim Pornography: depictions of women being bound, beaten, raped, mutilated, and, as often as not, begging for more. . . .

One can imagine the producers of Victim Pornography treating their models as though they were means only: as though they were not persons deserving of respect and consideration, as though their pain and humiliation were amusing or boring. Indeed, it is probably true that most producers of Victim Pornography *do* treat their models in this way.

However, this is not a *necessary* feature of the production of pornography, even of Victim Pornography. Although it would be naive to suppose that the producers of pornography typically show respect and consideration for their models, we can at least imagine a producer of pornography taking time to ensure that the model's job is no more painful than necessary; treating unpleasant aspects of her job *as* unpleasant aspects, rather than as opportunities for leering; treating the models as people doing a job for pay, rather than as so much meat. A producer of pornography who behaves in this way still treats the model as a means to making profits, and perhaps *only* as a means to making profits (and not as an artist, or as a friend, for example); but does not treat her as a means only, as though she were not an end in herself, as less than a person.

In other words, it is not a necessary feature of the production of Victim Pornography that the models be degraded. Certainly it *may* happen, and often *does* happen; and certainly it is morally reprehensible when it happens. But pornography, even Victim Pornography, can surely be produced without degradation to the models[2], and therefore the potential for degradation to models is not a reason to end the production of pornography. . . .

The hypothesis that the women who act in pornographic films and pose for pornographic magazines are necessarily treated as means only by the *patrons* of pornography, is even less plausible than the hypothesis that they are necessarily treated as means only by the producers of pornography.

It is doubtlessly the case that many people use pornography as a means of obtaining pleasure. The women who act in pornographic films and pose for pornographic magazines are, therefore, indirectly, instruments of pleasure for patrons of pornography. However, although it may follow that the patrons of pornography treat the models in pornographic material only as means to their own ends, it does *not* follow that they treat them as means *only*, as though they were not ends in themselves. The relationship between the patrons and the women who model for pornography is not, as such, sufficiently personal—they do not actually interact—to allow of this description.

In short, it is not true that women who serve as models for pornography are treated as means only, as less than persons, by consumers of pornography. On the other hand, although it may be true that these women are only treated as means, this is not in itself degrading to them.

It becomes apparent that any sort of degradation attaching to pornography will not occur on the personal level suggested by the hypotheses we have just considered. However, we have not yet considered the hypothesis that the pornography industry degrades women as a class rather than this or that individual woman.

The pornography industry regularly publishes material which, speaking conservatively, tends to contribute to the perpetuation of derogatory beliefs about womankind. Victim Pornography, in particular, depicts women not simply as ill treated, but as eager to be used and abused, totally lacking in human dignity: as more or less worthless for any purpose other than casual sexual intercourse. Many pieces of pornography depict *all* female characters in such negative ways.

Of course pornography is fiction, and does not purport to be anything other than fiction. However, fiction is not supposed to be devoid of all factual truth; indeed, fiction *should* contain truths about human nature, about motivation, about power, and so on. Consequently, although pornographic material may make no claim to be describing actual states of affairs, we might say that it offers a perspective on the actual nature of womankind. The perspective offered by Victim Pornography is that, in general, women are narcissistic, masochistic, and not fully persons in the moral sense.

I would not suggest that it is the *intention* of pornographers to convey the message that all women may be, or should be, or like to be treated as less than persons. This is almost surely false. Most pornographers are not at all interested in influencing behavior, or in conveying universal truths; their intention is to titillate. Nevertheless, because pornography trades in stereotypes, shunning any careful or serious character development (by its very nature; this is what makes it bad literature), and because the stereotypes that titillate (at least, that titillate the patrons of Victim Pornography) are derogatory ones—the nymphomaniac, the masochist, the mindless playmate—much of Victim Pornography supports the idea that all women fall into one or another of these categories, whether or not this is its intention. The genre of Victim Pornography, taken as a whole, implies that most women are mindless, masochistic nymphomaniacs. That is to say, this would be the logical conclusion to draw on the basis of the characterization offered in Victim Pornography.[3]

The point I want to make here is *not* that Victim Pornography is responsible for negative attitudes and/or violent behavior towards women. If pornography were eliminated from the culture, there would probably be no discernible change in beliefs about, or attitudes towards women, unless many of its spiritual cognates were eliminated simultaneously. Conversely, if all aspects of the tradition of treating women as less than persons *except* pornography were eliminated, pornography would become more or less innocuous, would be difficult to take seriously. In other words, I am inclined to be quite conservative in estimating the degree of potential pornography has, in and of itself, to actually plant the seeds of derogatory beliefs about, and subsequent violent behavior toward, womankind. Pornography only contributes to the nurture of the plant.

Again, the point is *not* that Victim Pornography has negative consequences for women. The point is that Victim Pornography contains implications that defame womankind. The perspective on women offered by Victim Pornography is not only derogatory, it is false. Most women are *not* mindless, masochistic nymphomaniacs. Most women do not enjoy being beaten and raped. Most women do not want, or expect, to be treated as less than persons by their sexual partners. (This may seem so obvious that it should not have to be said. Indeed, it should not have to be said. However, a look at what goes on at rape trials will show that it is not, unfortunately, obvious.)

Nevertheless, the pornography industry routinely publishes material that supports this view of womankind. The pornography industry does not care that this view is false. This is what sells, to the tune of $7 billion a year. In short, the pornography industry is quite willing to defame womankind for the sake of making a profit.

In so doing, the pornography industry degrades womankind. It treats the class of women as nothing more than a means to its own financial ends. It treats the class of women as though such a smearing of its reputation is unimportant, trivial. In other words, pornography degrades women because it treats them as members of a class which has no honor and is not entitled to respect. The pornography industry treats women as though the truth about their nature may be ignored or distorted with impunity. The point is not that pornography may incite men to rape women. The point is that the pornography industry blithely perpetuates derogatory myths, blithely lies, about the nature of women, for its own financial gain.

In publishing Victim Pornography, the pornography industry treats women, as a class, as less than persons. In my view, this is sufficient to support the claim that Victim Pornography is morally objectionable.

A word about the legal implications of this analysis:

The anti-pornography ordinances proposed in Indianapolis and Minneapolis suggest that the sale of pornography be viewed as a violation of women's civil rights. I think this is more promising than the old approach of objecting to pornography on grounds of obscenity. The champions of free speech characterize all obscenity laws as attempts to curtail the free exchange of ideas simply because the most sensitive members of society are offended by them. However absurd it may be to characterize Victim Pornography as an exchange of ideas, the civil libertarians do not seem likely to relinquish this position any time soon. The approach taken by MacKinnon and Dworkin has the advantage of not lending itself to this interpretation. Even a cursory reading of their defense will show that they are not bluestockings imposing their personal subjective standards of decency on the rest of society.

Furthermore, treating pornography as a violation of civil rights rather than as an affront to people who are offended by obscenity, entails that it cannot be dealt with, as Joel Feinberg (1980, 89) suggests, by noting that people do not have to read what offends them. In other words, if pornography were objectionable simply in the sense that it offends some people, it might be appropriate to conclude that censorship is not warranted. As Feinberg argues, if the material that offends one is easily avoided, as obscene books and movies are, the fact that they are offensive to some does not constitute reason to censor them. However, if pornography is not simply obscene, but a violation of civil rights, the suggestion that people who find it objectionable should simply avoid it, is hardly appropriate. Violations of civil rights are not corrected by ignoring them.

The MacKinnon/Dworkin appeal to the civil rights of women rests on equal rights statutes. Their hypothesis is that pornography is a discriminatory practice based on sex because its effect is to deny women equal opportunities in society. This approach has the disadvantage of having to appeal to highly controversial studies concerning the consequences of pornography: its success depends on the plausibility of the claim that when pornography is offered for sale, the result is a significant negative influence on people's beliefs about women, and a subsequent negative influence on people's behavior towards women. To date, this claim has been treated by the courts as not providing sufficient reason to curtail first amendment rights. Whatever negative consequences the sale of pornography might have—and these are minimized—they are not thought to be serious enough to warrant censorship.

My analysis of Victim Pornography as degrading suggests a different unpacking of the MacKinnon/Dworkin hypothesis that pornography violates the civil rights of women. On my account, Victim Pornography *libels* women as a class, in impugning the nature of women. This approach would not have to rely on controversial empirical studies concerning the consequences of pornography. Libel can be established without demonstrating actual damage to the plaintiff. Libel laws originated in a time when a person's honor and reputation were valued for their own sake, and not simply because of their business value. Therefore, in proving libel, it is enough to show that a defamatory statement about the plaintiff is false.

Furthermore, this approach does not constitute a new challenge to free speech. Libel has *never* been protected by the First Amendment, and it is unlikely that even the most liberal of civil libertarians would be tempted to argue that it should be.

Would a case against Victim Pornography as libel stand up in court?

There are precedents for treating defamatory statements concerning groups as libel. The rationale is that individuals can be harmed by defamatory statements about groups of which they are members as well as by defamatory statements about them as individuals. For example, repeated statements to the effect that all lawyers are dishonest obviously cause harm to individual lawyers. Although a particular lawyer may be hurt more by statements to the effect that she, in particular, is dishonest, than by statements to the effect that *all* lawyers are dishonest, the latter as well as the former certainly has the capacity to damage her reputation and business. In order to protect individuals, the law must prevent unwarranted defamation of groups as well as of specific individuals.

Group libel suits have been brought successfully by: an individual who was defamed as a member of a jury;[4] an individual who was defamed as a member of a board of County Commissioners;[5] an individual who was defamed as a member of a staff of doctors at a hospital;[6] an individual who was defamed as a member of a group of engineers employed by a construction company.[7] Historically, there has been some reluctance on the part of the judicial system to extend the principle of group libel to *large* groups, e.g., to defamatory statements about "all Jews," "all priests," "all blacks." Obviously, this would present an obstacle to finding the pornography industry guilty of libel against the class of women. However, it is reasonable to assume that individuals may be unjustly defamed by derogatory statements concerning *large* groups of which they are members, no less than by derogatory statements about *small* groups of which they are members (Reisman 1942, 770–771). Consequently, I do not think this obstacle is insurmountable.

The major difficulty I foresee in establishing that pornography libels women as a class is the problem of establishing that Victim Pornography does indeed imply that women are generally masochistic nymphomaniacs. The pornography industry will insist that it is dealing in fiction, that the material it sells depicting the degradation of women has nothing to do with reality; that its object is to entertain, not to inform.

It is beyond the scope of this paper to construct the legal case against pornography. I will only repeat that the fact that films or reading material are presented as fiction does not entail that they are supposed to be, expected to be, devoid of truth. Furthermore, it is not necessary to prove intent to injure in establishing libel; the fact that the producers of Victim Pornography do not intend to influence anyone's beliefs about the nature of women as a class (if it is a fact), is irrelevant. If the content of Victim Pornography carries the implication that, in general, women are masochistic, nymphomaniac, and not fully persons in the moral sense, the case for libel stands.

To conclude: The pornography industry makes a large share of its profit by selling material that displays a total lack of regard for the truth about womankind on the part of the industry. Pornographic material that depicts all or most women characters as masochists or nymphomaniacs or as mindless demi-persons, carries with it the implication that this is the nature of womankind, and therefore of all individual women. *Whether or not* anyone believes that this is true of women, or acts accordingly, as a result of reading pornographic books or watching pornographic films, the implication itself is defamatory. In marketing such material, the pornography industry treats all women as nothing more than means to its own financial gain. This is not a matter of the pornography industry excusably treating women only as means in the course of a very limited business relationship (in the way in which an employer might excusably treat an employee only as a means). The propagation of false and derogatory statements about a class of people, for the sake of profit, inexcusably treats all members of that class as though they were means only, as though they were not ends in themselves.

Many women are embarrassed even to acknowledge the existence of pornography. Many fear that they would only invite ridicule by openly objecting to it. Some women believe that pornography has nothing to do with them, or that it is harmless, or that censorship is a greater evil than pornography. Primarily for these reasons, many women make no objection to pornography.

I hope to have shown that pornography does concern all women. Whether or not pornography ever incites men to rape, or promotes depersonalized sex, all women are defamed by material that implies that typically, women like to be treated as less than persons by their sexual partners; and all women are degraded by the pornography industry's display of contempt for womankind in marketing such material.

Embarrassment and fear of ridicule are not good reasons to refrain from objecting to the sale of pornographic material that supports false and offensive beliefs about womankind. As we noted in Part 1, degradation should be taken seriously not only because it involves treating people as though they were less than people, but also because it involves an erosion of moral courage on the part of the degraded person. We cannot afford to pretend that pornography does not concern us. Only by expressing outrage at being used, can we hope to maintain self-respect.

NOTES

1. I should acknowledge that men as well as women can be, and sometimes are, portrayed in pornographic material as being degraded. Nevertheless, we would do well to keep in mind a few significant differences between pornography that portrays men as degraded, and pornography that portrays women as degraded: (1) Material in which men are the victims of sexually aggressive women is the exception rather than the rule; (2) Very little else in the culture reinforces the idea of men being degraded by women; and (3) The victimized men and aggressive women in such material are usually depicted as homosexual, and therefore not "really" men and not "really" women, respectively, by the standards of the material itself; thus, it is still quasi-women who are victimized and pseudo-men who are victimizers.

2. I am not suggesting, of course, that women who participate in making Victim Pornography are *less degraded than other women by the sale of pornography*, but only that they are not necessarily degraded in their role as models.

3. A word about the importance of context. If we lived in a culture in

which nothing supported the idea that women are less than full persons, I might be more reluctant to say that Victim Pornography has implications concerning the nature of womankind. If nothing in the culture supported the idea that women may be treated as though they were not ends in themselves, I might be willing to say that Victim Pornography is pure fantasy, no more to be taken seriously —no more to be generalized from—than a cartoon that portrays cats as indiscriminate eaters, or an advertisement that portrays auto mechanics as good natured and helpful, or a story that portrays men as enjoying abuse. But the fact is that there are many facets of our culture that tend to support the view that women like to be abused. Much of popular music romanticizes such relationships; advertisements tacitly give them a stamp of approval by describing abuse as the norm for the attractive upper-middle class family next door, or by giving it a slightly exotic flavor; some religious dogma openly prescribes treating women as less than persons. In light of this tradition, Victim Pornography can*not* be easily dismissed as mere fantasy, with no implications concerning the nature of women. Victim Pornography contributes to the tradition of viewing women as less than full persons, whatever the intention of its authors.

    4. *Byers* v. *Martin*, 2 Colo. 605, 25 Am.Rep. 755 (1875); *Welsh* v. *Tribune Publishing Co.*, 83 Mich. 661, 57 N.W. 562 (1890).

    5. *Wofford* v. *Meeks*, 129 Ala. 349, 30 So. 625 (1900); *Palmerlee* v. *Notage*, 119 Minn. 351, 138 N.W. 312 (1912); *Prosser* v. *Callis*, 117 Ind. 105, 19 N.E. 735 (1888).

    6. *Bornmann* v. *Star Co.*, 174 N.Y. 212, 66 N.E. 723 (1903). Contra: *Kassowitz* v. *Sentinel Co.*, 226 Wis. 468, 227 N.W. 177 (1938).

    7. *Hardy* v. *Williamson*, 86 Ga. 551, 12 S.E. 874 (1891).

REFERENCES

Berger, Fred. "Pornography, Sex, and Censorship." *Social Theory and Practice* 4 (1977): 183–210.

Dworkin, Andrea. *Pornography: Men Possessing Women.* New York: Perigee Books, 1981.

Feinberg, Joel. "Harmless Immoralities and Offensive Nuisances." In *Rights, Justice and the Bounds of Liberty.* Princeton: Princeton University Press, 1980.

Goldman, Emma. *Living My Life.* New York: Knopf, 1983.

Hentoff, Nat. "War on Pornography." *The Washington Post* (31 August 1984): A21.

Hill, Thomas. "Servility and Self-Respect." *The Monist* 57, 1 (1973): 87–104.

Reisman, David. "Democracy and Defamation: Control on Group Libel." *Columbia Law Review* 42, 5 (1942).

Shipp, E. R. "Federal Judge Hears Arguments on Validity of Indianapolis Pornography Measure." *New York Times* (31 July 1984): A10.

Styron, William. *Sophie's Choice.* New York: Random House, 1979.

13

Pornography and the Alienation of Male Sexuality

Harry Brod

Pornography is both an expression of men's public power and an expression of their lack of personal power. The argument of this paper is that pornography's image of male sexuality works to the detriment of men personally even as its image of female sexuality enhances the powers of patriarchy. . . .

[The editors include here that part of the essay discussing pornography's negative impact on men, and omit the author's analysis of pornography's oppression of women. Readers are urged to consult the full article, reprinted in *The Philosophy of Sex: Contemporary Readings,* second edition, ed. Alan Soble, Rowman & Littlefield, 1991, pp. 281–299.]

This paper is intended as a contribution to an ongoing discussion. It aims to augment, not refute or replace, what numerous commentators have said about pornography's role in the social construction of sexuality. . . . My primary focus is to examine pornography's model of male sexuality. . . . One reason I focus on the image of male sexuality in pornography is that I believe this aspect of the topic has been relatively neglected. In making this my topic here, I do not mean to suggest that this is the most essential part of the picture. Indeed, I am clear it is not. It seems clear enough to me that the main focus of discussion about the effects of por-

From *Social Theory and Practice* 14, no. 3 (Fall 1988): 265–284. Reprinted by permission of the publisher and the author.

nography is and should be the harmful effects of pornography on women, its principal victims. Yet, there is much of significance which needs to be said about pornography's representation, or perhaps I should more accurately say misrepresentation, of male sexuality. My focus shall be on what is usually conceived of as "normal" male sexuality, which for my purposes I take to be consensual, non-violent heterosexuality, as these terms are conventionally understood. I am aware of analyses which argue that this statement assumes distinctions which are at least highly problematic, if not outright false, which argue that this "normal" sexuality is itself coercive, both as compulsory heterosexuality and as containing implicit or explicit coercion and violence. My purpose is not to take issue with these analyses, but simply to present an analysis of neglected aspects of the links between mainstream male sexuality and pornography. I would argue that the aspect of the relation between male sexuality and pornography usually discussed, pornography's incitement to greater extremes of violence against women, presupposes such a connection with the more accepted mainstream. Without such a link, pornography's messages would be rejected by rather than assimilated into male culture. My intention is to supply this usually missing link.

My analysis proceeds from both feminist and Marxist theory. These are often taken to be theories which speak from the point of view of the oppressed, in advocacy for their interests. That they indeed are, but they are also more than that. For each claims not simply to speak for the oppressed in a partisan way, but also to speak a truth about the social whole, a truth perhaps spoken in the name of the oppressed, but a truth objectively valid for the whole. That is to say, Marxism is a theory which analyzes the ruling class as well as the proletariat, and feminism is a theory which analyzes men as well as women. It is not simply that Marxism is concerned with class, and feminism with gender, both being united by common concerns having to do with power. Just as Marxism understands class as power, rather than simply understanding class differences as differences of income, lifestyle, or opportunities, so the distinctive contribution of feminism is its understanding of gender as power, rather than simply as sex role differentiation. Neither class nor gender should be reified into being understood as fixed entities, which then differentially distribute power and its rewards. Rather, they are categories continually constituted in ongoing contestations over power. The violence endemic to both systems cannot be understood as externalized manifestations of some natural inner biological or psychological drives existing prior to the social order, but must be seen as emerging in and from the relations of power which constitute social structures. Just as capitalist exploitation is caused not by capitalists' excess greed but rather by the structural imperatives under which capitalism functions, so men's violence is not the manifestation of some inner male essence, but rather evidence of the bitterness and depth of the struggles through which genders are forged.[1]

For my purposes here, to identifiy this as a socialist feminist analysis is not, in the first instance, to proclaim allegiance to any particular set of doctrinal propositions, though I am confident that those I subscribe to would be included in any roundup of the usual suspects, but rather to articulate a methodological commitment to make questions of power central to questions of gender, and to understand gendered power in relation to economic power, and as historically, materially structured.[2] If one can understand the most intimate aspects of the lives of the dominant group in these terms, areas which would usually be taken to be the farthest afield from where one might expect these categories to be applicable, then I believe one has gone a long way toward validating claims of the power of socialist feminist theory to comprehend the totality of our social world. This is my intention here. I consider the analysis of male sexuality I shall be presenting part of a wider socialist feminist analysis of patriarchal capitalist masculinity, an analysis I have begun to develop elsewhere.[3]

As shall be abundantly clear, I do not take a "sexual liberationist" perspective on pornography. I am aware that many individuals, particularly various sexual minorities, make this claim on pornography's behalf. I do not minimize nor negate their personal experiences. In the context of our society's severe sexual repressiveness, pornography may indeed have a liberating function for certain individuals. But I do not believe an attitude of approval for pornography follows from this. Numerous drugs and devices which have greatly helped individual women have also been medical and social catastrophes—the one does not negate the other.

I shall be claiming that pornography has a negative impact on men's own sexuality. This is a claim that an aspect of an oppressive system, patriarchy, operates, at least in part, to the disadvantage of the group it privileges, men. This claim does not deny that the overall effect of the system is to operate in men's advantage, nor does it deny that the same aspect of the system under consideration, that is, male sexuality and pornography under patriarchy, might not also contribute to the expansion and maintenance of male power even as it also works to men's disadvantage. Indeed, I shall be arguing precisely for such complementarity. I am simply highlighting one of the "contradictions" in the system. My reasons for doing so are in the first instance simply analytic: to, as I said, bring to the fore relatively neglected aspects of the issue. Further, I also have political motivations for emphasizing this perspective. I view raising consciousness of the prices of male power as part of a strategy through which one could at least potentially mobilize men against pornography's destructive effects on both women and men. . . .

Alienated pornographic male sexuality can be understood as having two dimensions, what I call the objectification of the body and the loss of subjectivity. . . .

OBJECTIFICATION OF THE BODY

In terms of both its manifest image of and its effects on male sexuality, that is, in both intrinsic and consequentialist terms, pornography restricts male sensuality in favor of a genital, performance-oriented male sexuality. Men become sexual acrobats endowed with oversized and overused organs. . . . To speak noneuphemistically, using penile performance as an index of male strength and potency directly contradicts biological facts. There is no muscle tissue in the penis. Its erection when aroused results simply from increased blood flow to the area. All social mythology aside, the male erection is physiologically nothing more than localized high blood pressure. Yet this particular form of hypertension has attained mythic significance. Not only does this focusing of sexual attention on one organ increase male performance anxieties, but it also desensitizes other areas of the body from becoming what might otherwise be sources of pleasure. A colleague once told me that her favorite line in a lecture on male sexuality I used to give in a course I regularly taught was my declaration that the basic male sex organ is not the penis, but the skin.

The predominant image of women in pornography presents women as always sexually ready, willing, able, and eager. The necessary corollary to pornography's myth of female perpetual availability is its myth of male perpetual readiness. Just as the former fuels male misogyny when real-life women fail to perform to pornographic standards, so do men's failures to similarly perform fuel male insecurities. Furthermore, I would argue that this diminishes pleasure. Relating to one's body as a performance machine produces a split consciousness wherein part of one's attention is watching the machine, looking for flaws in its performance, even while one is supposedly immersed in the midst of sensual pleasure. This produces a self-distancing self-consciousness which mechanizes sex and reduces pleasure. (This is a problem perpetuated by numerous sexual self-help manuals, which treat sex as a matter of individual technique for fine-tuning the machine rather than as human interaction. I would add that men's sexual partners are also affected by this, as they can often intuit when they are being subjected to rote manipulation.)

LOSS OF SUBJECTIVITY

In the terms of discourse of what it understands to be "free" sex, pornographic sex comes "free" of the demands of emotional intimacy or commitment. It is commonly said as a generalization that women tend to connect sex with emotional intimacy more than men do. Without romantically blurring female sexuality into soft focus, if what is meant is how each gender consciously thinks or speaks of sex, I think this view is fair enough. But I find it takes what men say about sex, that it doesn't mean as much or the same thing to them, too much at face value. I would argue that men do feel similar needs for intimacy, but are trained to deny them, and are encouraged further 'to see physical affection and intimacy primarily if not exclusively in sexual terms. This leads to the familiar syndrome wherein, as one man put it:

> Although what most men want is physical affection, what they end up thinking they want is to be laid by a Playboy bunny.[4]

This puts a strain on male sexuality. Looking to sex to fulfill what are really nonsexual needs, men end up disappointed and frustrated. Sometimes they feel an unfilled void, and blame it on their or their partner's inadequate sexual performance. At other times they feel a discomfitting urgency or neediness to their sexuality, leading in some cases to what are increasingly recognized as sexual addiction disorders (therapists are here not talking about the traditional "perversions," but behaviors such as what is coming to be called a "Don Juan Syndrome," an obsessive pursuit of sexual "conquests"). A confession that sex is vastly overrated often lies beneath male sexual bravado. I would argue that sex seems overrated because men look to sex for the fulfillment of nonsexual emotional needs, a quest doomed to failure. Part of the reason for this failure is the priority of quantity over quality of sex which comes with sexuality's commodification. As human needs become subservient to market desires, the ground is laid for an increasing multiplication of desires to be exploited and filled by marketable commodities.[5]

For the most part the female in pornography is not one the man has yet to "conquer," but one already presented to him for the "taking." The female is primarily there as sex object, not sexual subject. Or, if she is not completely objectified, since men do want to be desired themselves, hers is at least a subjugated subjectivity. But one needs another independent subject, not an object or a captured subjectivity, if one either wants one's own prowess validated, or if one simply desires human interaction. Men functioning in the pornographic mode of male sexuality, in which men dominate women, are denied satisfaction of these human desires.[6] Denied recognition in the sexual interaction itself, they look to gain this recognition in wider social recognition of their "conquest."

To the pornographic mind, then, women become trophies awarded to the victor. For women to serve this purpose of achieving male social validation, a woman "conquered" by one must be a woman deemed desirable by others. Hence pornography both produces and reproduces uniform standards of female beauty. Male desires and tastes must be channeled into a single mode, with allowance for minor variations which obscure the fundamentally monolithic nature of the mold. Men's own subjectivity becomes masked to them, as historically and culturally specific and varying standards of beauty are made to appear natural and given. The ease with which men reach quick agreement on what makes a woman "attractive," evidenced in such things as the "1–10" rating scale of male banter and the reports of a computer program's success in predicting which of the contestants would be crowned "Miss America," demonstrates how deeply such standards have been internalized, and consequently the extent to which men are dominated by desires not authentically their own.

Lest anyone think that the analysis above is simply a philosopher's ruminations, too far removed from the actual experiences of most men, let me just offer one recent instantiation, from among many known to me, and even more, I am sure, I do not know. The following is from the *New York Times Magazine*'s "About Men" weekly column. In an article titled "Couch Dancing," the author describes his reactions to being taken to a place, a sort of cocktail bar, where women "clad only in the skimpiest of bikini underpants" would "dance" for a small group of men for a few minutes for about 25 or 30 dollars, men who "sat immobile, drinks in hand, glassy-eyed, tapping their feet to the disco music that throbbed through the room."

Men are supposed to like this kind of thing, and there is a quite natural part of each of us that does. But there is another part of us—of me, at least—that is not grateful for the traditional male sexual programming, not proud of the results. By a certain age, most modern men have been so surfeited with images of unattainably beautiful women in preposterous contexts that we risk losing the capacity to respond to the ordinarily beautiful women we love in our bedrooms. There have been too many times when I have guiltily resorted to impersonal fantasy because the genuine love I felt for a woman wasn't enough to convert feeling into performance. And in those sorry, secret moments, I have resented deeply my lifelong indoctrination into the esthetic of the centerfold.[7]

3. CONCLUSIONS

. . . I would like to conclude with some remarks on the practical import of this analysis. . . . [I]f the analysis of the relationship between pornography and consumerism . . . is correct, then a different conceptualization of the debate over the ethics of the feminist anti-pornography movement emerges. If one accepts, as I do, that idea that this movement is not against sex, but against sexual abuse, then the campaign against pornography is essentially not a call for censorship but a consumer campaign for product safety. The proper context for the debate over its practices is then not issues of free speech or civil liberties, but issues of business ethics. Or rather, this is the conclusion I reach remaining focused on pornography and male sexuality. But we should remember the broader context I alluded to at the beginning of this paper, the question of pornography's effects on women. In that context, women are not the consumers of pornography, but the consumed. Rather than invoking the consumer movement, perhaps we should then look to environmental protection as a model.[8] Following this line of reasoning, one could in principle then perhaps develop under the tort law of product liability an argument to accomplish much of the regulation of sexually explicit material some are now trying to achieve through legislative means, perhaps developing a new definition of "safe" sexual material.

Finally, for most of us most of our daily practice as academics consists of teaching rather than writing or reading in our fields. If one accepts the analysis I have presented, a central if not primary concern for us should therefore be how to integrate this analysis into our classrooms. I close by suggesting that we use this analysis and others like it from the emerging field of men's studies to demonstrate to the men in our classes the direct relevance of feminist analysis to their own lives, at the most intimate and personal levels, and that we look for ways to demonstrate to men that feminism can be personally empowering and liberating for them without glossing over, and in fact emphasizing, the corresponding truth that this will also require the surrender of male privilege.[9]

NOTES

1. I am indebted for this formulation to Tim Carrigan, Bob Connell, and John Lee, "Toward a New Sociology of Masculinity," in Harry Brod, ed. *The Making of Masculinities: The New Men's Studies* (Boston: Allen & Unwin, 1987).

2. For the *locus classicus* of the redefinition of Marxism as method rather

than doctrine, see George Lukács, *History and Class Consciousness: Studies in Marxist Dialectics,* trans. Rodney Livingstone (Cambridge, Mass.: MIT Press, 1972).

3. See my Introduction to Brod, *The Making of Masculinities.* For other recent books by men I consider to be engaged in essentially the same or a kindred project, see Jeff Hearn, *The Gender of Oppression: Men, Masculinity, and the Critique of Marxism* (New York: St. Martin's Press, 1987) and R. W. Connell, *Gender and Power* (Stanford, Calif.: Stanford University Press, 1987), particularly the concept of "hegemonic masculinity," also used in Carrigan, Connell, and Lee, "Toward A New Socilogy of Masculinity." Needless to say, none of this work would be conceivable without the pioneering work of many women in women's studies.

4. Michael Betzold, "How Pornography Shackles Men and Oppresses Women," in *For Men Against Sexism: A Book of Readings,* ed. Jon Snodgrass (Albion, Calif.: Times Change Press, 1977), p. 46.

5. I am grateful to Lenore Langsdorf and Paula Rothenberg for independently suggesting to me how this point would fit into my analysis.

6. See Jessica Benjamin, "The Bonds of Love: Rational Violence and Erotic Domination," *Feminist Studies* 6 (1980): 144–74.

7. Keith McWalter, "Couch Dancing," *New York Times Magazine,* December 6, 1987, p. 138.

8. I am indebted to John Stoltenberg for this point.

9. I attempt to articulate this perspective principally in the following: *The Making of Masculinities,* Introduction and "The Case for Men's Studies," *A Mensch Among Men: Explorations in Jewish Masculinity* (Freedom, Calif.: The Crossing Press, 1988), especially the Introduction; and "Why Is This 'Men's Studies' Different From All Other 'Men's Studies'?" *Journal of the National Association for Women Deans, Administrators, and Counselors* 49 (1986): pp. 44–49. See also generally the small men's movement magazines *Changing Men: Issues in Gender, Sex and Politics* (306 North Brooks St., Madison, WI 53715), *brother: The Newsletter of the National Organization for Changing Men* (1402 Greenfield Ave., #1, Los Angeles, CA 90025), and *Men's Studies Review* (Box 32, Harriman, TN 37748).

14

Pornography, Oppression, and Freedom: A Closer Look

Helen E. Longino

INTRODUCTION

The much-touted sexual revolution of the 1960s and 1970s not only freed various modes of sexual behavior from the constraints of social disapproval, but also made possible a flood of pornographic material. . . .

Traditionally, pornography was condemned as immoral because it presented sexually explicit material in a manner designed to appeal to "prurient interests" or a "morbid" interest in nudity and sexuality, material which furthermore lacked any redeeming social value and which exceeded "customary limits of candor." While these phrases, taken from a definition of "obscenity" proposed in the 1954 American Law Institute's *Model Penal Code*,[1] require some criteria of application to eliminate vagueness, it seems that what is objectionable is the explicit description or representation of bodily parts or sexual behavior for the purpose of inducing sexual stimulation or pleasure on the part of the reader or viewer. This kind of objection is part of a sexual ethic that subordinates sex to procreation and condemns all sexual interactions outside of legitimated marriage. It is this code which was the primary target of the sexual revolutionaries in the 1960s, and which has given way in many areas to more open standards of sexual behavior.

One of the beneficial results of the sexual revolution has been a growing acceptance of the distinction between questions of sexual mores and questions of morality. This distinction underlies the old slogan, "Make love, not war," and takes harm to others as the defining characteristic of immorality. What is immoral is behavior which causes injury to or violation of another person or people. Such injury may be physical or it may be psychological. To cause pain to another, to lie to another, to hinder another in the exercise of her or his rights, to exploit another, to degrade another, to misrepresent and slander another are instances of immoral behavior. Masturbation or engaging voluntarily in sexual intercourse with another consenting adult of the same or the other sex, as long as neither injury nor violation of either individual or another is involved, are not immoral. Some sexual behavior is morally objectionable, but not because of its sexual character. Thus, adultery is immoral not because it involves sexual intercourse with someone to whom one is not legally married, but because it involves breaking a promise (of sexual and emotional fidelity to one's spouse). Sadistic, abusive, or forced sex is immoral because it injures and violates another.

The detachment of sexual chastity from moral virtue implies that we cannot condemn forms of sexual behavior merely because they strike us as distasteful or subversive of the Protestant work ethic, or because they depart from standards of behavior we have individually adopted. It has thus seemed to imply that no matter how offensive we might find pornography, we must tolerate it in the name of freedom from illegitimate repression. I wish to argue that this is not so, that pornography is immoral because it is harmful to people.

WHAT IS PORNOGRAPHY?

I define pornography as *verbal or pictorial explicit representations of sexual behavior that,* in the words of the Commission on Obscenity and Pornography, *have as a distinguishing characteristic "the degrading and demeaning portrayal of the role and status of the human female . . . as a mere sexual object to be exploited and manipulated sexually."*[2] In pornographic books, magazines, and films, women are represented as passive and as slavishly dependent upon men. The role of female characters is limited to the provision of sexual services to men. To the extent that women's sexual pleasure is represented at all, it is subordinated to that of men and is never an end in itself as is the sexual pleasure of men. What pleases women is the use of their bodies to satisfy male desires. While the sexual objectification of women is common to all pornography, women are the recipients of even worse treatment in violent pornography, in which women characters are killed, tortured, gang-raped, mutilated, bound, and otherwise abused, as a means of providing sexual stimulation or pleasure to the male characters. It is this development which has attracted the attention of feminists and been the stimulus to an analysis of pornography in general. . .

Not all sexually explicit material is pornography, nor is all material which contains representations of sexual abuse and degradation pornography.

A representation of a sexual encounter between adult persons which is characterized by mutual respect is, once we have disentangled sexuality and morality, not morally objectionable. Such a representation would be one in which the desires and experiences of each participant were regarded by the other participants as having a validity and a subjective importance equal to those of the individual's own desire and experiences. In such an encounter, each participant acknowledges the other participant's basic human dignity and personhood. Similarly, a representation of a nude human body (in whole or in part) in such a manner that the person shown maintains self-respect—e.g., is not portrayed in a degrading position—would not be morally objectionable. The educational films of the National Sex Forum, as well as a certain amount of erotic literature and art, fall into this category. While some erotic materials are beyond the standards of modesty held by some individuals, they are not for this reason immoral.

A representation of a sexual encounter which is not characterized by mutual respect, in which at least one of the parties is treated in a manner beneath her or his dignity as a human being, is no longer simple erotica. That a representation is of degrading behavior does not in itself, however, make it pornographic. Whether or not it is pornographic is a function of contextual features. Books and films may contain descriptions or representations of a rape in order to explore the consequences of such an assault upon its victim. What is being shown is abusive or degrading behavior which attempts to deny the humanity and dignity of the person assaulted, yet the context surrounding the representation, through its exploration of the consequences of the act, acknowledges and reaffirms her dignity. Such books and films, far from being pornographic, are (or can be) highly moral, and fall into the category of moral realism.

What makes a work a work of pornography, then, is not simply its representation of degrading and abusive sexual encounters, but its implicit, if not explicit, approval and recommendation of sexual behavior that is immoral, i.e., that physically or psychologically violates the personhood of one of the participants. Pornography, then, is verbal or pictorial material which represents or describes sexual behavior that is degrading or abusive to one or more of the participants *in such a way as to endorse the degradation.* The participants so treated in virtually all heterosexual pornography are women or children, so heterosexual pornography is, as a matter of fact, material which endorses sexual behavior that is degrading and/or abusive to women and children. As I use the term "sexual behavior," this includes sexual encounters between persons, behavior which produces sexual stimulation or pleasure for one of the participants, and behavior which is preparatory to or invites sexual activity. Behavior that is degrading or abusive includes physical harm or abuse, and physical or psychological coercion. In addition, behavior which ignores or devalues the real interests, desires, and experiences of one or more participants in any way is degrading. Finally, that a person has chosen or consented to be harmed, abused, or subjected to coercion does not alter the degrading character of such behavior.

Pornography communicates its endorsement of the behavior it represents by various features of the pornographic context: the degradation of the female characters is represented as providing pleasure to the participant males and, even worse, to the participant females, and there is no suggestion that this sort of treatment of others is inappropriate to their status as human beings. These two features are together sufficient to constitute endorsement of the represented behavior. The contextual features which make material pornographic are intrinsic to the material. . . .

To summarize: Pornography is not just the explicit representation or description of sexual behavior, nor even the explicit representation or description of sexual behavior which is degrading and/or abusive to women. Rather, it is material that explicitly represents or describes degrading and abusive sexual behavior so as to endorse and/or recommend the behavior as described. The contextual features, moreover, which communicate such endorsement are intrinsic to the material; that is, they are features whose removal or alteration would change the representation or description. . . .

PORNOGRAPHY: LIES AND VIOLENCE AGAINST WOMEN

What is wrong with pornography, then, is its degrading and dehumanizing portrayal of women (and *not* its sexual content). Pornography, by its very nature, requires that women be subordinate to men and mere instruments for the fulfillment of male fantasies. To accomplish this, pornography must lie. Pornography lies when it says that our sexual life is or ought to be subordinate to the service of men, that our pleasure consists in pleasing men and not ourselves, that we are depraved, that we are fit subjects for rape, bondage, torture, and murder. Pornography lies explicitly about women's sexuality, and through such lies fosters more lies about our humanity, our dignity, and our personhood.

Moreover, since nothing is alleged to justify the treatment of the female characters of pornography save their womanhood, pornography depicts all women as fit objects of violence by virtue of their sex alone. Because it is simply being female that, in the pornographic vision, justifies being violated, the lies of pornography are lies about all women. Each work of pornography is on its own libelous and defamatory, yet gains power through being reinforced by every other pornographic work. The sheer number of pornographic productions expands the moral issue to include not only assessing the morality or immorality of individual works, but also the meaning and force of the mass production of pornography. . . .

The entrenchment of pornography in our culture also gives it a significance quite beyond its explicit sexual messages. To suggest, as pornography does, that the primary purpose of women is to provide sexual pleasure to men is to deny that women are independently human or have a status equal to that of men. It is, moreover, to deny our equality at one of the most intimate levels of human experience. This denial is especially powerful in a hierarchical, class society such as ours, in which individuals feel good about themselves by feeling superior to others. Men in our society have a vested interest in maintaining their belief in the inferiority of the female sex, so that no matter how oppressed and exploited by the society in which they live and work, they can feel that they are at least superior to someone or some category of individuals—a woman or women. Pornography, by presenting women as wanton, depraved, and made for the sexual use of men, caters directly to that interest. The very intimate nature of sexuality which makes pornography so corrosive also protects it from explicit public discussion. The consequent lack of any explicit social disavowal of the pornographic image of women enables this image to continue fostering sexist attitudes even as the society publicly proclaims its (as yet timid) commitment to sexual equality.

In addition to finding a connection between the pornographic view of women and the denial to us of our full human rights, women are beginning to connect the consumption of pornography with committing rape and other acts of sexual violence against women. Contrary to the findings of the Commission on Obscenity and Pornography, a growing body of research is documenting (1) a correlation between exposure to representations of violence and the committing of violent acts generally, and (2) a correlation between exposure to pornographic materials and the committing of sexually abusive or violent acts against women.[3] While more study is needed to establish precisely what the causal relations are, clearly so-called hard-core pornography is not innocent.

From "snuff" films and miserable magazines in pornographic stores to *Hustler,* to phonograph album covers and advertisements, to *Vogue,* pornography has come to occupy its own niche in the communications and entertainment media and to acquire a quasi-institutional character (signaled by the use of diminutives such as "porn" or "porno" to refer to pornographic material, as though such familiar naming could take the hurt out). Its acceptance by the mass media, whatever the motivation, means a cultural endorsement of its message. As much as the materials themselves, the social tolerance of these degrading and distorted images of women in such quantities is harmful to us, since it indicates a general willingness to see women in ways incompatible with our fundamental human dignity and thus to justify treating us in those ways.[4] The tolerance of pornographic representations of the rape, bondage, and torture of women helps to create and maintain a climate more tolerant of the actual physical abuse of women.[5] The tendency on the part of the legal system to view the victim of a rape as responsible for the crime against her is but one manifestation of this.

In sum, pornography is injurious to women in at least three distinct ways:

1. Pornography, especially violent pornography, is implicated in the committing of crimes of violence against women.

2. Pornography is the vehicle for the dissemination of a deep and vicious lie about women. It is defamatory and libelous.

3. The diffusion of such a distorted view of women's nature in our society as it exists today supports sexist (i.e., male-centered) attitudes, and thus reinforces the oppression and exploitation of women.

Society's tolerance of pornography, especially pornography on the contemporary massive scale, reinforces each of these modes of injury: By not disavowing the lie, it supports the male-centered myth that women are inferior and subordinate creatures. Thus, it contributes to the maintenance of a climate tolerant of both psychological and physical violence against women.

PORNOGRAPHY AND THE LAW

> Congress shall make no law respecting the establishment of religion, or prohibiting the free exercise thereof; or abridging the freedom of speech, or of the press; or the right of the people peaceably to assemble, and to petition the Government for a redress of grievances.
>
> —FIRST AMENDMENT, BILL OF RIGHTS
> OF THE UNITED STATES CONSTITUTION

Pornography is clearly a threat to women. Each of the modes of injury cited above offers sufficient reason at least to consider proposals for the social and legal control of pornography. The almost universal response from progressives to such proposals is that constitutional guarantees of freedom of speech and privacy preclude recourse to law.[6] While I am concerned about the erosion of constitutional rights and also think for many reasons that great caution must be exercised before undertaking a legal campaign against pornography, I find objections to such a campaign that are based on appeals to the First Amendment or to a right to privacy ultimately unconvincing.

Much of the defense of the pornographer's right to publish seems to assume that, while pornography may be tasteless and vulgar, it is basically an entertainment that harms no one but its consumers, who may at worst suffer from the debasement of their taste; and that therefore those who argue for its control are demanding an unjustifiable abridgment of the rights to freedom of speech of those who make and distribute pornographic materials and of the rights to privacy of their customers. The account of pornography given above shows that the assumptions of this position are false. Nevertheless, even some who acknowledge its harmful character feel that it is granted immunity from social control by the First Amendment, or that the harm that would ensue from its control outweighs the harm prevented by its control.

There are three ways of arguing that control of pornography is incompatible with adherence to constitutional rights. The first argument claims that regulating pornography involves an unjustifiable interference in the private lives of individuals. The second argument takes the First Amendment as a basic principle constitutive of our form of government, and claims that the production and distribution of pornographic material, as a form of speech, is an activity protected by that amendment. The third argument claims not that the pornographer's rights are violated, but that others' rights will be if controls against pornography are instituted.

The privacy argument is the easiest to dispose of. Since the open commerce in pornographic materials is an activity carried out in the public sphere, the publication and distribution of such materials, unlike their use by individuals, is not protected by rights to privacy. The distinction between the private consumption of pornographic material and the production and distribution of, or open commerce in, it is sometimes blurred by defenders of pornography. But I may entertain, in the privacy of my mind, defamatory opinions about another person, even though I may not broadcast them. So one might create without restraint—as long as no one were harmed in the course of preparing them—pornographic materials for one's personal use, but be restrained from reproducing and distributing them. In both cases what one is doing—in the privacy of one's mind or basement—may indeed be deplorable, but immune from legal proscription. Once the activity becomes public, however—i.e., once it involves others—it is no longer protected by the same rights that protect activities in the private sphere.

In considering the second argument (that control of pornography, private or public, is wrong in principle), it seems important to determine whether we consider the right to freedom of speech to be absolute and unqualified. If it is, then obviously all speech, including pornography, is entitled to protection. But the right is, in the first place, not an unqualified right: There are several kinds of speech not protected by the First Amendment, including the incitement to violence in volatile circumstances, the solicitation of crimes, perjury and misrepresentation, slander, libel, and false advertising. That there are forms of proscribed speech shows that we accept limitations on the right to freedom of speech if such speech, as do the forms listed, impinges on other rights. The manufacture and distribution of material which defames and threatens all members of a class by its recommendation of abusive and degrading behavior toward some members of that class simply in virtue of their membership in it seems a clear candidate for inclusion on the list. The right is therefore not an unqualified one.

Nor is it an absolute or fundamental right, underived from any other right: If it were there would not be exceptions or limitations. The first ten amendments were added to the Constitution as a way of guaranteeing the "blessings of liberty" mentioned in its preamble, to protect citizens against the unreasonable usurpation of power by the state. The specific rights mentioned in the First Amendment—those of religion, speech, assembly, press, petition—reflect the recent experiences of the makers of the Constitution under colonial government as well as a sense of what was and is required generally to secure liberty.

It may be objected that the right to freedom of speech is fundamental in that it is part of what we mean by liberty and not a right that is derivative from a right to liberty. In order to meet this objection, it is useful to consider a distinction explained by Ronald Dworkin in his book *Taking Rights Seriously*.[7] As Dworkin points out, the word "liberty" is used in two distinct, if related, senses: as "license," i.e., the freedom from legal constraints to do as one pleases, in some contexts; and as "independence," i.e., "the status of a person as independent and equal rather than subservient," in others. Failure to distinguish between these senses in discussions of rights and freedoms is fatal to clarity and understanding.

If the right to free speech is understood as a partial explanation of what is meant by liberty, then liberty is perceived as license: The right to do as one pleases includes a right to speak as one pleases. But license is surely not a condition the First Amendment is designed to protect. We not only tolerate but require legal constraints on liberty as license when we enact laws against rape, murder, assault, theft, etc. If everyone did exactly as she or he pleased at any given time, we would have chaos if not lives, as Hobbes put it, that are "nasty, brutish, and short." We accept government to escape, not to protect, this condition.

If, on the other hand, by liberty is meant independence, then freedom of speech is not necessarily a part of liberty; rather, it is a means to it. The right to freedom of speech is not a fundamental, absolute right, but one derivative from, possessed in virtue of, the more basic right to independence. Taking this view of liberty requires providing arguments showing that the more specific rights we claim are necessary to guarantee our status as persons "independent and equal rather than subservient." In the context of government, we understand independence to be the freedom of each individual to participate as an equal among equals in the determination of how she or he is to be governed. Freedom of speech in this context means that an individual may not only entertain beliefs concerning government privately, but may express them publicly. We express our opinions about taxes, disarmament, wars, social-welfare programs, the function of the police, civil rights, and so on. Our right to freedom of speech includes the right to criticize the government and to protest against various forms of injustice and the abuse of power. What we wish to protect is the free expression of ideas even when they are unpopular. What we do not always remember is that speech has functions other than the expression of ideas.

Regarding the relationship between a right to freedom of speech and the publication and distribution of pornographic materials, there are two points to be made. In the first place, the latter activity is hardly an exercise of the right to the free expression of ideas as understood above. In the second place, to the degree that the tolerance of material degrading to women supports and reinforces the attitude that women are not fit to participate as equals among equals in the political life of their communities, and that the prevalence of such an attitude effectively prevents women from so participating, the absolute and fundamental right of women to liberty (political independence) is violated.

This second argument against the suppression of pornographic material, then, rests on a premise that must be rejected, namely, that the right to freedom of speech is a right to utter anything one wants. It thus fails to show that the production and distribution of such material is an activity protected by the First Amendment. Furthermore, an examination of the issues involved leads to the conclusion that tolerance of this activity violates the rights of women to political independence.

The third argument (which expresses concern that curbs on pornography are the first step toward political censorship) runs into the same ambiguity that besets the arguments based on principle. These arguments generally have as an underlying assumption that the maximization of freedom is a worthy social goal. Control of pornography diminishes freedom —directly the freedom of pornographers, indirectly that of all of us. But again, what is meant by "freedom"? It cannot be that what is to be maximized is license—as the goal of a social group whose members probably have at least some incompatible interests, such a goal would be internally inconsistent. If, on the other hand, the maximization of political independence is the goal, then that is in no way enhanced by, and may be endangered by, the tolerance of pornography. To argue that the control of pornography would create a precedent for suppressing political speech is thus to confuse license with political independence. In addition, it ignores a crucial basis for the control of pornography, i.e., its character as libelous speech. The prohibition of such speech is justified by the need for protection from the injury (psychological as well as physical or economic) that results from libel. A very different kind of argument would be required to justify curtailing the right to speak our minds about the institutions which govern us. As long as such distinctions are insisted upon, there is little danger of the government's using the control of pornography as precedent for curtailing political speech.

In summary, neither as a matter of principle nor in the interests of maximizing liberty can it be supposed that there is an intrinsic right to manufacture and distribute pornographic material.

The only other conceivable source of protection for pornography would be a general right to do what we please as long as the rights of others are respected. Since the production and distribution of pornography violates the rights of women—to respect and to freedom from defamation, among others—this protection is not available.

CONCLUSION

I have defined pornography in such a way as to distinguish it from erotica and from moral realism, and have argued that it is defamatory and libelous toward women, that it condones crimes against women, and that it invites tolerance of the social, economic, and cultural oppression of women. The production and distribution of pornographic material is thus a social and moral wrong. Contrasting both the current volume of pornographic production and its growing infiltration of the communications media with the status of women in this culture makes clear the necessity for its control. Since the goal of controlling pornography does not conflict with constitutional rights, a common obstacle to action is removed.

Appeals for action against pornography are sometimes brushed aside with the claim that such action is a diversion from the primary task of feminists—the elimination of sexism and of sexual inequality. This approach focuses on the enjoyment rather than the manufacture of pornography, and sees it as merely a product of sexism which will disappear when the latter has been overcome and the sexes are socially and economically equal. Pornography cannot be separated from sexism in this way: Sexism is not just a set of attitudes regarding the inferiority of women but the behaviors and social and economic rules that manifest such attitudes. Both the manufacture and distribution of pornography and the enjoyment of it are instances of sexist behavior. The enjoyment of pornography on the part of individuals will presumably decline as such individuals begin to accord women their status as fully human. A cultural climate which tolerates the degrading representation of women is not a climate which facilitates the development of respect for women. Furthermore, the demand for pornography is stimulated not just by the sexism of individuals but by the pornography industry itself. Thus, both as a social phenomenon and in its effect on individuals, pornography, far from being a mere product, nourishes sexism. The campaign against it is an essential component of women's struggle for legal, economic, and social equality, one which requires the support of all feminists.

NOTES

1. American Law Institute *Model Penal Code,* sec. 251.4.

2. *Report of the Commission on Obscenity and Pornography* (New York: Bantam Books, 1979), p. 239. The Commission, of course, concluded that the demeaning content of pornography did not adversely affect male attitudes toward women.

3. Urie Bronfenbrenner, *Two Worlds of Childhood* (New York: Russell Sage Foundation, 1970); H. J. Eysenck and D. K. B. Nias, *Sex, Violence and the Media* (New York: St. Martin's Press, 1978); and Michael Goldstein, Harold Kant, and John Hartman, *Pornography and Sexual Deviance* (Berkeley: University of California Press, 1973); and the papers by Diana Russell, Pauline Bart, and Irene Diamond [included in Lederer (ed.), *Take Back the Night* (New York: William Morrow and Company, Inc., 1989)].

4. This tolerance has a linguistic parallel in the growing acceptance and use of nonhuman nouns such as "chick," "bird," "filly," "fox," "doll," "babe," "skirt," etc., to refer to women, and of verbs of harm such as "fuck," "screw," "bang" to refer to sexual intercourse. See Robert Baker and Frederick Elliston, " 'Pricks' and 'Chicks': A Plea for Persons," in *Philosophy and Sex* (Buffalo, N.Y.: Prometheus Books, 1975).

5. This is supported by the fact that in Denmark the number of rapes committed has increased while the number of rapes reported to the authorities has decreased over the past twelve years. See *Women Against Violence in Pornography and Media Newspage,* Vol. II, No. 5, June, 1978, quoting M. Harry, "Denmark Today—The Causes and Effects of Sexual Liberty" (paper presented to The Responsible Society, London, England, 1976). See also Eysenck and Nias, *Sex, Violence and the Media* (New York: St. Martin's Press, 1978), pp. 120–124.

6. Cf. Marshall Cohen, "The Case Against Censorship," *The Public Interest,* No. 22, Winter 1971, reprinted in John R. Burr and Milton Goldinger, *Philosophy and Contemporary Issues* (New York: Macmillan, 1976), and Justice William Brennan's dissenting opinion in *Paris Adult Theater* I v. *Slaton,* 431 U.S. 49.

7. Ronald Dworkin, *Taking Rights Seriously* (Cambridge: Harvard University Press, 1977), p. 262.

15

Defamation and the
Endorsement of Degradation

Alan Soble

1. INTRODUCTION

In one of the more significant papers in the feminist anti-pornography collection *Take Back the Night,* Helen Longino advances two arguments for the censorship of pornography.[1] Longino argues that much pornography defames women (it is libelous), and that it endorses the degradation of women. Pornography defames women by telling lies about the nature of women and women's sexuality; in particular, it maliciously asserts that women naturally cater to the sexual needs of men and that women enjoy being sexually degraded. And by endorsing the degradation of women, pornography promotes that degradation and contributes causally to acts harmful to women. . . .

In Section 2 it will be argued that the defamation argument fails because pornography is nonpropositional, and that even though much pornography is in some sense false, it does not promulgate lies about women. In Section 3 . . . the accusation that pornographic materials degrade women is discussed, an accusation that is common to the defamation and endorsement arguments. Finally, in Section 4, I argue that the endorsement

From "Pornography: Defamation and the Endorsement of Degradation," *Social Theory and Practice* 11, no. 1 (Spring 1985): 61–87. Reprinted by permission of the publisher and the author.

argument fails because a depiction of degradation is not by itself an endorsement of that degradation.

2. PORNOGRAPHIC FANTASY IS NONPROPOSITIONAL

. . . Suppose that the main function served by pornography for the consuming male is to induce sexual arousal. We can safely say, on the basis of what feminists and others have described as the content of much pornography, that the fantasies contained in pornographic material depict a world in which sexual activity for its own sake, sex without commitments, prohibited or scorned types of sexual activity, sexually attractive bodies, and sexually adventurous women are more plentiful than they are in the lives of the consumers. If the function of pornography is to provide stimuli that enable men to imagine that women fully accommodate to their sexual desires (either by being passive attendants, or by being active seekers of their own pleasure, whichever works at the time for the individual), then any thesis about the propositional content of pornography will be irrelevant; it will simply not be grappling with what is central to the phenomenon. If pornography is consumed primarily for the sexual arousal it induces, and if this arousal is generated by fantasies contained in and provoked by pornographic depictions, then the issue of what might be asserted by pornography drops out.[2] Pornography does not arouse by advancing arguments, defending theses, or laying out a metaphysics, and it is not consumed for any arguments, theses, or metaphysics it might just happen to contain. It is, in fact, a common complaint about pornography that it is made by men, and that as a result it is nothing but a one-sided man's fantasy of a woman's fantasy, a projection that "says" something only about the men who produce and consume it. This observation has merit. But if we are going to be this sophisticated about pornography, then we are already acknowledging that men's fantasies do not assert anything about women and therefore could not defame them.

Pornographic fantasies go beyond the merely factually false to the grossly unrealistic, and things in this category are not usefully seen as propositional. In *some* sense, all fantasies *are* false, and so it is quite right to claim that pornography does not depict the actual state of the world or the nature of women's sexuality. All fantastic literature fails to correspond with reality. Indeed, the failure of pornographic fantasy to match reality probably contributes to its ability to generate sexual arousal; if women in reality always accommodated to the sexual desires of men, if women were in fact full sexual slaves, then the depiction of their accommodation in pornography might not arouse. But fantasy material is not false in the same way that nonfantasy material (a disproven scientific theory) is false. Pornography is false in some weak sense, in whatever sense, say, science fiction is false. Fantasy material never purports to be telling the truth about its subject matter; *Star Wars* is false, but as fantasy its falsity is beside the point. Men consume pornography because they find that entering its fantasy world is enjoyable, not because it is sexually arousing to perpetuate discredited theories about the nature of women. Similarly, the massive consumption of romance novels by women is motivated by the enjoyment of contemplating a fantasy world in which everlasting loves are more plentiful than they happen to be; these novels hardly depict men as they are, yet they are not defamatory.[3] The key here is that to engage in pretense is not to disseminate lies. Pornography is understood better by analogy with playing cops and robbers, than by analogy with a piece of journalism.

The suggestion that pornography is a vehicle of fantasy, and therefore perhaps not legally-speaking speech, pleases conservatives who use it to defend the legal prohibition of pornography. Harry Clor, for example, insists that pornography ("obscenity") does not "espouse or discuss opinions," but invites its audience "to experience sensations" and "wallow" in degradation.[4] Clor is right insofar as what is psychologically and socially important about pornography is its sexual function and not its possible propositional content. From this perspective, an item of pornography is more like a bit of technology such as contraceptive foam (both contribute to sexual enjoyment) than it is a religious pamphlet. It is more like a piece of machinery like a vibrator (both are "sexual aids") than it is a scandal sheet. Thus, those who wish to oppose the prohibition of pornography can avail themselves of other Constitutional protections, perhaps by invoking arguments based on the privacy considerations related to the Ninth Amendment.[5] Note that it is not being claimed that pornography "is a purely sexual activity" and, therefore, is not legally speech. That argument is easy enough to refute; and to refute it does not establish that pornography *is* speech.[6] It is also insufficient to point out that

> Since men of intelligence do not generally disagree over nothing, one would suppose that some question of perceived social importance is at issue. It is difficult to conclude that a book which generates such a serious dispute presents or represents no ideas, is nothing.[7]

But there have been heated debates about all sorts of things that could never be construed as speech and which are perceived as socially important; abortion is a sexual technology about which the debate goes on and on.

3. DEGRADATION: THREE APPROACHES

The defamation and endorsement arguments presuppose that pornography degrades women, or at least that specific items of pornography degrade women. The former holds that pornography defames women by telling the lie that women enjoy being sexually degraded; the latter holds that pornographic depictions of the degradation of women endorse and thereby promote that degradation. Let us assume that if there are sexual acts that are degrading to women, and these are depicted by pornography, then pornography is degrading to women. But which sexual acts are degrading to women, and how frequently are these degrading acts depicted by pornography? Consider two descriptions of pornography, the first by Griffin, the second by Kathleen Barry:

> If all the literature of pornography were to be represented by one performance, and if that performance were to move into its most dramatic moments, the scenes . . . which would embody the entire action and meaning of the play . . . would have to be the moments (which are inevitable in the pornographic *oeuvre*) in which most usually a woman, sometimes a man, often a child, is abducted by force, verbally abused, beaten, bound hand and foot and gagged, often tortured, often hung, his or her body suspended, wounded, and then murdered.[8]

> The most prevalent theme in pornography is one of utter contempt for women. In movie after movie women are raped, ejaculated on, urinated on, anally penetrated, beaten, and, with the advent of snuff films, murdered in an orgy of sexual pleasure.[9]

These claims are factually false.[10] That both summaries mention murder suggests that these writers got carried away; it is a gross exaggeration to say that most pornography produced today is a variation on the theme of de Sade's *120 Nights*.[11] One can agree that pornographic depictions of rape and abuse are degrading, because these acts are degrading, without being committed to the view that most pornography is degrading or that other sexual acts are degrading to women. In particular, anal penetration and the smearing of the ejaculate (or their depictions) are not clearly degrading.

It is useful to distinguish three ways of understanding the claim that pornography degrades women. First, the *definitional* approach: pornography degrades women because pornography *is* sexually explicit material that degrades women. Although a number of feminists, among others, define pornography in these terms,[12] it is not an ideal definition. It works persuasively to make a defender of pornography look like a cad, and it closes the door immediately on serious investigation into the extent of degradation in the content of pornography.[13]

Second, there is the *descriptive* approach. Pornography is defined, say, as sexually explicit material designed to induce sexual arousal, and then some of it can be described, in virtue of its content, as degrading to women. If there are criteria for the presence of degradation in pornography, the descriptive approach can provide important information. However, one standard view, common among liberals, is that descriptions of the degrading content of pornography are subjective or presuppose essentially contestable values. This view, I think, is empty when applied to depictions of brutal sexual assault; Barry's claim that rape is degrading does not involve a malignant sort of subjectivism. The reason is that this judgment—brutal assault is degrading—is based on a nearly universal consensus. At the same time, because there is no such consensus about anal penetration or the smearing of the ejaculate, Barry's claim that these acts are degrading to women does succumb to the liberal critique. Consider, too, Rosemarie Tong's claim that sexual activity without love is quite acceptable and that only degrading pornography should be censored.[14] The pope agrees that degradation is immoral, depicted and in practice, but also claims that it is degrading for any woman to engage in sexual activity outside of the proper context. If the defamation and endorsement arguments are to avoid probably unresolvable debates about what counts as degradation, they must be severely qualified, claiming at most that universally condemned brutality is degrading and that only pornographic depictions of brutality are to be censored.[15]

Third, there is the *metaphysical* approach. When examining pornography we could focus on the "deeper" messages that can be teased out of it. To investigate degradation in pornography we would examine it intellectually, somewhat like doing dream analysis or literary interpretation.[16] Claims like Griffin's (see her expression, the "meaning of the play") and Barry's do not have to be taken as true by definition, as largely false descriptions, or as essentially contestable evaluations. They could be understood as attempts to probe beneath the surface of pornography in order to reveal its latent meaning. In this approach, nonbrutal scenes can be read as violent at a deep level, and superficially violent acts can be read as symbolic of something else altogether. Because metaphysical readings are plastic, it will be difficult to substantiate the claim that nonviolent items of pornography, for example, scenes of the smearing of the ejaculate, are degrading. In her review of Angela Carter's *The Sadeian Woman*, Robin Morgan rejects Susan Sontag's interpretation of pornography "as a metaphor for political and aesthetic freedom," and applauds Carter's view that pornography's "attitude . . . is the profound hatred of the mother, not in a simplistic Freudian sense, but as a metaphor for disgust with life itself. . . ."[17] Arguments, such as Morgan's, that one interpretation is superior to another, will be delicate at best and speculative at worst. But even if it can be demonstrated that the deep meaning of an item of pornography is the degradation of women, that demonstration will not help the defamation and endorsement arguments. For those arguments refer only to degradation that is immediately and easily witnessed by viewers of pornography. Those who consume pornography are not concerned with the deep interpretations of the material they are using to achieve sexual arousal. If the degrading content of pornography is located only in the metaphysical level, it will not be successful in defaming women for these people, or in endorsing the degradation of women for them. . . .

4. HOW CAN A DEPICTION ENDORSE?

The endorsement argument can be understood[18] as admitting that pornography contains and elicits fantasies of what the male consumers think of as a better sexual world. As fantasy, pornography is a vision of the way things ought to be or could be, regardless of the way things actually happen to be. Pornography cannot be charged with falsely and maliciously describing women and, therefore, avoids the defamation argument. The endorsement argument picks up the slack: as a depiction of the way things ought to be, pornography endorses that things be the way they are depicted, and by endorsing these values, pornography causally helps to bring these states of affairs into existence. "Pornography, especially violent pornography, is implicated in the committing of crimes of violence against women" and it "supports sexist . . . attitudes, and thus reinforces the oppression and exploitation of women."[19]. . .

Why has the endorsement argument been popular lately?[20] What is the motivation behind the insistence that pornography endorses what it depicts . . . ? Part of the answer is that feminists have been hard pressed to find convincing arguments against pornography. But if in virtue of endorsing the abusive treatment of women, pornographic depictions promote that degradation, contribute to the oppression of women, or undermine their civil rights, then a good case can be made for the legal control of pornography. There is, however, more to the story.

Longino is one of the few writers on pornography who credit it with reliable harmful causal effects; her argument against pornography turns on a causal connection between pornographic endorsements of acts harmful to women and the occurrence of acts harmful to women. Now, when pornography is charged with causing behavior that would otherwise not occur, *not* by endorsing that behavior but in some other way (for example, through mere imitation), any such causal claim is quickly undercut by the existence of multiple factors that determine whether one does copy a behavior one views or reads about.[21] To claim that pornography *per se* is causally responsible for imitative harm is as unsupportable as claiming that newspapers can be attributed causal responsibility for imitative harm. Perhaps, then, the motivation behind the endorsement argument is this: if pornographic depictions *endorse* what they depict, it might be more plausible that there is a causal connection between pornography and acts harmful to women, a causal connection that goes beyond mere imitation. Newspapers get off the causal hook, since they depict or describe harm without endorsing it.[22]

The assumption here is that endorsing an act is an especially effective way to increase the frequency of that act. However, the assumption is probably false. Quite often, whether my endorsing X gets others to do X depends on factors out of my control: they already believe X should not be done, or they already do X and my endorsement is superfluous, etcetera. (Football players endorse after-shave; newspapers endorse candidates; the *Nihil Obstat* endorses. Are these effective?) I can often be successful in getting others to do X without endorsing it: I can give orders, coerce, bribe, threaten, cajole, or plead in order to influence their behavior. Or I can simply do X and hope that others will copy it. None of these methods of increasing the frequency of an act is consistently more efficient than the others; at the very least, I know of no reason to suppose that endorsements, in particular, are any more effective than the other methods. If so, an argument against pornography that turns on a connection between endorsements and harmful consequences is as weak as any other causal-consequences argument against pornography.

But this does not mean that Longino must abandon ship. The endorsement argument can be maintained even when there is no evidence of pornography's harmful effects. If attempting but failing to perform a criminal act is itself criminal, and if encouraging others to commit crimes is itself a crime even when the encouragement fails, then there is some reason to say that the endorsement of acts harmful to women is criminal, even if those endorsements are known to be unsuccessful in causing the actions endorsed or cannot be proved to be successful. This argument against pornography, that is, might be subsumed under the law of attempts, encouragement, and conspiracy. This is the hidden beauty of the endorsement argument, apparently overlooked by its sponsors: it does not necessarily depend on contentious claims about the causal effects of pornography.

The issue, then, is whether depictions of degradation can endorse what they depict, and if so, what conditions must be satisfied for a depiction to be an endorsement. . . . In explaining how pornography endorses degradation, Longino begins with:

> . . . the degradation of the female characters is represented as providing pleasure to the participant males and . . . to the participant females, and there is no suggestion that this sort of treatment of others is inappropriate. . . . These two features are together sufficient to constitute endorsement of the represented behavior.[23] . . .

It is not obvious, however, that depicting degradation as pleasurable or depicting a happy adulterer is to endorse degradation or adultery. A corollary of the suggested principle would seem to be that depicting degradation as unpleasurable or adulterers as unhappy is to disapprove of these behaviors. But consider John Barth's *The End of the Road*; does linking extramarital sex and abortion with a tragic death amount to disapproving of extramarital sex and abortion? Or consider Judith Rossner's *Looking for Mr. Goodbar*; does linking barhopping with calamity amount to a condemnation of barhopping? No. From Barth one could just as easily extract the advice that if one is going to engage in extramarital sex, one should use efficient birth control, or that if one is going to have an abortion, one should avoid quacks. And from Rossner one could just as easily extract the idea that barhopping is safe fun, as long as one is adequately attuned to the psychological complexities of potential sex partners. I use the word "extract" quite intentionally, for it focuses attention not on the mysterious ability of a depiction to implicitly endorse, but on the ability of the viewer of the depiction to construct a commentary from it.[24]

The centrality of the characteristics of the audience is easy to illustrate. Consider the old documentary film, "Reefer Madness," which was intended to disapprove of marijuana by linking the smoking of marijuana with immoral sexual behavior, crime, and insanity. Audiences today howl with laughter at this film, which shows that depicting a behavior as a disaster of unhappiness is not sufficient for endorsing its avoidance. Similarly, for audiences today of scenes of a happy nuclear family (as in "Ozzie and Harriet"), the happiness linked to that structure hardly serves to endorse the nuclear family. In both cases, even if the depictions are meant as endorsements, they are not taken as endorsements. Further, for the conservative, the pleasure and ecstasy recorded in pornography—the depiction of a woman happily and guiltlessly engaging in sexual activity —does not make the depiction an endorsement of her behavior, but is proof of the woman's depravity, and even proof that sexual activity corrupts. In this case, a depiction of a pleasurable X does not endorse X but condemns it. Similarly, for some audiences that view the happily depicted nuclear family in reruns of "Ozzie and Harriet," that the persons are depicted as being happy serves to condemn *them*, not to praise their arrangement. There is nothing special, then, about linking X with pleasure or happiness that makes a depiction of X an implicit endorsement rather than a disapproval.

I have not claimed that depictions and their appendages never implicitly or explicitly endorse, although I do think that the sponsors of the endorsement argument have not adequately explained how implicit endorsement, in particular, is possible. But even if both implicit and explicit endorsement of degradation by pornography are possible, they do not seem to be possible in a manner required by the endorsement argument. If the endorsement of degradation is explicit, then it is not the item of pornography itself that does the endorsing, but nonessential material or a framing device, and these explicit endorsements can be eliminated, or the pornography accompanied by explicit disclaimers, in which case the force of the endorsement argument is avoided. (Indeed, there is already very little if any pornography that explicitly endorses anything.) On the other hand, if the endorsement of degradation is implicit, the endorsement can be overridden by a more powerful explicit disclaimer, and the argument will succeed in prohibiting no pornography at all. Further, even though an item of pornography might endorse *in part* in virtue of its essential content, whether the item does implicitly endorse depends *also* on the nature of the audience.

The fact that whether an item of pornography implicitly endorses degradation is partially a function of the nature of the audience creates an unanticipated complication for the endorsement argument. The pornography that Longino wishes to have censored is that which *endorses* degradation. The pornography to be censored, then, is that which *accomplishes* the endorsement of degradation, or that which is *successful* as an endorsement. I do not mean that the pornography to be censored must be causally successful in bringing about an increase in the frequency of the acts depicted and endorsed; that is a different sense of "successful endorsement" and a sense not necessarily presupposed by the endorsement argument (as I argued earlier). Rather, the pornography must at least succeed in *being* an endorsement, even if it doesn't have any causal effects. But whether an item of pornography succeeds in being an endorsement depends on whether it is taken as an endorsement (rather than, say, ignored or even laughed at) by its audience. If the censorship of pornography turns on being able to show that it succeeds in being an implicit endorsement for an audience, there will be too many counterexamples to satisfy the goal of the argument. That a depiction is intended or meant to implicitly endorse degradation is not sufficient for it to succeed in being an implicit endorsement, in which case proving success in being an implicit endorsement will be difficult. . . .

NOTES

1. Helen Longino, "Pornography, Oppression, and Freedom: A Closer Look," in L. Lederer, ed., *Take Back the Night* (New York: William Morrow, 1980), pp. 40–54. Rosemarie Tong, in "Feminism, Pornography, and Censorship," *Social Theory and Practice,* 8 (1982): 1–17, elaborates Longino's defamation argument.

2. It is unconvincing for Susan Lurie to claim *both* that pornography asserts an "insidious lie" about women and that it "articulates the fantasy" that women accommodate to male sexual desires ("Pornography and the Dread of Women," in *Take Back the Night,* pp. 159–73, at p. 160 and 171, respectively).

3. Does children's literature, in which women are portrayed stereotypically as mothers, nurses, and grade-school teachers, *defame* women? Is it *because* many children's books were defamatory that they are now more carefully constructed? I think the answer to both questions is "no." First, children's literature that portrays women in their stereotypical roles depicts them in a favorable light. Second, for one large section of our society, to portray a woman as naturally taking on nurturant roles hardly counts as defamatory. (To say, as some feminists do, that domesticity is silly business for women, comes close to defaming those women who have made it their lives.) Third, it is not the case that the old children's literature was defamatory in virtue of lying; after all, most women *are* mothers, nurses, and so on. Indeed, children's literature that depicts an equal number of men and women engineers, doctors and lawyers is false if taken as propositional. This fact helps us answer the second question. The new books for children are stories meant to promote the conditions required for their depictions to come true; they are thought to have some chance of working because young minds are malleable. (I have more difficulty deciding whether the Westerns of the 1950s defame Indians—or even the cowboys.)

4. Harry M. Clor, *Obscenity and Public Morality* (Chicago: University of Chicago Press, 1970), pp. 52 and 234, respectively.

5. See Joel Feinberg "Pornography and the Criminal Law," *University of Pittsburgh Law Review,* 40 (1979): 567–604, especially pp. 579–81.

6. William Brigman argues that pornography is speech partly on the grounds that the claim that pornography is a purely sexual activity "cannot stand up under scrutiny," in his "Pornography as Political Expression," *Journal of Popular Culture,* 17 (1983): 129–34, at p. 129.

7. Al Katz,"Free Discussion v. Final Decision: Moral and Artistic Controversy and the *Tropic of Cancer* Trials," *Yale Law Journal* 79 (1969): 209–52, at p. 214.

8. Susan Griffin, *Pornography and Silence* (New York: Harper and Row, 1979), p. 46.

9. Kathleen Barry, *Female Sexual Slavery* (Englewood Cliffs, N.J.: Prentice-Hall, 1979), p. 175.

10. Pat Califia's response to Dworkin's claim that "the eroticization of murder is the essence of pornography," is that Dworkin selects the worst examples (for example that infamous "snuff" film) and unfairly takes them as representative ("The New Puritans," *The Advocate,* April 17, 1980, pp. 14–18, at p. 16).

11. There is bad faith in Sally Wagner's writing that "male violence is an ever present potential in pornography, waiting in the wings to make its appearance . . ." ("Pornography and the Sexual Revolution," in R. Linden *et al.,* eds., *Against Sadomasochism: A Radical Feminist Analysis* (East Palo Alto, CA: Frog in the Well, 1982) pp. 23–44, at p. 24). In the absence of explicit brutality, Wagner forces the case against pornography by reading the violence into it.

12. For example, Diana E. H. Russell, "Pornography and Violence: What Does the New Research Say?," in *Take Back the Night,* pp. 218–38, at p. 218.

13. Fred Berger provides a number of compelling arguments against this definition in his "Pornography, Feminism, and Censorship," in R. Baker and F. Elliston, eds., *Philosophy and Sex,* 2nd edition (Buffalo, N.Y.: Prometheus, 1984), pp. 327–51, at p. 333–34.

14. Tong, "Feminism, Pornography, and Censorship," p. 3.

15. Here the arguments face the difficult case of radical feminist lesbian sadomasochistic literature, for example Samois, eds., *Coming to Power* (Palo Alto, CA: Up Press, 1981), much of which is pornographic.

16. Brigman, for example, claims that pornography "expresses a philosophical viewpoint," namely, naturalism ("Pornography as Political Expression," pp. 129, 131). This is amusing unless it is meant as a deep interpretation. (See also fn. 11, above; Wagner might be reading pornography metaphysically when she claims that it always contains male violence.)

17. *The New Republic,* September 1 and 8, 1979, pp. 31–33, at pp. 31 and 32. . . .

18. I say "can be," and I also mean "should be," because this is not the way the argument is expressed by Longino. She conflates the defamation and endorsement arguments when she says that pornography lies because it recommends that women should be subservient to the sexual needs of men. To recommend a state of affairs, even an obnoxious one, is not to tell a lie.

19. Longino, "Pornography, Oppression, and Freedom," p. 48.

20. See also Judith Wagner DeCew, "Violent Pornography: Censorship, Morality and Social Alternatives," *Journal of Applied Philosophy*, 1 (1984): 79–94, at p. 86: "The only unconditional conclusion that all violent pornography is wrong is based on the claim that every portrayal endorsing or recommending treatment of human beings in a way disregarding their dignity and worth is immoral." In her essay "Pornography and Freedom of Expression," Susan Wendell uses the disjunction "recommends, condones, or portrays" over a dozen times, never stopping to ask whether, or when, a portrayal recommends (in D. Copp and S. Wendell, eds., *Pornography and Censorship*, Buffalo, N.Y.: Prometheus, 1983, pp. 167–83).

21. The showing of the movie "The Burning Bed" on television in October, 1984, had, apparently, a number of effects: one man in Wisconsin burned his wife, a woman in Ohio shot her sleeping boyfriend, some men beat their wives who insisted on watching the movie, and crisis centers were flooded with calls from possibly abused women. (See *Fargo Forum*, October 12, 1984, p. B1; October 14, p. C4; the Minneapolis Star and Tribune, October 10, p. 20A.) The point is that it would be too quick to blame this feminist-endorsed movie as the cause of the death of the Wisconsin woman; after all, as the jury will conclude, her husband made the decision to imitate the movie.

22. Similarly, DeCew relies on endorsement to distinguish violent pornographic films and the feminist anti-pornography documentary *Not a Love Story* ("Violent Pornography," p. 83).

23. Longino, "Pornography, Oppression, and Freedom," pp. 43–44.

24. See Jonathan Miller, "Censorship and the Limits of Permission," in M. Yaffe and E. Nelson (eds.), *The Influence of Pornography on Behavior* (London: Academic Press, 1982), pp. 27–46, at p. 41 ("He who extracts from pornography an endorsement of his tendency to exploit another . . . is already crippled . . ."); Robert Fullinwider, "Feminism and Pornography: Discussion Review," *Report from the Center for Philosophy and Public Policy* 3 (1983): 12–14, at p. 14 (this issue of the *Report* is not numbered); and Berger, "Pornography, Feminism, and Censorship," pp. 336–37.

Part Three
Libertarian Perspectives

16

Feminist Moralism, "Pornography," and Censorship

Barbara Dority

The issue of "pornography" has engendered an intense debate within the feminist movement. Will feminism, having achieved some significant gains, continue to capitulate to moralistic forces, or will it wake up and take a stand for the liberation of women in all domains, including the difficult and often contradictory domain of sexual expression?

Two separate issues are involved in this debate: first, the moralistic feminist condemnation of "pornography"; and, second, the translation of that condemnation by nearly all feminist leaders into calls for various kinds of legislation which would effectively ban "pornographic" imagery and words. Both issues are alarming.

As a feminist secular humanist and a card-carrying member of the American Civil Liberties Union, I believe the writers of the First Amendment meant every word exactly and literally: "Congress shall make no law . . . abridging the freedom of speech or of the press. . . ." No law means *no law*.

The First Amendment does not say there is to be freedom of speech and press provided they are not sexually explicit, offensive, dangerous, or degrading. The authors of the Bill of Rights had learned firsthand why it

From *The Humanist* 49 (November–December 1989):8–9, 46. Reprinted by permission of the publisher.

was absolutely necessary to permit all manner of ideas to be expressed in the new republic. They knew this guarantee could not be confined to the expression of ideas that are conventional or shared by the majority but must include even those ideas considered repugnant or socially undesirable.

In the words of Justice William O. Douglas: "This demands that government keep its hands off all literature. There can be no freedom of expression unless all facets of life can be portrayed, no matter how repulsive these disclosures may be to some people." Justice Douglas later added that, in addition to freedom from government intervention, all manner of literature must remain available in the marketplace of ideas or the purpose of free expression is defeated. In other words, if we protect only the right to publish and then limit availability, we are still limiting freedom of speech.

The moralistic pro-censorship mind-set has remained the same throughout the history of civilization. The censors aim at protecting us from the perceived harmful effects of what we read, see, and hear. Historically, they did this to protect our souls from blasphemy or society from alien political, social, or economic ideas. Today, it is being done to protect us from explicit sexual imagery and words. The justification, however, remains the same: it is best for us and best for society.

The highly subjective term *pornography* is grossly overused and abused. A wide range of materials has been so classified by feminists and summarily condemned, boycotted, picketed, and even banned.

The definition of *pornography* from Webster is: "The depiction of erotic behavior (as in pictures or writing) intended to cause sexual excitement." The blanket condemnation of all such materials is cause for grave concern. Obviously, this would include a great deal of advertising, network television, art, film, and a vast array of magazines, books, and videos. Indeed, many feminists have condemned most mainstream advertising and film as degrading and harmful to women. Most members of the feminist movement endorse and promote Minneapolis-style "anti-pornography" ordinances. Many feminists are committed full-time to these pursuits.

Despite their claims to a mandate, these women do not speak for all feminists. Scores of women and men dropped out (or were forced out) of the feminist movement when the Equal Rights Amendment was defeated and attention shifted to moralizing and "pornography." We will never know how many feminists were lost to activism, or never activated, as a result of this departure from our basic goals and principles.

Many of us believe that feminism and civil liberties are inextricable. We remind our sisters that history has repeatedly shown that censorship and suppression work directly against feminist goals and are always used to limit women's rights in the name of protection. If such censorship laws are passed, we would create the illusion that something is being done to end sexism and sexual violence—a harmful effect in itself.

We ask: whose definitions shall we use? Who will decide? Who will make all the necessary individual judgments? Who will distinguish "dehumanizing, objectifying, degrading" materials from "erotica"?

Many leaders in the feminist movement assert that the message of all "pornography," even "soft-core," is that women are slaves whose bodies are for sale and available to be used and degraded. Again, this is not the only feminist view. For example, many feminists do *not* believe that *Playbody* and *Penthouse* are sexist, or that the presentation of the naked female body, whether or not in "inviting positions," is intrinsically sexist. We do not believe that sexually explicit photos and words are intrinsically exploitative, degrading, or objectifying.

Many feminist leaders tell us that "pornography" is sex discrimination and hate literature against women—a violation of women's civil rights. But the history and intent of civil rights law and case law are clear: discrimination is not what people say or write about other people; it is what people *do* to other people. Individuals cannot be persecuted, censored, or condemned for their ideas. In a free society, there are no crimes of thought—only crimes of action.

Certainly some materials are offensive and degrading to many women, and few would claim that sex discrimination and oppression of women no longer exist in our culture. But many materials are offensive and degrading to *men,* blatantly promoting not only their oppression but their brutalization. There are aspects of our culture that oppress Indians, Hispanics, Asians, and homosexuals. Anti-Semitic literature is inarguably harmful to Jews, as is racist literature to blacks. Are we going to offer men and racial, ethnic, and religious minorities a civil right to suppress speech which they find objectionable?

Many feminists tell us that "pornography" *causes* sexism and violence against women. But this claim draws on simplistic behaviorist psychology and has been repeatedly discredited by reputable specialists in sexual behavior. Even the notorious Meese commission reported that no such causal link can be substantiated. Sexist and violent materials are *symptoms* of a sexist and violent society—not the causes.

The claim that certain forms of expression are dangerous and an incitement to violence has been used time after time to try to prohibit speech that some people don't like. Although some of us do not support this exception to the First Amendment, the notion of "a clear and present danger" was evolved to address this threat. For "pornography" to be suppressed under this test, we would have to demonstrate that any viewer is likely to be provoked to sexual violence immediately upon seeing it.

Anecdotal stories of sex offenders who are found to possess "pornography" are often cited. As Sol Gordon has pointed out, a large percentage of these offenders are also found to possess milk in their refrigerators. Sporadic incidents do not prove a correlation, nor does a correlation prove causation.

Even if it is assumed that a small percentage of people are "encouraged" to engage in sexist behavior or commit violent acts after exposure to certain books or films, this still would not justify suppression. Such a "pervert's veto" would threaten a broad range of literature and film. A free society must accept the risks that come with liberty.

People receive different messages from sexually explicit material, and it is ridiculous and dangerous to conclude that a picture or an idea will have the same effect on all viewers or readers. Charles Manson testified that he was inspired by the biblical Book of Revelations to commit multiple murders. Youths involved in interracial street fights have said that viewing *Roots* led them to commit their crimes. John Hinckley testified that he knew he had to kill Ronald Reagan after reading *Catcher in the Rye.*

If viewing and reading sexually explicit and violent materials caused people to become sex criminals, all the members of the Meese commission would now be dangerous sexual predators. The same would be true of the many sociologists who study this material, countless persons who create, publish, and disseminate it, mental health professionals who work with sex offenders, and all the moralists—on the right and the left—who pore over these materials as they analyze them for the rest of us.

In many repressive countries—whether in Central America, Asia, Africa, eastern Europe, or the Middle East—there is practically no "pornography." But there is a great deal of sexism and violence against women. In the Netherlands and Scandinavia, where there are almost no restrictions on sexually explicit materials, the rate of sex-related crime is much lower than in the United States. "Pornography" is virtually irrelevant to the existence of sexism and violence.

Nor does a causal relationship exist between an increase in the availability of "pornography" and inequality for women. While "pornography" has increased over the past fifty years, the rights of women have jumped dramatically.

"Violent pornography" is viewed by many as the most offensive form of expression. But it can be seen in two ways: as the depiction of consensual sadomasochism or as the depiction of actual coercion and violence against nonconsenting persons. If the latter, the *actual perpetrators of the violence or coercion* have broken the law and should be prosecuted to its full extent. However, not everyone sees the degradation of women in depictions of "violent" sexual activity. What some find degrading, others may find erotic.

Human sexual behavior is very complicated. In our society, and all over the world, consenting adults exist who like to engage in sadomasochistic activity and who do so of their own free will. They enjoy publications which depict or describe this behavior. For them, these activities are not designed to degrade or promote violence against women *or men* but, rather, to satisfy a sexual need of the participants. It is not a crime or an issue subject to moral judgment to fantasize about rape, or even for two consenting adults to choose to enact a pretend rape. It is not anyone's right to judge the private sexual fantasies, inclinations, or activities of other consenting adults.

We are told we must especially condemn materials depicting (usually simulated) violence to prove that we are opposed to violence against women. We must, many feminists say, condemn nearly all sexually explicit materials as degrading to women and label "pornography" a principal cause of women's oppression in order to retain our credentials as feminists.

Many feminist humanist women and men refuse to do this. We believe it is possible to be feminists dedicated to equal rights and the elimination of violence against women while defending the freedom of all kinds of sexual expression. It is a tragedy that the feminist movement has been drawn into an anti-sex stance, condemning "deviant" sexual representation and expression. We are horrified by the assertion of many feminists that male sexuality is inherently destructive, violent, and "pro-rape." We are appalled by the condemnation of men who enjoy "pornography" as sexist and anti-humanist or, in the case of women, by the assertion that they are "brainwashed by patriarchy."

This Victorian imagery—pure women controlling the vile, lustful impulses of men and being unable to think for themselves—is a feminine stereotype we should be working against. In this analysis, women cannot ever freely choose to have sex with men or use "male-identified" imagery in their sexual fantasies or practices. Certainly they cannot freely choose to earn their living by inviting the rapacious male gaze or providing sexual services to men.

Many feminist women and men believe it is moralistic, insulting, and inaccurate to maintain that no "normal" woman rationally chooses or consensually participates in the sex industry. This moralistic position alienates not only women in the sex industry but also women who create their own sexual pleasure without regard for its "political correctness."

We believe that this moralism and the attendant calls for censorship have seriously undermined the integrity of our movement. Being a feminist means being against sexism—not sex. In *Against Sadomasochism,* feminist Ti Grace Atkinson says, "I do not know any feminist worthy of that name who, forced to choose between freedom and sex, would choose sex." This is the choice being presented to feminist women and men. In so doing, the movement betrays its principles and destroys its credibility.

Many of us insist on the right to choose *both* freedom *and* sexuality. We call upon other feminist humanists to do likewise.

Author's note: The access of minors to sexually explicit material is a complex issue which would require another article for proper examination. The Supreme Court has held that minors' access to legally "obscene" materials is not protected by the First Amendment. The Court's nebulous and subjective definition of *obscenity* raises even more definitional problems, and a vast array of materials are currently restricted on the basis of this seriously flawed definition. These restrictions, instituted to protect minors, inevitably affect the freedom of adults. *Legally,* the burden of preventing the exposure of children to offensive or "pornographic" materials *should* rest with parents; as a *practical* matter, parents *must* assume this responsibility.

17

Pornography as Representation: Aesthetic Considerations

Theodore A. Gracyk

I

Recent arguments against pornography are being translated into action, with several American cities adopting or considering ordinances aimed at removing pornography from society. Many of the supporting arguments try to establish a causal link between pornography and direct harm to women. One objection is that the attitude taken toward women in pornography is inculcated in its audience, at least some of whom then translate this attitude into actions that directly harm women. Because the existence of such a causal chain has been questioned, some attacks on pornography simply hold that pornography systematically degrades women, that to degrade persons on the basis of contingent class membership is to strip them of their rightful human dignity, and so pornography should be censored because "it is defamatory and libelous."[1] But both the causal chain and defamation arguments hold that pornography is a certain sort of objectionable content and that that content can and should be censored.

I wish to challenge the viability of these arguments and ordinances against pornography by taking an aesthetic standpoint and questioning

From *Journal of Aesthetic Education,* 21, no. 4 (Winter 1987): 103–121. Copyright © 1987 by the Board of Trustees of the University of Illinois. Reprinted by permission of the publisher and the author.

their understanding of pornography as a certain represented content. Ethical objections to such ordinances often begin with their conflicts with the First Amendment or by questioning whether they will significantly reduce violence against women. I will consider neither of these matters, but restrict my discussion to the question of whether those who are attempting to combat pornography with a civil rights approach have adequately identified what makes representations pornographic. While I accept that much pornography is morally objectionable because it defames or degrades women, I submit that proponents of this view generally provide misleading and unacceptable criteria for pornography. I suggest that they should focus less on the proper definition of 'pornography' and should concentrate more on finding criteria for what I call "the pornographic attitude." The pornographic attitude is the real locus of the defamation argument against pornography. I do not assume that all material that is commonly classified as pornographic manifests the pornographic attitude.

I will focus on a so-called "model pornography law" (hereafter referred to as the Dworkin/MacKinnon law for its authors)[2] and will argue that its characterization of pornography fails because it overly simplifies pornography as a certain content.[*] I take this law to summarize the more general analysis and strategy that some recent writers have advocated. If the offered definition does not capture what is genuinely pornographic, the law will not succeed in its goal; and if it captures material that is not pornographic, the law constitutes unjustified censorship. I fear that the proposed law captures a great deal that is neither pornographic nor morally objectionable, because it takes a commonsensical but misleading view of pornography as a certain represented subject matter.

My concern is with "trafficking in pornography" as unlawful under the ordinance. Other portions of the law require proof of actual harm to specific persons; because the trafficking clause deals only with the *content* of the material, it allows for censorship of representational works without proof that the works have the harmful effects claimed for pornography. I take it that the defamation argument provides the strongest reason for this blanket prohibition of trafficking in pornography, since it finds pornography unacceptable apart from any specific effects on its audience. However, a mistaken characterization of pornography thereby poses a threat to the free production, display, and sale of sexually explicit materials of artistic value that are not pornographic.

[*See this volume pages 56 and 154 for a brief description of the ordinance—Eds.]

II

While it is commonly assumed that representational art succeeds by "copying" perceptual objects, many recent aestheticians have emphasized that "there is no innocent eye." Nelson Goodman presents this viewpoint in *Languages of Art,* forcefully arguing that "faithful representation" is an impossible ideal no matter what medium is employed. Realistic representation depends "upon inculcation" and not just upon accurate depiction. E. H. Gombrich argues for much the same position.[3]

But if the production of representations is always confined by some set of conventions, so is our ability to interpret a representation. Ordinances such as the Dworkin/MacKinnon law implicitly assume that there *is* an innocent eye, or at least they downplay the problems inherent in determining the content of visual and literary representations. In its nine conditions defining pornographic representations as ones that include the "graphic sexually explicit subordination of women," the ordinance offers standards for determining what is and isn't pornographic.

My objections stem from the fact that the ordinance is aimed at "graphic" and "sexually explicit subordination of women through pictures and/or words" and stipulates that at least one of nine further elements must be "presented" to make a work pornography. Requiring that materials must be "graphic" means that they must be "vivid" and "lifelike" as representations.[4] But no representation, either literary or visual, is straightforwardly "lifelike." Failure to acknowledge that interpretation hinges on the training and prejudices of the interpreter leads to genuine difficulties with the ordinance, particularly because it tries to capture something that cannot be graphically presented in terms of what *is* graphically presented.

The attempt to define pornography in terms of specific represented content therefore carries with it various difficulties which are inherent in the nature of representation. No matter how carefully the ordinance describes the content that exploits and dehumanizes women, those who implement the law may not recognize the intended proper content when presented with it. We cannot assume that only those in sympathy with the law will do the interpreting, nor can we assume that even those in sympathy with it will be competent to do so. Worse yet, attempts to pass a version of the law in Indianapolis suggest that some supporters hope to use the ordinance to prohibit trafficking in any sexually explicit materials.[5]

Turning to specifics, consider condition (iii) of the ordinance, which prohibits graphic depiction of women as experiencing "sexual pleasure in being raped." It follows, then, that it would be perfectly legal for someone to *advocate* rape, or to express the view that women enjoy being raped, so long as the representation is not "graphic." This makes about as much sense as considering *Mein Kampf* inoffensive while objecting to Leni Riefenstahl's film *Triumph of the Will*. But what the law is trying to do is clear enough; it tries to identify works that take the wrong attitude toward rape by reducing that attitude to a specific represented subject matter.[6]

Suppose, however, that we present a graphic situation in which women are raped but which do not indicate or show the victim's reaction. We evidently cannot count it as pornography, even if the context somehow indicates that women *deserve* rape or that men should be allowed to rape women. Condition (iii) does protect Giovanni Bologna's *The Rape of the Sabines* and Bernini's *Appollo and Daphne*, since in each the woman appears to protest. But what about Reubens's *The Rape of the Daughters of Leukippos*? One of the two daughters has a facial expression which might be an indication of pleasure. Representations of pain and of sexual ecstasy look very much alike. Does the law prohibit exhibition of the painting because the woman could be taken to be enjoying rape? Do we improve upon Reubens's painting by retouching it so that she is clearly protesting? Would it really make any difference if she was clearly protesting?

In holding that only the portrayal of rape as pleasurable to the victim is pornographic, the law conflates the subject matter depicted with the moral attitude expressed. The law tries to ban representations that take the wrong attitude toward rape. Mere trafficking in pornography is outlawed, so a work need not be proven to cause or incite anyone to practice rape or sexual discrimination but need only in itself be discriminatory by conveying the wrong message. But if anything is difficult to determine when one deals with representational art, it is the attitude taken toward the subject matter. Here we arrive at the crux of the matter. Condition (iii) tries to avoid this difficulty by reducing the work's attitude to an attitude represented in the work. It focuses on pornography as a represented subject matter, but that isn't what pornography is.[7] Pornography is a certain use of sexual images, and our focus should be directed to the conditions under which such images adopt a reprehensible attitude.

It is one thing for a work of art to depict a subject graphically, another thing graphically to depict someone expressing an attitude, and quite another thing for the *work* to *express* an attitude. Let me clarify these distinctions. In the film *A Clockwork Orange*, a group of young thugs brutally beat a drunken tramp. Let us call this an element of the film's represented subject matter. But part of this subject matter is the graphic depiction of the attitude of the youths as they beat the man; they are represented as enjoying their act of brutality. However, what I will call the content of a film often contains something further. Accompanying the represented subject matter is the film's attitude toward its subject matter. This element is not represented *in* the film. It cannot be graphically depicted. Instead, it is expressed *by* the film. Expression is supervenient on other properties of a work of art. The point I am making is that the content of representational art usually contains both a represented subject matter and an attitude expressed towards the subject matter.[8] In the case of *A Clockwork Orange,* director Stanley Kubrick seems to aim at a vision of the moral corruption and instability that inevitably strike a free society.[9] Of course, it is easier to determine without ambiguity the subject matter than the attitude, but the latter is usually what we treasure most.

Consider Roman Polanski's classic film *Repulsion* (1965). The heroine is repeatedly shown being raped, and at one point she is shown as taking pleasure in the rape. The film is pornographic under the law; but is it really? How much of the film do we consider? While the film contains a depiction of rape, the broader context of the film indicates that these events are purely the imaginings of a mentally ill woman. Furthermore, her mental illness seems caused by her mistreatment by a sexist society. So the woman's pleasure in rape can be construed as an element of mental illness. What, then, is the film's attitude toward rape? Do we view the film as pornographic?

I have twice viewed *Repulsion* with an audience of college students, some of whom failed to realize that the rapes were only delusions. Even when faced with the reasoned explanation of why the rapes were not "real" but only the woman's delusions, some viewers persisted in believing that their reading was correct and that the woman is raped in the film. *Repulsion* is a difficult film, as many good films are, and not everyone is equally prepared to interpret it fairly. I can imagine many communities where most of the audience would not be able to evaluate it appropriately and where its exhibition would count as trafficking in pornography under the Dworkin/MacKinnon law. I will even grant that, if a few minutes of the film were shown outside the context of the whole film, perhaps shown at a bachelor party, those minutes of the film would be pornography in the altered context. But they do not adopt the pornographic attitude within the context of the whole film.[10]

III

The role of context in determining a work's expressed attitude is particularly acute in conditions (i) and (vi) of the ordinance. Condition (i) covers cases where "women are presented dehumanized as sexual objects, things, or commodities." How does one graphically represent dehumanization? Certainly not in the same sense that we might represent a freight train or a bowl of fruit. Condition (i) clearly requires a judgment about both what is expressed by a work about its subject and what is represented in the work. Yet a work could easily present a woman's treatment as a commodity (e.g., she is presented as a prostitute or slave) while she is not necessarily being dehumanized. The depiction of a slave's or prostitute's role in society is often used to emphasize the humanity of the oppressed. Dehumanization is a matter of the total work's attitude toward persons in those societal circumstances.

To take a specific case, the film *The Pawnbroker* (1963) was condemned by the Legion of Decency. The reason for the C ("condemned") rating was that, at one point in the film, a prostitute shows her breasts to the protagonist in an effort to entice him. This is hardly a gratuitous element in the film, since it sets the stage for the pawnbroker's remembrance of his wife's dehumanization in a Nazi concentration camp. The unjustified C rating was later withdrawn, the entire incident doing much to destroy the power of the Legion of Decency.[11] How does the same film fare under the proposed law? We clearly have a sexually explicit presentation of a woman as a commodity. The problematic question is whether the prostitute is dehumanized. Given that her action parallels the wife's dehumanizing treatment, the film seems to express the attitude that the prostitute has dehumanized herself by her action. To those who believe that prostitution is an inherently dehumanizing profession, there can be no question but that the film would be pornographic under the Dworkin/MacKinnon law.

While the requirement of dehumanization makes it clear that condition (i) turns on the work's attitude, not just on its represented subject matter, (i) is hardly less problematic than (iii). Suppose that puritanical censors do a little homework in art history. In *The Nude*, Lord Kenneth Clark argued that we must distinguish between "the naked" and "the nude." The former is just a figure devoid of clothing, while the latter is something very different: "the body re-formed."[12] A key to Clark's interpretation of the nude comes in the book's subtitle, "A Study in Ideal Form." By its very nature, the nude as a subject of visual representation takes the naked body as "no more than the point of departure,"[13] even when it is a photograph. The nude differs from the naked in the work's attitude toward the unclothed body. Naked bodies are themselves not very interesting or appealing, Clark contends, and artists seldom even attempt to present the human form in a genuinely "lifelike" manner. On the side of the viewer, only proper training allows proper appreciation. Faced with a nude, one must not "judge it as a living organism, but as a design."[14] In other words, the body must be viewed as an object; one must stop seeing it as a naked human person. Since the best nudes also preserve the body's presence as a sexual object, I take it that any nude of aesthetic merit is pornographic under the ordinance's first condition.

We obviously don't want to make it illegal to exhibit or sell reproductions of Matisse's *Blue Nude* and a host of other works. Perhaps I miss the sense of 'object' or 'thing' that the authors intend; perhaps they mean that the woman is made into *nothing but* an object. Women are not to be "dehumanized" in the sense of representing them as not being subjects of free choice with respect to their own sexuality, and it is only this sense of 'object' which constitutes the pornographic attitude.[15] But if that is meant, we have a condition that, like most of the other conditions, prohibits representation of a certain subject matter. The cost of such a move is that a great deal of the pornography which might fall under this condition, such as photographs (e.g., *Playboy* centerfolds that present women as objects for voyeurism), would no longer count as pornographic. Photographs do not themselves reveal action, so they reveal neither choice nor a lack of choice. They cannot make women 'objects' in the sense that someone whose free choice is restricted is an object.

I submit that such photographs *do* present the pornographic attitude, but only because of their broader context in such magazines. The context, not just the subject matter, tells us to view these women as nothing but objects for male use (I amplify this notion of context below). We again find that the material is objectionable in terms of its expressed attitude, a function of context and not just represented subject matter. Attempts to refine the specification of subject matter that is always offensive pornography will always allow some objectionable materials to fall outside the criteria. However one interprets the dehumanization of women as "objects," the characterization fails. One interpretation captures much fine art that is not pornographic, while the other fails to capture atemporal representations that express the pornographic attitude.

This problem also arises for condition (vi), prohibiting cases where women are "reduced to" any of their body parts. This condition may prohibit "soft" pornography while saving Matisse's *Blue Nude*, but we now stand to lose any number of other nonpornographic artworks, such as those viewing the body from a perspective restricted to the buttocks and back, a common perspective for representing nudes.[16] It also rules out some feminist art, such as Judy Chicago's famed *Dinner Party*, which apparently reduces women to reproductive organs. Chicago herself claims that her focus on women's genitalia is to be understood as metaphorical for various other things, but other women who pursue a similar emphasis on sex organs downplay any symbolic reading and claim that they are reclaiming their bodies from male artists.[17] These women seem to intend that their reductionist paintings have a positive, liberating effect on viewers.

However, some photographs that appear in magazines such as *Playboy* and *Penthouse* are close-ups of genitalia that differ little from the work of some feminist artists in terms of what is depicted. If these photographs were displayed in a gallery, surrounded by feminist art, would we grant them the same charity of interpretation that we grant to Judy Chicago's work? One might be tempted to claim that Chicago's pronouncements about her work constitute the context determining that her work, while sexually explicit, does not involve sexually explicit subordination. But that route subscribes to the intentional fallacy, leaving defenders of *Playboy* photographs the option of proclaiming that their intention is the glorification, not degradation, of women. An artist's claims and disclaimers about a work are insufficient to distinguish what is objectionable from what is not. We must locate a broader context to identify why women are defamed or degraded in specific cases.

The crucial role of context in determining what is pornographic is precisely what the Dworkin/MacKinnon law fails to address. American obscenity laws are now close to useless, but remember that their gradual alteration came about because courts recognized that isolated passages had to be interpreted within the context of the total work. James Joyce's *Ulysses* was, of course, a pivotal case, but the historical emphasis on literature and film provides too narrow an understanding of the context required to evaluate representational works.

A great deal of contemporary pornography consists of still photographs, often published in magazines. In many respects, paintings pose the same difficulties as individual photographs; all parts of the work can be seen at a glance, with no fixed temporal ordering established among the parts. Establishing a coherent order falls to the audience more fully than with literature and film. In a film or novel, the sequence of events preceding and following a specific portion of the action guides our interpretation of the events portrayed. *Repulsion* and *The Pawnbroker* are clear examples of how the other parts of a film provide a context for interpreting individual scenes. Individual paintings and photographs offer fewer such clues, so their interpretation becomes particularly crucial in light of attempts to prohibit materials with a specific content.

Let me turn to several paintings in order to clarify the idea of context which might, if incorporated into the Dworkin/MacKinnon law, make that law appropriately sensitive to the context required for photos and paintings. First, consider Magritte's painting *The Rape*, wherein "the woman's face turns with frightful clarity into the 'genital face' whose blind, mute, and pathetic sexuality has a truly Sadeian character."[18] Among images produced in this century, it is one of the most graphic subordinations of a woman to an object, for it reduces her to genitalia. However, while it meets condition (i) of the Dworkin/MacKinnon law, it is not pornographic. On the contrary, as one major critic remarks, it is "a magnificent protest against fixation and fetishization."[19] Part of this interpretation rests on the relationship between the work and its title, which conveys a need to understand the work symbolically, not simply as the reduction of the woman to body parts. But our understanding of the work's relationship with its title depends on our familiarity with both Magritte's other work and its broader context, Surrealism, which together provide a tradition wherein images carry complex social messages.

These same factors account for the shock and outrage which initially greeted Manet's *Olympia*. To those of us who admire French painting of the late nineteenth century, it is not the least bit disturbing. But that is because we cannot regain its original context of artistic conventions, when nudes were placed in mythological and exotic settings to diffuse their erotic character. As Clark observes, "for almost the first time since the Renaissance a painting of the nude represented a real woman in probable surroundings."[20] With this radical break from established tradition, Manet emphasized that the naked woman in the painting was to be interpreted simply as a naked woman. It is *subsequent* paintings of naked figures that provide the full context for appreciating Manet's achievement instead of regarding the *Olympia* as a perverse fluke in the history of painting.

Given, then, that reasonable interpretation of a graphic image depends on a context that includes other works, both of the same artist and of relatively contemporary artists, no work is inherently pornographic simply on the basis of the represented image. A photograph of genitalia may be educational when printed in a medical textbook, or it may carry political overtones when displayed in a feminist art gallery. The same photo, printed beside others in *Playboy*, may be defamatory in that context. I take it that condition (v) aims to prohibit "soft porn" in outlawing images that present women "in postures or positions of sexual . . . display." But whether or not a sexually explicit "display" is offensive depends on the context of interpretation. A good case of this variability of interpretation is offered by the paintings of Mel Ramos. The painting *You get more salami with Modigliani*, for instance, imitates the glossy look of a *Playboy* photograph.[21] But given its title, its borrowing of pose from Modigliani's *Nude, Lying*

(1917–1918), and its pop-art style, Ramos's painting is a witty commentary on both conventional nudes in recent art and on the conventions of the pornography business itself. On the other hand, if Ramos's primary outlet for his work were *Playboy* rather than art galleries, the same painting, retitled, might well be pornographic.

As it stands, under condition (v) Ramos's work may be banned as pornographic for its sexual display of women. Likewise, under condition (vi) almost anything that exaggerates one part of the body as its focus risks being banned as pornographic because it "reduces" women to that body part. Similar problems arise for all of the other conditions of the proposal, but there is little point in generating further examples. Clearly, however, such approaches to defining pornography capture much art that is not pornographic. The problem is compounded if we stress the conditions' emphasis on the attitude taken towards *women*. Since the objectionable representations typically present the dehumanization of a specific woman, the pornographic nature of the representation seems additionally to require contexts where the specific woman represented clearly stands for women in general. But when does this or that woman come to stand for all women? Does Shakespeare's Ophelia represent all women, or does Hamlet's mother? What about Lady Macbeth? This complication is a further example of the general contextual problem that I have aimed at identifying.

IV

Perhaps you will think that I am only entertaining hypothetical problems that will never really result in the censorship I have imagined. Let me therefore draw a connection between sexual discrimination, which this ordinance attacks, and racial discrimination, a form of discrimination that is equally offensive and which is often discussed in tandem with sexism. Suppose we draft a similar ordinance, to ban materials which are graphically racist. At this point we no longer need to think hypothetically; well-meaning citizens who are troubled by racism have recently tried to remove racist literature from library shelves. One of the books that is repeatedly singled out and banned as racist is Mark Twain's *Adventures of Huckleberry Finn*.[22]

Consider two sentences from *Huck Finn* that might prompt charges that the book is racist. First, we find Huck as narrator saying, "I see it warn't no use wasting words—you can't learn a nigger to argue."[23] Second, after pulling a practical joke on Jim, Huck says, "It was fifteen minutes before I could work myself up to go and humble myself to a nigger."[24] While the book thus depicts racist attitudes within its subject matter, the second of the two sentences also points to the *book's* real attitude, "Huck's growth in social awareness."[25] The book abhors racist practices, but adopts Huck's point of view so that we can share his increasing horror at prevailing morals and his gradual release from the prejudices of his time and place. In chapter sixteen, Huck struggles with the question of whether to turn in Jim after Jim reveals his plan to kidnap his own children and free them from slavery. Ironically, although Huck has learned to appreciate Jim's humanity, he has not yet come to grips with the idea that blacks must never be regarded as property.[26]

The important point is that it seems inconceivable that anyone could say that the book itself is a racist work. As one commentator has noted, the "controversy is a perfect example of how one can read a book and not really *read* the book."[27] Sensitive readers should recognize that Twain's novel indicts racism. Point of view is so essential to any representational work that no audience can fail to appreciate its contribution to the work. Or so we assume. It remains true that many well-meaning people have failed to appreciate this obvious component in evaluating *Huck Finn* and so have tried to block "trafficking" in the work. Some of those who seek to remove it from library shelves do appreciate its true content, but are afraid to let others read it because those others will misread it and be led to practice racial discrimination. I cannot say which of these two reasons for banning the book is the more disturbing.

Huck Finn illustrates the obvious fact that one effective way to attack an attitude is to present it graphically. Magritte's *The Rape* takes such an approach to sexism. But we must not conflate representing an attitude (as part of the represented subject matter) with the attitude expressed about that attitude. If I have understood them correctly, the Dworkin/MacKinnon law and others like it insist that this tool of attack cannot be used, since one depicts the very thing that one attacks. Viewing pornography as a specific represented subject matter does not allow us to take into account the subtle shades of meaning employed in the best art, but instead focuses on one element of content. There is no reason to believe that the mere representation of the reduction of a woman to an object or a whore or body parts cannot serve a legitimate artistic need or even be a means of expressing attitudes that should be expressed or cannot be put into a context where it makes an important statement. Gertrude Stein said that "rose is a rose is a rose is a rose," and ordinances of this sort proceed as if depiction of women as whores or objects is wrong because it depicts them as whores or objects. But in an aesthetic context a rose is sometimes something more than a rose, and a graphic depiction of a woman enjoying rape may be something far more complex.

I believe that proponents of the law also recognize the distinction I am stressing, but they tend to lose sight of it when it comes to identifying materials which degrade or dehumanize women in sexual contexts. Honestly set into law, the definition of pornography might say that it is any sexually oriented material that degrades or dehumanizes when the total context is considered. But that definition is extremely vague, and so the ordinance replaces the definition with a more precise list of materials that usually or often appear in pornography, as though that subject matter is what makes it pornographic. Essentially, this law presents a heuristic list as a set of sufficient conditions.

Furthermore, if we agree that pornography is morally repugnant for the attitude it takes towards women, attempts to define the pornographic in terms of represented subject matter will be counterproductive to the goal of restricting materials that defame or degrade women. More specifically, because the Dworkin/MacKinnon law does not simply specify a certain attitude as pornographic, it will remove few of the materials that express the pornographic attitude. For instance, Japan has strict restrictions on pornography and sexually explicit material, so much so that some erotic classics of Japanese art cannot be displayed in their country of origin. Yet this has made no difference; sadistic comic-book pornography is extremely common and popular. Japanese comics often depict the brutal rape of women and young girls. Although genitalia are never shown and so the comics are technically not explicit, they brutally convey the message that male rape of women is an acceptable sexual pleasure. (Clearly, then, material can adopt the pornographic attitude without being sexually explicit.) Fine art is censored while pornographic comics are perfectly legal. But if we recognize that pornography is reprehensible for its defamatory attitude, not its subject matter, it becomes clear that the Japanese restrictions have failed precisely because they only prohibit certain represented subject matter.

Proponents of legislation against pornography might object that prohibiting an expressed attitude makes it too difficult to prove that a work is pornographic. If so, the loss of a few works of art is a small price to pay in order to end the discrimination and suffering created by the pornography business. But there is no reason to believe that only a limited amount of art will be involved. To clarify my own position, I am *not* saying that fine art and pornography are mutually exclusive categories. Fine art can be pornographic and pornographic art should not be sacrosanct. My point is that nonpornographic art often treats of sexually explicit subject matter and that an overly simplistic characterization of pornography as a certain objectionable content threatens nonpornographic fine art, particularly when that work is new.

Through its oversimplification of what makes an image pornographic, the ordinance leaves it up to local courts to determine what would be censored. Keep in mind that when the Armory Show was exhibited in Chicago in 1913, the president of the Chicago Law and Order League said of Matisse's paintings: "The idea that people can gaze at this sort of thing without it hurting them is all bosh. This exhibition ought to be suppressed."[28] The show was then investigated by the Illinois Vice Commission. This negative, horrified reaction to Matisse's work was to be expected, given the artistic context of 1913 America. If Matisse now shocks hardly anyone, it is because the artistic context has changed and not because we are aesthetically more sophisticated in any absolute sense.

The same forces that led to shock at Matisse's nudes are in operation today; new works generally take time for the development of a climate in which they can be given a fair evaluation. But the Dworkin/MacKinnon law does not provide the luxury of time necessary to formulate a reasoned evaluation of new work. Instead, it serves as a roadblock for artists whose work involves sexually explicit materials. Few artists can afford to have their livelihood become the invitation to frequent court battles. George Orwell, for instance, edited sexual material from his own writings, even to the extent of making nonsense of his plot lines, in order to avoid any possibility of litigation.

Let me mention one last example. In *Less Than Zero*, the best-selling first novel of Bret Easton Ellis, one of the characters keeps a twelve-year-old girl drugged and tied to a bed, available for gang-rape by him and his friends. When asked if this is right, he replies, "What's right? If you want something, you have the right to take it. If you want to do something, you have the right to do it."[29] This scene is fairly typical for the novel. Given condition (iv), prohibiting cases where "women are presented as sexual objects tied up, . . ." *Less Than Zero* is pornographic. Consensus is divided about the value and meaning of this recent novel, but one critic sees in it a "sense of vague, timeless, and inevitable sin" and as presenting a portrait of the moral confusions of contemporary young Americans.[30] This review is by no means atypical and, given time, the novel may turn out to be another *Catcher in the Rye* as a portrait of coming of age. Or it may simply become valuable as the first novel of a talented writer who later turns out to be another Dickens or Faulkner. Given the Dworkin/MacKinnon law, however, we would not be afforded the time to find out. Publishers would not risk making the book available without first requiring drastic revisions, demanding changes that would dilute its total impact.[31] Its potential social value (not to mention its aesthetic integrity) would be lost.

Whatever legal and moral reasons may be offered against such laws, we must wonder how much society really benefits when we dictate by law what artists can or cannot portray. The cultural revolution in China and the Stalin years in the Soviet Union hardly constituted the flowering of the arts in those societies. There is no evidence that censorship accomplishes all that its proponents claim for it or that censors can be trusted to judge prudently. When censors are chosen for their grasp of ideology, not their knowledge of art history, we can expect them to judge imprudently. In those cases where we do find it necessary to adopt censorship, we must take great care to place clear limitations on the powers of the censors.

V

If my analysis has been correct, then proponents of the ordinance cannot get around the problems I have noted by redefining 'pornography' in an attempt to secure more workable criteria. Instead, attention must shift to the fact that pornography is being singled out because it provides a highly visible symptom of the mistreatment of women and other groups. Racism and sexism are morally reprehensible, and the degradation or defamation of persons because of their race or sex is one manifestation of such behavior. More to the point at hand, if racism and sexism can occur by one person's saying degrading things about another, it is equally wrong to express the same attitudes in representational works. But sexually explicit materials are just one forum for degrading women in images. A degrading attitude can and does occur in representations which are not sexually explicit (e.g., in advertisements and some popular novels). The pornographic attitude can be found in any number of representations or images that express contempt for women as sexually autonomous, equal persons. The pornographic attitude does not accompany only sexually explicit representations, just as many sexually explicit representations that are commonly labeled "pornographic" (e.g., sexually explicit films of homosexual or lesbian lovemaking) need not express the pornographic attitude.[32]

The real goal, then, is to distinguish objectionable pornography from the sexual explicit *per se* (to distinguish the pornographic from, say, the erotic) while providing for restriction of the former but not the latter. The situation is comparable to analyses of what is morally wrong with rape that stress that, while rape has a sexual component, the wrong of the offense lies not in its sexual nature but in the assault and lack of consent, that is, in its denial of the victim's personhood.[33] Any materials challenged as pornographic must be examined in light of the distinction between sexual activity as a subject matter and the attitude expressed toward that subject matter. A failure to appreciate the distinction between subject matter and attitude can be seen in many other attempts at censorship, as when persons have tried to remove *Romeo and Juliet* from American classrooms for "advocating sexual freedom." *The Three Little Pigs* has come under similar attack for "promoting witchcraft because the pigs danced gleefully in a circle while the big bad wolf burned in flames."[34] In both cases, as in the earlier case of *Huck Finn*, the attack's only plausibility depends on interpreting an isolated aspect of the work's subject matter as decisive in fixing the work's expressed attitude. Just as having the pigs dance around a fire need not mean that the work endorses witchcraft, so showing a woman enjoying rape need not mean that the work endorses rape as pleasurable to women.

Although those who would ban *Huck Finn* and *Romeo and Juliet* are motivated by social good, their efforts take root in the mistaken notion that representational art is equally accessible to any audience. This notion, however democratic, is false; only those with adequate training can reasonably interpret complex works. The error underlying this censorship thus follows from the discredited assumption that visual representations unproblematically "copy" their subject; but now the assumption has been extended to literature, too. My point is that just as there can be illiteracy in English or French or any other spoken language, without training one remains illiterate with respect to a wide range of representational art. And just as we find degrees of fluency in spoken languages, there are levels of interpretative ability for representations. Two conclusions follow.

First, we cannot trust mere societal consensus to determine which representations express the pornographic attitude. Doing so makes no more sense than following an engineering blueprint by majority vote when most of those voting are not very good at reading blueprints. Letting juries and judges decide what is objectionable trusts to the luck of the draw, despite the high probability that the evaluators will be unqualified for the job. (Juries and judges are competent to decide questions of obscenity, since all members of a community are equally capable of deciding whether something violates prevailing community standards. But we are not dealing with the issue of community standards here.) Some mechanism should ensure that those with an adequate background take part in evaluating works accused of being pornographic or, more properly, of expressing the pornographic attitude. For instance, film theorists, established critics, and film historians should be involved in the decision of whether, say, *Repulsion* is objectionable.

Second, looking at the long term, there is some hope that unfounded calls for censorship of nonobjectionable works can be mitigated, although they will never be silenced. Given that a concentrated effort to teach basic reading skills to all citizens of the United States still results in a substantial illiteracy rate, consider the current "illiteracy rate" for more complex writing (e.g., the novel *Huck Finn*) and for other means of communication (e.g., paintings and films). I have already argued that many of the more questionable calls for censorship stem from the fact that many people deal with art on a rather elementary level. Aesthetic education, therefore, should not be dismissed as an educational luxury; aesthetic education is necessary for any improvement in aesthetic literacy. If such education were taken more seriously and if everyone had a better introduction to the complexities and range of representational art, we might spend less time arguing over the more spurious charges brought against a wide range of materials and could better face the issue of which representations are genuinely objectionable.

Society has some responsibility to preserve and to protect fine art from unjustified censorship. However, assuming the case for censorship of some objectionable representations, one final problem remains. I have argued that countless sexually explicit works are threatened when society does not take account of an appropriately broad context of interpretation and does not recognize that an objectionable attitude toward persons is the real basis for censorship. We must abandon the attempt to fix, in a list of conditions, which elements unqualifiably make a work unacceptable, any more than we should expect to be able to anticipate in advance all the things that would make a book "religious" or a film "fascist." Who would have predicted in 1922 that T. S. Eliot's *The Wasteland* would later be widely interpreted as containing a significantly religious outlook?

Yet there is some price to pay if ordinances against pornography are altered in the ways I have suggested. Just as those who viewed the Armory show in 1913 could not have been expected to appreciate Matisse, we cannot say just yet what to make of *Less Than Zero*. Aesthetic judgment and art interpretation are generally trustworthy once we gain some hindsight, but they are notoriously uncertain regarding contemporary works. I have already suggested that we can facilitate a charitable interpretation of new works by providing an education that includes exposure to a wide range of art, but even the most sympathetic audience will take years to assimilate and understand some new works.

How, then, do we handle those works whose interpretation is still highly questionable? When we have such a work and it is accused of expressing the pornographic attitude (e.g., suppose we were judging Picasso's *Les Demoiselles D'Avignon* in 1907), we should resist restricting its exhibition or sale merely because it *might* be objectionable. As I argued in section IV, artists, publishers, and other members of the art world would become overly cautious about what they made public if they were not protected from the constant threat of litigation. We should therefore restrict only those works which do, beyond a reasonable doubt, express the pornographic attitude. Unclear and borderline cases should not be censored until subsequent evidence, such as the artist's subsequent work, tips the scales against the work in question. But to hold off on a censorship decision until we obtain a clear picture of the developing tradition that surrounds a new work seems to undercut the goals of an ordinance aiming to block trafficking in pornography. Fortunately, this is not a serious problem.

Separating the issue of defamation from the sexually explicit character of works already minimizes the number of problematic cases. Individual scenes of a work will become less important. Rather than immediately challenging the films *Repulsion* and *A Clockwork Orange* because they contain brutal rape scenes, debate will shift to the general attitude toward women in these works. Those who might use the Dworkin/MacKinnon ordinance as a means of challenging any work merely because it is sexually explicit or contains some offensive scenes would lack a case. Despite the violent mistreatment of women in some scenes in *Less Than Zero*, the novel takes the same critical attitude toward males and females of a certain age and social class, and so we have little reason to hold that the work is sexist and degrading to women.

Furthermore, pornography is only one element of the more complex problem of sexism, hence censorship alone will not create a more egalitarian society. Some censorship may be necessary to mitigate sexism, but it is hardly sufficient to do the job. Thus, our difficulties in evaluating some works are not a major setback. Advocates of censorship will recognize that societally entrenched attitudes toward women will not change unless *positive* attitudes toward women replace those which today express the pornographic attitude. In addition to censorship, we must therefore pressure artists, museums, publishers, filmmakers, and so on, to produce and present works that acknowledge women as equal human beings. In particular, we must encourage works which positively present women in control of their sexual lives. There is nothing original in this recommendation, but it suggests that, if censorship is appropriately balanced by support of works taking a positive attitude toward women, it will hardly matter that a few objectionable works will slip through the cracks. Should we censor those works which clearly express the pornographic attitude and should a work whose interpretation is uncertain later turn out to be reprehensible, its intervening availability is not particularly distressing if society otherwise makes it clear that sexism is not acceptable.

In conclusion, it may be possible to adopt limited censorship of pornography, but only if such censorship is directed at the pornographic attitude. In this way, we may be able to avoid censorship of sexually explicit but nonobjectionable works. It is unreasonable, however, to prohibit any specific represented subject matter. By calling attention to the pornographic attitude and unambiguously indicating that such attitudes violate the principles of our society, we can gradually lessen the present need to take legal action against sexist materials.[35]

NOTES

1. Helen E. Longino, "Pornography, Oppression, and Freedom: A Closer Look," *Take Back the Night*, ed. Laura Lederer (New York: Morrow, 1980), p. 48. Rosemarie Tong offers a variation of the same argument: Rosemarie Tong, "Feminism, Pornography and Censorship," *Social Theory and Practice* 8, no. 1 (1982): 1–18.

Criticism of this approach is offered by Fred R. Berger, "Pornography, Feminism, and Censorship," in *Philosophy and Sex*, 2nd ed., ed. Robert Baker and Frederick Elliston: (Buffalo, New York: Prometheus Books, 1984), pp. 327–51; and by Alan Soble, "Pornography: Defamation and Endorsement of Degradation," *Social Theory and Practice* 11, no. 1 (1985): 61–87. My analysis covers the aesthetic components of the issue in a way that is only occasionally suggested by Berger and Soble.

2. Mary Kay Blakely, "Is One Woman's Sexuality Another Woman's Pornography?" *Ms.*, April 1985, pp. 46–47. The model law referred to in this article is essentially identical to the Minneapolis ordinance; both are the work of Andrea Dworkin and Catherine MacKinnon.

3. Nelson Goodman, *Languages of Art* (Indianapolis: Hackett Publishing, 1976), pp. 7–8, 38. See also E. H. Gombrich, *Art and Illusion* (Princeton, N.J.: Princeton University Press, 1961).

4. *The Compact Edition of the Oxford English Dictionary* (Oxford: Oxford University Press, 1971), p. 1191.

5. Lisa Duggan, "Censorship in the Name of Feminism," *The Village Voice* 29 (16 October 1984): 11–42.

6. Some writers have equated advocacy of rape with the narrower category of material that endorses rape, with pornography taken as representations of sexual behavior that both degrades one of the participants and recommends such

degradation. See Longino, "Pornography, Oppression, and Freedom," p. 43. Tong similarly holds that objectionable or "thanatic" pornography is that which *encourages* violation of someone's rights as a sexual being; see Tong, "Feminism, Pornography and Censorship," p. 4.

However, works can defame or degrade without also recommending or encouraging that the audience follow suit. I can libel or defame some persons by saying heinous things about them, and I thereby wrong them even if I do not go on to encourage others to wrong them likewise. Thus, if women are degraded by a work, the work is offensive whether or not it also encourages such degradation. This error in Longino's and Tong's analysis merely reintroduces the idea that pornography is wrong by virtue of its *causal* role in the mistreatment of women and as such is not essential to a definition of pornography as subordination of women through sexually explicit representations. My analysis does not assume that the degradation of women involves some encouragement or recommendation of sexism.

Soble notes that the defamation and endorsement arguments are independent, but his analysis of how pornography might be thought to degrade women overlooks the difference between "content" and expressed attitude which underlies my discussion. As a result, his criticisms of the defamation argument are inconclusive. See Soble, "Pornography: Defamation and the Endorsement of Degradation."

7. Of all those authors who defend restrictions on pornography for "feminist" reasons, I can find only one who recognizes the point I am making. Helen Longino says that "whether or not [something] is pornographic is a function of contextual features," so it is pornographic only if it endorses degradation in sexual encounters (Longino, "Pornography, Oppression, and Freedom," p. 43). But the Dworkin law ignores Longino's analysis, and even Longino herself quickly tries to outline the specific content which always constitutes a degrading attitude.

Berger notes that context is crucial whether or not pornography includes degrading messages about women, but Berger does not pursue or explain the idea. See Berger, "Pornography, Feminism, and Censorship," pp. 336–37.

8. These distinctions are not meant to be original, and roughly parallel those found in Virgil C. Aldrich, *Philosophy of Art* (Englewood Cliffs, N.J.: Prentice-Hall, 1963), pp. 35–50.

Ann Gary and Alan Soble ignore the complexities of what each calls the "content" of representational art. See Ann Gary, "Pornography and Respect for Women," *Social Theory and Practice* 4, no. 1 (1978): 395–421, at p. 396, and Soble, "Pornography: Defamation and the Endorsement of Degradation," at pp. 68–70.

9. Admittedly, Kubrick's film is open to multiple interpretations; see Eric Rhode, *A History of the Cinema from Its Origin to 1970* (New York: Hill and Wang, 1976), pp. 613–14.

10. The ordinance does contain a clause to the effect that "isolated passages or isolated parts" cannot be singled out under the law. I take it that defenders

of the ordinance do not mean that a book is not pornographic if, for instance, only some of its chapters violate the nine conditions. *Quantity* of pornographic content surely does not decide what is and isn't pornographic. But the nine clauses defining pornography therefore prohibit in whole any material which, for instance, contains (as even a small portion) a scene where a woman enjoys rape, even if the work as a whole puts this scene into a context which shows that only a sick person could react in this way.

The clause prohibiting action against isolated parts of a work does not protect works, as one might assume, but makes it easier to censor artistic and literary works.

11. Corolyn See, *Blue Money* (New York: David McKay, 1974), p. 159; Rhode, *A History of the Cinema*, p. 336.

12. Kenneth Clark, *The Nude* (New York: Doubleday Anchor Press, 1956), p. 23. If my arguments are correct, then the sale of Clark's book constitutes "trafficking in pornography" under the ordinance.

13. Clark, *The Nude*, p. 27.

14. Ibid.

15. Gloria Steinem, for instance, seems to make lack of free or equal choice the basis for distinguishing between the pornographic and the erotic; Gloria Steinem, "Erotica and Pornography : A Clear and Present Difference," in *Take Back the Night*, p. 37. This explanation of "objects" is also offered by Tong, "Feminism, Pornography and Censorship," p. 4.

16. E.g., Clark, *The Nude*, pp. 22, 26, 28, 210, and 215.

17. Rozsika Parker and Griselda Pollock, *Old Mistresses* (New York: Pantheon, 1981), pp. 126–30.

18. Robert Hughes, *The Shock of the New* (New York: Knopf, 1981), p. 249.

19. Ibid.

20. Clark, *The Nude*, p 224.

21. Terry Measham, *The Moderns: 1945-1975* (Oxford: Phaidon, 1976), p. 77.

22. Michael Patrick Hearn, "Expelling Huck Finn," *The Nation*, 7–14 August 1982, p. 117.

Fred Berger offers the same comparison, noting another case where Twain's novel was removed from a library as "racist." See Berger, "Pornography, Feminism, and Censorship," p. 339.

23. Mark Twain, *Adventures of Huckleberry Finn, The Complete Novels of Mark Twain*, ed. Charles Neider, vol. 1 (New York: Doubleday, 1964), p. 801, chap. 14.

24. Twain, *Adventures*, p. 860, chap. 15.

25. Claude M. Simpson, "Introduction," *Twentieth-Century Interpretations of Huckleberry Finn*, ed. Charles M. Simpson (Englewood Cliffs, N.J.: Prentice-Hall, 1968), p. 4.

26. Twain, *Adventures*, p. 808, chap. 16.

27. Hearn, "Expelling Huck Finn," p. 117.

28. Quoted in Russell Lynes, *The Tastemakers* (New York: Harper, 1954), p. 219.

29. Bret Easton Ellis, *Less Than Zero* (New York: Simon and Schuster, 1985), p. 189.

30. See Eliot Fremont-Smith, "The Right Snuff," *The Village Voice* 30 (7 May 1985).

31. "More and more books are being censored" by their publishers in recent years to avoid the threat of legal battles; see Anne C. Roark, "Libel Lawyers Wield Blue Pencils on Books," *Los Angeles Times*, 26 June 1986, sec. 1, pp. 1, 26, and 27.

32. To illustrate the possibility of nonpornographic materials displaying the pornographic attitude, readers of *Ms.* magazine have accused it of publishing advertisements that exploit and dehumanize women. "Several hundred" letters of protest were directed against a recent ad for "Obsession" perfume. The ad includes a photograph of a man caressing the seminude torso of a woman. Her head and arms are eliminated by the cropping of the photo. One letter protested, "What better way to objectify a woman than to render her faceless. Truly she is the *object* of this man's sexual obsession." The editors of *Ms.* defended the ad as "sensuous" but not offensive because the man is portrayed as "emotional and vulnerable." See "Letters to the Editors," *Ms.*, July 1986, p. 10, and "Obsession" advertisement, *Ms.*, April 1986, p. 18.

For an example of a potentially objectionable image which is not sexually explicit, consider another ad that appeared in *Ms.* Promoting beer, it shows an attractive woman attired in exercise tights, leaning back in a chair, and holding a beer. There is little reason for the pose and attire except to make her body an object of sexual display. Since no "emotional and vulnerable" man is present to mitigate the message, this ad should probably be seen as expressing the pornographic attitude. See *Ms.*, July 1986, p. 9.

A classic example of offensive material that is not sexually explicit is the ad for "Black and Blue," an album by The Rolling Stones. The ad shows a woman bound with rope, arms over her head and her legs pulled wide apart by the ropes. Between her legs is a copy of the record album. Her lace gown is torn at the breast area. See "Black and Blue" advertisement, *Rolling Stone*, 1 July 1976, p. 79.

33. See Susan Brownmiller, *Against Our Will: Men, Women, and Rape* (New York: Simon and Schuster, 1975).

34. Keith Richburg, "A Holy War for Young Minds," *The Washington Post*, 30 December 1985, part A, pp. 1 and 6.

35. Earlier drafts of this paper were presented at California State University, San Bernardino, and at the Pacific Division Meetings, American Philosophical Association, Los Angeles, 1986. My thanks to Stephanie Ross and Linda Carr-Lee for their comments on previous drafts.

18

The Case Against Censorship of Pornography

William A. Linsley

THE MARKET

The publication of sexually explicit material is a multi-billion dollar annual business in America. From the public's patronage of bookstores and movie theatres to the use of videocassette recorders (VCRs), telephones, and computers to bring pornography into the home, the evidence of its acceptance and impact on the economy is indisputable. Despite efforts to censor pornography, the market for it demonstrates the appetite, or at least the indulgence, of a staggering number of people.

An estimated 165,000 people are involved as producers, distributors, retailers, writers, or photographers of sexually explicit materials. Twenty million adult magazines are bought by us per month. Sexually explicit films account for 10 percent–15 percent of the videocassette market. A 1985 Gallup poll of 1,020 adults found X-rated films account for one-fifth of all video sales, and 9 percent of all Americans (40 percent of all VCR owners) bought or rented an X-rated cassette within the year prior to the poll.[1] Every week Americans buy more than 2 million tickets to X-rated movies, representing

Edited and published with permission of the author, William A. Linsley, from "The Case Against Censorship of Pornography," in *Pornography: Research Advances and Policy Considerations* edited by Dolf Zillmann and Jennings Bryant (Hillsdale, N.J.: Lawrence Erlbaum Associates, Inc., 1989).

a box office in excess of $500 million annually. Pornography is big business and our friends, neighbors, relatives, and colleagues make it so. Those who protest how terrible "this stuff" is, such as the *Attorney General's Commission on Pornography, Final Report* (1986) (hereinafter referred to as The Commission Report),[2] also unwittingly contribute to the publicity that calls attention to the business and makes it big.

In 1986, on a Tuesday in June, voters in the traditionally conservative state of Maine answered this question: "Do you want to make it a crime to make, sell, give for value, or otherwise promote obscene material in Maine?" Although remote from the influence of urban America and lobbied heavily by church activists, Maine voted decisively (3-1) against the question. It remains to be determined if their rejection of censorship rather than smut can be interpreted as indicative that "as Maine goes so goes the nation."

The size of the market and the reticence to ban sexually explicit material as demonstrated by both surveys and ballots hardly constitute a mandate for only the chosen few to see and judge what everyone else can not even look at. The public does not always get what the public wants; but when the few attempt to dictate what the many can see, hear, read, and sense, the issues that address the oppression come into sharper focus: Should adults be permitted to receive explicit sexual messages and judge them for themselves or should the state censor "sinful" messages in order to "save us from ourselves"? Is the right to know the corollary of the right to speak or publish? Should government by regulatory power sit in judgment of tastes or beliefs? Is there a definable class of sexually oriented expression that may be suppressed totally without also proscribing constitutionally protected expression?

These questions are answered differently by those on both sides who see themselves as sincere, decent, rational individuals dedicated to bringing out the best in each of us. One explanation for these differences may be that what causes a person to be startled by nude bodies in a movie or a magazine reflects only a neurosis not shared by others. But the real reason probably lies in the trust or distrust characteristic of those who believe we can or cannot be the best judges of what is in our own best interest. Unfortunately *pornography* is so negatively connotated that it defies openminded objective investigation to see which side can advance the most logically persuasive arguments about self-reliance, trust, and individual worth. The advocates bring to the fray, in addition to personal experience, their religious, ethical, social, and professional bias. As Becker and Levine, commissioners for the *Attorney General's Commission on Pornography* (1986) state in the commission's final report: "To some a discussion of pornography raises concerns of sincerely and deeply felt moral imperatives; to others it is a feminist issue of violence against women; and still to others, it is a lightning rod attracting debates about First Amendment guarantees with the threat of censorship seen as the overriding danger."[3]

On the law and order side of the confrontation with civil libertarians are the self-righteous, the indignant, and the outraged who sincerely believe that today's flood of pornography assuredly will portend the downfall of Western civilization. This group is constituted of police and prosecutors, preachers and church-goers, and those others who know in their hearts that people left to their own devices surely will destroy themselves by succumbing to lust or deviant moral behavior. To these moral police, pornography in all of its "abhorrent" forms—cusswords, nudity, suggestive lyrics, female degradation, natural or simulated sex acts—must be exposed and purged before the debauchery of fragile individuals occurs. Smut must be banned before it defiles either the young and the unwilling or the mature and the consenting. Private individuals in this camp may be quite susceptible to a prurient appeal and even innocently lured into a moment of lust. But when called upon to render a judgment in their role as citizens, they assertively protest appeals to prurient interest.

The opposite camp, made up of free expressionists who are paradoxically intolerant of intolerance, contends that the identification and preservation of safe societal norms is assured best by unrestrained discussion and debate which cannot take place under the censor's axe. This group regards censorship as thought control that keeps people ignorant and denies them the opportunity for responsible choice. Censorship is seen as a cancer that spreads and defies corrective therapy once a good suppression becomes established. Obscenity is seen as a hodgepodge, undefinable with precision, but sufficient when indulged in to send people to jail for violating standards that they cannot understand, construe, and apply. This is a "monstrous" consequence according to Supreme Court Justice William Douglas who lamented that such a restraint can exist in a nation dedicated to fair trials and due process.[4]

The range of social control over objectionable, sexually explicit expression is broader than governmental censorship. Even constitutionally protected material may be regulated by societal groups not under the aegis of the First Amendment's constraint that "Congress shall pass no law." Therefore, the case against censorship is not exclusively a case against state regulation but a broader one where the anti-censorship arguments draw strength from the same premises whether oppressive action is taken by the state or by quasi-legal control groups that enforce their dictates through pressure exerted on obedient followers. Consequently, we have long sought a way to reconcile freedom for citizens to speak out in public and in print with assurance that the content will be pure enough to gratify all who, by whatever regulatory means, guard us from anti-social thought and action.

Three premises must coalesce their elements to enable censorship of the sexually offensive and still appease those who fear capricious abuse of fundamental freedoms:

Premise 1. The work is definably pornographic.

Premise 2. The pornography causes identifiable harm.

Premise 3. The censorship of the pornographic cause preserves traditional guarantees of expression rights.

To require less, without identification or connection or respect for individual rights, is to permit everything objectionable to be banned even if we cannot agree on what it is or what it does or whether the forfeiture of free choice is worth the price.

THE UNDEFINABLE

Censorship fails initially as a means to preserve preferred morality standards if we must settle for a definition of pornography based solely on a case by case objection to the content of ideas as judged differently from one person to another. However, to hold us to a shared meaning for the pornographic depends on the myth that the nature of offensive material is so common to everyone's experience, that its pornographic essence speaks for itself. This simplistic belief perpetuates a kind of vagueness about obscenity that deprives individuals of the fair warning that keeps them out of prison and saves them from being fined for conduct they could not know was criminal.

The line that separates the obscene, the pornographic, the licentious, the lewd, the libidinous, the prurient, the lascivious, the indecent, the smutty, and the filthy from each other is imperceptible and controversial. Because these words have no meaning in themselves and are merely symbols that stand for something other than themselves, little significance can be attached to any one of these symbols for its accepted meaning or intended implications. The "obscene" and the "pornographic" routinely are used interchangeably without pretense that they stand for more than the "offensive," which represents how people individually use devil terms rather than how symbols are chosen to achieve universal understanding. Nevertheless, for the sake of argument we can proceed to examine other dimensions of the censorship act without being deceived by the ambiguity of that language, the meaning of which we only pretend to understand. The troublesome question remains however: How does a rational person censor that which can be defined only with such imprecision that in frustration one admits to only being able to "know it when he sees it"[5] or finds it self-exposed when "the grossest of the gross"[6] occurs?

The Supreme Court has worked hard to define obscenity and has failed.[7] Supreme Court Justice William Brennan contends that a class of obscene speech is "incapable of definition with sufficient clarity to withstand attack on vagueness grounds," and therefore fair notice to persons who create and distribute sexually oriented material cannot be provided. Brennan concluded in *Paris Adult Theatre I* v. *Slaton* (1973) that although the Supreme Court has assumed that obscenity does exist "we are manifestly unable to describe it in advance except by reference to concepts ['prurient interest,' 'patent offensiveness,' 'serious literary value'] so elusive that they fail to distinguish clearly between protected and unprotected speech."[8]

Society, like the Supreme Court, has worked hard to define obscenity, and it, too, has failed. Art and literature reflect tastes and feelings. Tastes, like beliefs, are too personal, too emotional, and too vague to define. These intangibles defy precise definition and provide compelling argument for why "obscenity," because it is undefinable, should be protected in whatever guise it is perceived.[9]

The 1970 report of the Commission on Obscenity and Pornography sensed the problem with words and disdained use of the term *pornography*. They said the word lacked legal significance and commonly denoted subjective disapproval of certain materials, rather than a recognition of their content or effect. *The Commission Report* (1986) noted that marking the boundaries of *pornography* is essentially a "futile" task, but this did not keep them from trying. So what did they mean when referring to pornographic materials? Operationally they announced such to be "predominantly sexually explicit and intended primarily for the purpose of sexual arousal."[10] Given our dependence on sexual arousal for perpetuation of the species, the fear that arousal may occur is questionably an antisocial disadvantage, at least on select occasions pertinent to assuring that the species does not become extinct. Few would argue the social harm of sexual desires that lead to normal and not anti-social behavior; but many of these same people would, nevertheless, censor the prurient to protect against anti-social behavior while concurrently preempting a stimulus that triggers fulfillment of imperative biological needs.

At most, obscenity is the expression of offensive ideas.[11] But that someone proclaims to be offended is not enough. The offensiveness standard gives the censor unbridled authority to declare smut to be garbage and select from all the available garbage, be it essentially even political or social, what shall be suppressed. As Supreme Court Justice Douglas pointed out in the *Paris* (1973) case:

> [People are] offended by political pronouncements, sociological themes, and by stories of official misconduct. The list of activities and publications and pronouncements that offend someone is endless. . . . Life in this crowded modern technological world creates many offensive statements and many offensive deeds. There is no protection against offensive ideas, only against offensive conduct.[12]

To define obscenity as the offensive is so vague that fair notice of what is forbidden cannot be provided. Besides, statutory vagueness becomes even less tolerable because of its potentially inhibiting effect on constitutionally protected speech. We should not be required to act at our peril where the free dissemination of ideas may be the loser. We should not have to risk imprisonment by having to guess whether society will be traumatized if we express taste and feeling. It is unconscionable to force a choice between silence and speech when the statute prohibiting conduct is too vague to give guidance.[13]

Thus the question: Can obscenity be defined with sufficient precision so we can know how not to violate the law? Apparently this is not possible if we accept Justice Brennan's position in the *Paris* case:

> Even the most painstaking efforts to determine in advance whether certain sexually oriented expression is obscene must inevitably prove unavailing. For the insufficiency of the notice compels persons to guess not only whether their conduct is covered by a criminal statute, but also whether their conduct falls within the constitutionally permissible reach of the statute. The resulting level of uncertainty is utterly intolerable, not alone because it makes bookselling a hazardous profession but as well because it invites arbitrary and erratic enforcement of the law.[14]

In addition to the stress placed on the accused, when the line separating protected from unprotected speech is extremely vague, identification of the obscene places considerable institutional stress on the courts. Almost every obscenity case before the Supreme Court has resulted in a marginal separation of the protected from the unprotected. The system is forced, therefore, each time to take on a constitutional challenge of exceptional difficulty. The problem for the accused, who lacks guidance because he cannot find the vague line, as well as for the courts that must draw the line, is mired in the ambiguity of definition—a seemingly irreconcilable problem.

The first blow for the case against censorship of the pornographic, therefore, is struck with the realization that the premise that requires before-the-fact definition of material to be censored cannot be gratified. Everyone should be able to know with certainty what constitutes a crime. No such certainty exists with obscenity. . . .

THE UNCONNECTED

Even if for the sake of argument *pornography* can find widespread meaning, the causal connection to whatever it is that pornography incites must be established or we fail to remove the real causes for the disapproved effects. To millions of Americans the porno-causes-harm assumption makes reasonable the banning of books, magazines, and video displays. But the censorship of "dirty" pictures is a "red herring" that leads us away from finding the real causes of the harms and the real solutions for those harms. During our early history and in particular before X-rated movies, provocative centerfolds, and commercial erotica, men raped women and molested children. Violence and sexual deviance flourished even when violators of social norms saw no pornography and read nothing. At the very least the spectre of as yet unidentified multiple causes for anti-social behavior should produce caution in those who isolate blame by observation and verification rather than by emotion and haste.

Even if we believe that mass communication has delivered incitement to the pervert's door, how, given the vast overlap in content between mass communication channels, do we isolate the offending channel for censorship? As Judge Frank reminds us in *U.S.* v. *Roth* (1956) "The daily press, television, radio, movies, books, and comics all present their share of so-called 'bad' material. . . . It is virtually impossible to isolate the impact of one of these media on a population exposed to all of them."[15]

When an effect (anti-social behavior) is all out of proportion to its supposed cause (pornography), might there be other factors of greater force at work? Could it be that the source of influence lies not in the published material that attracts our attention but in those other influences which everyone concedes can produce harmful reaction? Can a democratic society survive if it governs by taboo, whim, and anecdote, rather than deliberation, reason, and science? How frequently does it warrant repeating that in the discovery of the obscene and its assumed consequences we do not have all the facts, not even most of them; and therefore, even if a connection with the obscene is accepted as asserted, how can evil behavior be identified and condoned by a censor's choice from the simple absolutes of right–wrong or good–bad? Irving Brant, Bill of Rights interpreter and scholar, aptly addressed the folly of this choice when he wrote: "There is no greater fallacy than the belief that government can or ought to separate truth from error. Error, protected by freedom of speech, may outlive truth. But freedom dies when error is repressed by law, and error multiplies when freedom dies."[16]

"If we were certain that impurity of sexual thoughts impelled to action," punishment of the distributors of sex literature would be on less dangerous ground according to Justice Douglas in *Roth* v. *U.S.*[17] But the lack of dependable information about the effect of obscene literature on human conduct bothered Douglas who believed "it should put us on the side of protecting society's interest in literature, except and unless it can be said that the particular publication has an impact on action the government can control."[18] The Supreme Court, twelve years later, pointed out in *Stanley* v. *Georgia* (1969) that "there appears to be little empirical basis" for the assertion that "exposure to obscene materials may lead to deviant sexual behavior or crimes of sexual violence."[19] Then in 1970 the Commission on Obscenity and Pornography, which produced findings that startled its sponsors, found no empirical research to verify that exposure to explicit sexual material causes delinquent or criminal behavior among youth or adults. Instead, they noted that explicit sexual materials are sought as a source of entertainment and information by substantial numbers of American adults, apparently without harm.

A critical concern of the Attorney General's Commission on Pornography in 1986, sixteen years after the inability to determine causality defeated any effort by the commission's predecessors to recommend censorship, was to measure and assess pornography's role in causing anti-social behavior.

By vaguely defining pornography as sexually explicit material that does not foster traditional family values, and by giving equal credence to fundamentalist preachers, anti-porn zealots, and porn victims as given to scientific research, the commission found a relationship between exposure to certain kinds of pornography and acts of sexual violence. In one sense, the manufactured impression of a causal link disguised the absence of hard evidence. Nevertheless, commission members Becker and Levine in The Commission's *Report* regard human behavior as complex and multicausal. "To say that exposure to pornography in and of itself causes an individual to commit crime is simplistic, not supported by the social science data, and overlooks many of the other variables that may be contributing causes."[20] Becker, a psychiatrist, claimed that she had worked with sexual offenders for ten years without seeing any causal link between pornography and sex crimes.

Although the commission struggled mightily, according to Becker and Levine, it never did "agree on definitions of such basic terms as pornography and erotica. . . . This failure to establish definitions acceptable to all members severely limited our ability to come to grips with the question of impact. . . . In fact, the commission failed to carve out a mutually satisfactory definition of anti-social behavior."[21] Becker and Levine stressed that the social science research presented to the commission "has not been designed to evaluate the relationship between exposure to pornography and the commission of sex crimes." The evidence "does not speak to harm, on which the commission report focuses" but to the "relationship among variables or effects that can be positive or negative."[22] As The Commission *Report* itself points out: "In many respects, research is still at a fairly rudimentary stage, and with few attempts to standardize categories of analysis, self-reporting questionnaires, types of stimulus materials, measurement of effects and related problems."[23]

Other than the quantity of materials consumed, we really know very little about the relationship of pornography to adolescents and young adults. Indeed the moral and ethical implications of conducting sex-related experiments on them, and adults too, to discover causal relationships, may forever prevent the impact of pornography from being scientifically determined. Thus, unless you can sell the dubious notion of inherency, namely, that there is "stuff" that is obscene because it exists, as The Commission's *Report* seems to say, obscenity censorship depends on the unproved and possibly unprovable assumption that the obscene is a significant cause of sexual deviation from identifiable community standards. Conclusive research findings do not exist to allow the conclusion that obscenity is *the* or even *a* causal factor in sexually deviant behavior. It is equally plausible, based on the evidence introduced to date, that multiple and as yet unidentified causes prompt the misbehavior of man. . . .

The key question thus becomes: Do you censor out of a presumptive hunch about causality or refrain from censorship for lack of demonstrably valid evidence of harm? The contagion theory, based on the presumptive hunch, tells us that anti-social behavior is caught from books, films, and videotapes. Significantly, however, the commissioners of the Attorney General's 1986 inquiry failed to become sex criminals as they apparently survived exposure to pornography in all of its infectious forms. . . .

The second blow for the case against censorship of the pornographic, therefore, is struck with the realization that the premise that requires that discernible obscenity causes identifiable harm fails because the causality is unverified and probably unverifiable.

THE TRADITION

The case against censorship is not complete, however, without testing whether a proscription of this nature is consistent with the protection generally afforded expression.

On occasion, citizens' decency boards, textbook selection committees, religious groups, and assorted other guardians of human morals have proscribed, among numerous other works, Hemingway's *For Whom the Bell Tolls,* Whitman's *Leaves of Grass,* Dreiser's *An American Tragedy,* Steinbeck's *The Grapes of Wrath,* Joyce's *Ulysses,* Lawrence's *Lady Chatterley's Lover,* the Bible, and various dictionaries. Review boards have banned films, and censors have prohibited the mailing of magazines. Convenience stores have been intimidated into withdrawing publications from store shelves, and school authorities have conditioned the publication of school newspapers on the use of officially approved content. Although all rule-making, norm-creating bodies are not governed by the First Amendment, the rationale behind the "Congress shall make no law" guarantee of expression rights supports tenets so basic that the necessity for their respect and adoption, even outside government circles, is self-evident if the democratic nature of our self-governing society is to survive with respect for the dignity of man.

Supreme Court Justice Hugo Black believed that there are prohibitory absolutes in our Bill of Rights that were purposely put there by men who knew what words meant; and, therefore, the phrase "Congress shall make no law," contains plain, easily understood words. Black, in *Smith v. California* (1959), spelled out how there is no room for modification and discretion of this absolute which prohibits the regulation of speech:

> Certainly the First Amendment's language leaves no room for inference that abridgements of speech and press can be made just because they are slight. That Amendment provides, in simple words, that "Congress shall make no law . . . abridging the freedom of speech, or of the press." I read "no law . . . abridging" to mean *"no law abridging."* The First Amendment, which is the supreme law of the land, has thus fixed its own value on freedom of speech and press by putting these freedoms wholly "beyond the reach"

of federal power to . . . subordinate speech and press to what they think are "more important interests."[24] (pp. 157–159)

*   *   *

The debate persists over whether the courts should interpret the First Amendment in accord with the views of those who sponsored and adopted it or in accord with subsequent views that remove protection from offensive expression and through controls banish it. Those, however, who interpret the Constitution to gratify their own needs must accept the ambiguity, division, and inconsistency created by their self-serving ways when they act without regard for the guidance provided by men like James Madison and Thomas Jefferson whose statements show no sympathy for allowing censorship of the offensive.

When James Madison offered the Bill of Rights to Congress in 1789 he looked at the First Amendment's limitation on the federal government and declared: "The right of freedom of speech is secured; the liberty of the press is expressly declared to be *beyond the reach of this Government*."[25] Ten years later Madison, in an address to the General Assembly of Virginia, said the "free range of the human mind is injuriously restrained" when the truth of opinion is subject to imprisonment by those of a different opinion, and it would subvert the First Amendment to make a "distinction between the freedom and the licentiousness of the press."[26] Previously he had written that "a man has property in his opinions and the free communication of them," and a government that "violates the property which individuals have in their opinion . . . is not a pattern for the United States."[27]

Jefferson, in his Second Inaugural Address in 1805, declared that "no inference is here intended, that the laws, provided by the State against false and defamatory publications should not be enforced. . . . [T]he press, confined to truth, needs no other legal restraint . . . and no other definite line can be drawn between the inestimable liberty of the press and its demoralizing licentiousness."[28]

The right to speak does not depend on a judgment about the quality or content of speech to be tolerated. The restraint of expression cannot be justified by the purpose or character of expression but only by falling outside "freedom of speech and press" or by constituting a regulation that is not in fact an "abridgment." Therefore, the regulation of offensive expression becomes an abridgment of the quality and content, purpose, or character of expression, long regarded as above regulation. But even to refrain from textual and semantic considerations is insufficient because the First Amendment dictates that "government should be concerned with anti-social conduct not with utterances."[29] Utterances thus became absolutely free whereas conduct alone is controlled.

The overriding purpose in ratifying the Bill of Rights was to secure for the people of the United States greater freedom of religion, expression, assembly, and petition than was then prevalent in England. Ratified while the memory of English restrictions on basic liberties was still fresh, the First Amendment cannot reasonably be interpreted as approving existing English oppressions. In particular, it is evident that English restrictions such as those against the press, in force when the Constitution was adopted, never were accepted by the American colonists.

Therefore, those in the twentieth century who would censor the obscene have an attitude toward free expression that arguably does not concur with that of the framers of the First Amendment but rather arises from mid-nineteenth-century Victorian morality that preached a "faith that you could best conquer evil by shutting your eyes to its existence."[30] The prudery of the purely verbal Victorian code, hypocritically at odds with the actual conduct of some of the code's advocates, clearly was not the moral code of those who framed the First Amendment.

Opposition to the censorship of pornography seeks to preserve open and robust debate about the content and quality of expression created by uninhibited and unfettered writers and artists. The legacy for these rights carries with it a philosophy that does not protect speech only for "decent" people with sanitized messages. The words of Judge Cuthbert Pound in *People* v. *Gitlow* (1921) appropriately make the point: "Although the defendant may be the worst of men . . . the rights of the best of men are secure only as the rights of the vilest and most abhorrent are protected."[31]

To permit censors to judge the content and quality of offensive expression is to endorse guardians for public morals who are not charged with ignoring basic rights but are permitted to grant them selectively when their elitist code is not offended. The regulation of offensive material, either as conduct itself or that which presumptively stimulates disapproved conduct, is contradictory to our traditional guarantees of expression which must allow protests against our moral code of the day if First Amendment speech guarantees are to mean anything. Indeed, the protections inherent in the First Amendment are inconsequential if used only to assure continued expression of the inoffensive and the noncontroversial. If the controversial, the objectionable, and the offensive, customarily thought of as things which provoke the need for censorship, are to be proscribed, then the freedom to differ becomes limited to things that do not bother much.

THE NEW CENSORS

Although dismissed by many as a scholarly embarrassment that produced conclusions no self-respecting investigator could possibly accept, The Commission *Report* has rekindled the hopes of those who are encouraged to renew the struggle to suppress speech that generates bad attitudes. Armed with a license to flush out targets and hunt them down, within three months of the commission's final report Attorney General Edwin Meese turned federal attorneys loose across the country to encourage local law enforcement to mop up the incitement to sexual deviation. The commission could have repudiated, as did its predecessor commission in 1970, the constraints of obscenity regulation and let consenting adults read and see what they choose without interference from moral vigilantes who summarily seek to save man from himself. Instead of encouraging affirmative alternative speech and preserving self-control over the development and expression of one's own intellect, interests, tastes, and personality, the commission instead reinforced the need for censorship.

Whether the recommendations of the commission (1986) are seen as hypocritical to the free expressionist or long awaited gospel to the moral police, some of the ideas expressed and language used by the commission warrant exposure, at least for those who decline to wade through 1,959 pages of text. The following passages do not elevate the case for censorship above an intuitive, unreasoned, presumptive rationalization for oppressive action against a perceived sociological aberration:

> Issues of human dignity and human decency, *no less real* for their lack of scientific measurability, are for many of us central to thinking about the question of harm. And when we think about harm in this way, there are acts that must be condemned . . . *because conscience demands it.*[32]

> Few if any judgments of causality or danger are ever conclusive, and a requirement of *conclusiveness is much more rhetorical device than analytical method.*[33]

> Finding a link between aggressive behavior towards women and sexual violence, whether lawful or unlawful, requires assumptions not found exclusively in the experimental evidence. *We see no reason, however, not to make these assumptions.*[34]

> Materials depicting sexual violence seem *intuitively likely* to bear a causal relationship to sexual violence. . . .[35]

> We deal in an area in which *a great deal must be taken on faith,* including descriptions of stimulus materials, descriptions of experimental environments,

questionnaire design, and description of what may or may not have been told to subjects.[36]

Only *a well-founded intuition* that direct depictions of sexual violence are more likely to produce such violence allows us to conclude that they are more "harmful" than non-violent materials.[37]

THE THREAT

The danger in censoring the obscene lies in bending the popular mind to new forms of conformity. If any governing body seeks to establish a moral tone by prescribing what its constituency cannot read or see, does it not follow that in pursuit of that same objective they can decree what must be read or seen? The alternative is to risk the consequences of tolerance that may lead to the robust as well as the ribald. But that is the risk taken by recognizing civil rights which allow citizens to define their own moral tone. To treat censorship as preferable to this risk is to mistake what constitutes needed rights in a free society.

To install a few fallible mortals as artistic censors over taste and feeling is to empower them to ban mediocre books as obscene today while tomorrow stifling originality as they ban a work of genius. What kind of imagination do we unleash if an author must write with one eye on prosecutors and juries? It would be a dark day for America if the inhibition of creativity and not its rewards becomes our destiny. Indeed, in a larger sense, much good and little harm can result if we err on the side of free expression but much harm and little good can result if we err on the side of oppression. . . .

NOTES

1. "The War against Pornography," *Newsweek* (March 18, 1985): 58–62.
2. U.S. Department of Justice, *The Attorney General's Commission on Pornography: Final Report* (Washington, D.C.: Government Printing Office, 1986).
3. *The Commission Report*, p. 197.
4. *Miller* v. *California*, 413 U.S. 15 (1973), pp. 43–44.
5. *Jacobellis* v. *Ohio*, 378 U.S. 184 (1964).
6. *Redrup* v. *New York*, 386 U.S. 767 (1967).
7. *Miller* v. *California*, p. 37.
8. Ibid., p. 84.
9. *Paris Adult Theatre I* v. *Slaton*, 413 U.S. 49 (1973), p. 70.
10. *The Commission Report*, pp. 228–229.

11. *Paris Adult Theatre I* v. *Slaton,* p. 71.

12. Ibid.

13. *Smith* v. *California,* 361 U.S. 476 (1959), p. 151; *United States* v. *Harris,* 347 U.S. 612 (1954), p. 617.

14. *Paris Adult Theatre I* v. *Slaton,* p. 87.

15. 237 F.2d 796 (1956), p. 815.

16. I. Brant, *The Bill of Rights* (Indianapolis, Ind.: Bobbs-Merrill, 1965), p. 506.

17. *Roth* v. *U.S.,* 354 U.S. 476 (1957), p. 510.

18. Ibid., p. 511.

19. *Stanley* v. *Georgia,* 394 U.S. 557 (1969), p. 566.

20. *The Commission Report,* p. 206.

21. Ibid., p. 200.

22. Ibid., p. 204.

23. Ibid., p. 207.

24. *Smith* v. *California,* 361 U.S. 147 (1959), pp. 157–159.

25. James Madison. *The Debates and Proceedings in the Congress of the United States* (1789), Vol. 1, pp. 757–777. (Washington, D.C.: Gales and Seaton, 1834), p. 766.

26. S. K. Padover. *The Complete Madison* (New York: Harper, 1953), pp. 295–296.

27. Ibid., 267–269.

28. S. K. Padover. *The Complete Jefferson* (Freeport, N.Y.: Books for Libraries Press, 1943), pp. 413–414.

29. *Roth* v. *U.S.,* pp. 512–513.

30. C. Wingfield-Stratford, *Those Earnest Victorians* (New York: Morrow, 1930), p. 151.

31. *People* v. *Gitlow,* 195 App. Div. 773 (1921), p. 773.

32. *The Commission Report,* p. 303 (italics added).

33. Ibid., p. 307 (italics added).

34. Ibid., p. 325 (italics added).

35. Ibid., p. 337 (italics added).

36. Ibid., p. 350 (italics added).

37. Ibid., p. 173 (italics added).

19

Redefining Obscenity

Rita C. Manning

. . . Helen Longino gives the following definition of pornography.

> Pornography is not just the explicit representation or description of sexual
> behavior which is degrading and/or abusive to women. Rather, it is material
> that explicitly represents or describes degrading and abusive sexual behavior
> so as to endorse and/or recommend the behavior as described. The contex-
> tual features, moreover, which communicate such endorsement are intrinsic
> to the material; that is, they are features whose removal or alteration would
> change the representation or description.[1]

This sexual behavior may be depicted either verbally or pictorially.[2] She con-
trasts pornography with erotica on the one hand and moral realism on the
other. Erotica includes explicit depiction of sexual behavior but without the
degrading and abuse of women. Moral realism can include both but endorses
neither. Pornography endorses the degradation and abuse of women in two
ways, by showing the male participants as experiencing pleasure through such
activity and by depicting the females as enjoying such treatment.

The other definition I want to evaluate is the *Ordinance* [drafted by
Andrea Dworkin and Catherine MacKinnon and], introduced in Indianapolis and Minneapolis. It defines pornography as follows:

From *Journal of Value Inquiry* 22 (1988): 193–205. Copyright © 1988 by Kluwer Publishing
Group (Netherlands). Reprinted by permission of the publisher.

Pornography shall mean the graphic sexually explicit subordination of women, whether in pictures or in words, that also includes one or more of the following:

(1) Women are presented as sexual objects who enjoy pain or humiliation; or

(2) Women are presented as sexual objects who experience sexual pleasure in being raped; or

(3) Women are presented as sexual objects tied up or cut up or mutilated or bruised or physically hurt, or as dismembered or truncated or fragmented or severed into body parts; or

(4) Women are presented being penetrated by objects or animals; or

(5) Women are presented in scenarios of degradation, injury, abasement, torture, shown as filthy or inferior, bleeding, bruised, or hurt in a context that makes these conditions sexual;

(6) Women are presented as sexual objects for domination, conquest, violation, exploitation, possession, or use, or through postures or positions of servility or submission or display.[3]

The Ordinance and Longino share two features. They both define pornography by appeal to the harmfulness of some sexually explicit material, and their main concern is with harm to women. They also differ in two related ways. The Ordinance describes in much greater detail than Longino what kind of material would be pornographic; Longino merely says that behavior depicted must be degrading and abusive to women in order to count as pornographic. I'm not convinced that this is a criticism of Longino, because I'm not sure that any list could be complete and I think that the Ordinance list includes more than it should. In addition, the Ordinance does not insist that prohibited depictions be endorsed before they are deemed pornographic. This is the great failing of the Ordinance. The problem is that audiences weaned on pornography are likely to see all sexually explicit material as "presenting women as sexual objects." Because it does not insist on endorsement of prohibited depictions, it is far too broad, and protects neither erotica nor moral realism. The advantage of Longino's definition is that it protects both. In what follows, I will focus attention on the Longino definition.

If we accept the harm principle [restrictions of liberty are justified to protect against public harm], we must argue for censorship on the grounds that pornography is harmful, and that the harm is serious enough to justify interference. How serious the harm must be depends upon what we are interfering with. If we are interfering with an important exercise of expression, as some allege we do when we censor obscenity, the harm must be both serious and imminent. If we are interfering with something less than expression in the First Amendment sense, the harm needn't be as serious or as likely. I will return to this discussion.

Several different kinds of harms have been alleged to occur as a result of pornography. First, some have argued that pornography is harmful to the female participants involved. While I suspect that such participation is harmful, given that these women are asked to depict situations in which women are systematically degraded, I don't think that this constitutes a sufficient justification for censorship. Participation is not in most cases coerced. (Though there are many who would disagree about this.[4]) I would agree that many of these women are indirectly coerced, e.g., through economic conditions. The solution to this kind of coercion is not the censorship of pornography but a restructuring of our economic system. The complaints about genuine coercion and unhealthy working conditions can be handled through other legal channels.

A more serious charge is that pornography harms all women because it reinforces sexist models of interaction. Brownmiller offers the following thought experiment to illustrate the claim that pornography sustains a climate in which women are devalued. She invites us to imagine a possible world in which all the bookstores and movie theaters around 42nd St. were devoted to "a systematized commercially successful propaganda machine depicting the sadistic pleasures of gassing Jews or lynching Blacks," and that such displays generated little protest.[5] She thinks that we would draw two conclusions about such a society: that Jews and Blacks were despised by many and that such displays reinforced this attitude. She invites us to draw the analogous conclusion about women in our society. I think that Brownmiller is right about this. Since women have a legitimate interest in achieving and protecting a status of equal and independent person, anything which reinforces sexist stereotypes is harmful to all women.

This leads me to the last alleged harm, sexual violence. Robin Morgan writes, "Pornography is the theory and rape is the practice."[6] A modest version of her claim is that rapists are encouraged in their actions by pornography. If this is true, we would have a justification for the censorship of pornography. Crimes of sexual violence are a serious infringement of fundamental rights, to life, against bodily harm, to bodily integrity. The results of early studies (prior to mid 1970s) were mixed,[7] but later research indicates that the harm is fairly clear.[8] The harm documented includes (1) creation of calloused attitudes towards women in general;[9] (2) change in beliefs about rape, including an increase in willingness to believe that most women would enjoy being raped and that it would be a sexually stimulating experience for the rapist;[10] (3) male subjects' acceptance of interpersonal violence against women;[11] (4) increased aggression against women;[12] (5) increase in rape.[13]

These later studies did distinguish between erotica and pornography and, within pornography, between more and less violent depictions. (Most early studies lump these together.) The later studies suggest that nonaggressive pornography does not increase violence against women, though it does encourage both men and women to trivialize rape.[14] The evidence also indicates that violent pornography which portrays a victim who enjoys such treatment is more likely to lead to aggression against women than any other type of sexually explicit material.[15] This material has two of the features which Longino's definition picks out; it depicts behavior which is degrading and abusive to women, and it endorses such behavior.

Edward Donnerstein, who has done a great deal of this recent research, reviewed much of the later studies and remarked, "We have now seen that there is a direct causal relationship between exposure to aggressive pornography and violence against women."[16]

If the harm is clear, censorship would be compatible with the harm principle as long as the harm being prevented were judged to be more serious than the harm censorship would cause. The interests which censorship is alleged to invade include the pornographer's interest in making a profit from his work, the audience's interest in watching pornography, and the interests we all have in free expression. A balance must be struck here between the interests of women in protecting bodily integrity and political independence and the interests of the pornographer, the audience, the artist, and the community's interest in free expression. . . . [I]t seems clear that the interest of women will weigh more heavily than the interests of the pornographer and the audience. The interests of the artist and the community in free expression are more serious. If one reads the history of censorship, one sees that these interests have often been invaded.

Critics of censorship have insisted that this balancing be recognized as more than a balancing of competing interests. They have insisted that free expression ought to be accorded special status. They have argued that censorship is incompatible with the First Amendment protection of speech and press. (Some would also argue that it is incompatible with the Fourth and Fourteenth Amendments' protection of privacy. The areas of privacy recognized by the Court have been restricted to sexual relations, procreation decisions, and the viewing of obscenity in one's home. Since the Court has refused to recognize other areas of privacy and because pornography is not typically produced, distributed, or viewed in private, I am ignoring this argument.) For this reason and because any definition of pornography must be shown to be compatible with the First Amendment, I will focus on whether Longino's definition is compatible with the First Amendment. . . .

Absolutists would argue that the First Amendment should be taken at face value as rejecting all infringements of press and speech "Congress shall make no law respecting an establishment of religion, or prohibiting the free exercise thereof; or abridging the freedom of speech or of the press; or the right of the people peaceably to assemble, and to petition the government for a redress of grievances."

The Supreme Court has not accepted the absolutist position, however. They have included obscenity along with libel and fighting words as unprotected speech (*Chaplinsky* v. *New Hampshire*,[17] decided in 1942). There are two arguments which could be given for this exclusion.

Longino cites Ronald Dworkin's distinction between liberty as license and liberty as independence.[18] Liberty as license is the freedom to do whatever one pleases and liberty as independence refers to "the status of a person as independent and equal rather than subservient." Restrictions on mere whims needn't be justified by a showing of harm, but one is obligated to justify interference with independence liberty, though, and such a justification must show that your action harms others. Longino argues that the liberty to make and destribute pornography is an example of liberty as license, and this license violates the independence liberty of women because they are harmed in the ways discussed above.

Alexander Meiklejohn offers a similar argument for excluding utterances from First Amendment protection. The purpose of the First Amendment is to protect political speech because such discussion is necessary in a democracy.[19] Presumably, pornography is not political speech and hence is not protected by the First Amendment. Feinberg suggests that obscenity is not expression at all, but akin to "chemical aphrodisiacs and mechanical sex aids."[20] Interestingly enough, the argument that pornography might be both expression and political expression at that comes from defenders of censorship. For example, Andrea Dworkin offers the following analysis. "The major theme of pornography is male power, its nature, its magnitude, its use, its meaning. Male power, as expressed in and through pornography, is discernible in discrete but interwoven, reinforcing strains: the power of self, physical power over and against others, the power of terror, the power of naming, the power of owning, the power of money, and the power of sex. . . . Male power is the *raison d'être* of pornography: the degradation of the female is the means of achieving this power."[21] However we decide to analyze political speech, presumably we would want to include discussions of the allocation of political power. On this view, Dworkin is committed to saying that pornography is political speech.

I don't think that Longino falls into this trap. Her definition focuses on the degradation and abuse of women in some sexually explicit material. One might use the depiction of degradation and abuse to enhance one's political power, but it does not follow that all expressions of degradation and abuse are political expression. This is not to say that Longino's definition is without fault. In what follows, I will discuss three objections.

First, one might argue that this definition will not allow us to censor child pornography.[22] I'm not disturbed by this objection because I think that we can handle child pornography through other legal channels (e.g., laws which protect children). In *New York* v. *Ferber*, 1983,[23] the Supreme Court ruled that sexually explicit material which used child models need not be obscene in order to be banned.

Second, it is vague. Specifically, one wonders what will count as behavior degrading and abusive to women, and what will count as an endorsement of it. While I am inclined to agree that there will be clear cases, I think that there will be many cases which will be less clear. Andrea Dworkin suggests that a piece of erotica which involved only women and which did not depict the degradation or abuse of the women would still be pornographic because it would be viewed by an audience which would see it as degrading and abusive to women. I suspect that she is right about this. I would not want to censor this material, and it is clear that Longino would agree with me. The problem is to define pornography in such a way that such material would be protected. Longino tries to do this by making clear what kind of acts would count as abusive and degrading, but it would be impossible to give a complete list. She also makes explicit that the endorsement and recommendation of this behavior includes (only?) the suggestion that both the male and female participants enjoy the behavior depicted. But again, Dworkin would argue that our audience, weaned on a diet of degrading pornography, might see even a sensitive work by a feminist who is trying to create erotica as endorsing the degradation of women. We might get around this objection by including a mention of the intention of the producer of the pornography, (and this is what Longino tries to do with the distinction between pornography and moral realism) but doing so will make it extremely difficult to get convictions. Even the most degrading pornography is probably not intended to endorse degradation of women. It simply caters to a market which enjoys such material. A better response to Dworkin would be that it is really not so hard to tell if the depicted behavior is endorsed, especially given that Longino tells us what endorsement consists of, *viz.*, the depiction of a satisfied male and an ultimately willing victim. The more serious worry about vagueness is that the use of Longino's definition could have a chilling effect on artists, because even a great work would be unprotected if it contained sexually explicit material and it endorsed the degradation and abuse of women. I don't think that Longino would want to remedy this defect by adopting the LAPS standard [according to the LAPS standard, an offensive work could be banned only if, taken as a whole, it lacked "serious literary, artistic, political or scientific value"], and the LAPS standard is objectionable on other grounds. The LAPS standard creates a chilling effect of another kind. Here the artist must be sure that he is creating a masterpiece if he wants to depict explicit sexual behavior. Longino's definition is better than this standard because it attempts to protect more pedestrian work, but the artist must still worry about whether he is endorsing the degradation and abuse of women, even if he is convinced that he is creating a masterpiece. She could add here a modified LAPS standard and a clause which says that the work should be taken as a whole. I suspect that she would have reservations about doing either, and for good reason. If pornography is genuinely harmful to women, it will be harmful whether or not it turns up in a "masterpiece." (One wonders, by whose standards such a work would be judged a masterpiece.) Preventing the harm is here taken to be more important than protecting art. . . . One might argue, instead, that a reasonable conception of art ought to rule out as art a work which depicted and endorsed the degradation of persons. Another worry about vagueness is that it might protect the genuine pornographer. One wonders if a simple footnote condemning the treatment of women would suffice to protect the work.

The third worry is that the sexual explicitness of the material seems almost accidental. Longino is primarily objecting to the depiction of the degradation and abuse of women. But if this is what is objectionable, why should we stop at censoring pornography? Some would view the suggestion that we censor far more than pornography as a perfectly reasonable one. Their argument would be that if we are concerned to protect from harm, then we should be willing to censor all the harmful material. If slasher films (e.g., *Halloween* ad nauseum) are harmful in the same way as pornography, out they go. But many more would view the reasonableness of this suggestion as a reductio of Longino's position. The worry here would be that too much censorship would be an infringement of liberty and privacy as well as being a costly use of legal machinery better put to some other use. The other fear is that our intuitions about what ought to be censored don't jibe with this broader conception (censor everything harmful). (For example, *Swept Away*, which was shown to have a powerful negative effect on men's attitudes about rape, is seen by many as art.[24] I think that this is a very real worry. My hunch is that sexual explicitness should be a necessary condition for censorship, but I'm unable to come up with very compelling arguments in support of this intuition. Nevertheless, let me sketch five less than compelling arguments in support of this.

The first is that there is already a strong connection between sex and harm in our culture.[25] One need only watch music videos and listen to much of today's popular music to see how the juxtaposition of sex and violence has entered the popular culture. Since there is already an acceptance, on some level, of sexual violence, endorsements of it will not fall on deaf ears. A receptive audience is more likely to act upon such endorsements. . . .

The second argument involves an appeal to a public harm principle. Women are disturbed by the thought that pornography has an audience, and worry translates into a reluctance to trust any men that they do not know extremely well. This worry has consequences for the relationships which women have (or don't have). Both men and women are affected by these fears. If we take it that we have an interest in promoting the possibility of generally decent relationships, sexual and nonsexual, between the sexes, then we have a special reason for objecting to depictions of sexual violence. (Unfortunately, this argument gives us a reason to object to moral realism as well as pornography.)

The third argument is that if we restrict censorship to sexually explicit material, we will be less likely to inadvertently censor ideas. I suspect that this argument figures in the Supreme Court's insistence that material must appeal to prurient interest before it can be a candidate for censorship. The First Amendment is designed to protect the free expression of ideas. A feature of material which contains ideas is that it appeals primarily to the intellect, while sexually explicit material appeals primarily to prurient interest. I don't find this a very compelling argument. On one reading, the claim that sexually explicit material appeals to prurient interest is simply analytic; sexually explicit material is simply defined as material which appeals to prurient interest. On another reading, the claim is empirical; this type of material seldom engages us at an intellectual level. But even if it is true that it engages us at some lower level (e.g., our emotions), it doesn't follow that our intellect is bypassed entirely. Much of the work on emotion suggests that all emotions have a cognitive component.[26] There is another reason why we would want to reject this argument. The research on pornography suggests that it can have a real effect on beliefs about women. This implies that the material appeals beyond prurient interest.

Another argument is offered by Barry Sapolsky, a psychologist who has researched the causal relationship between pornography and sexual violence.[27] He argues that exposure to erotica creates "residues of excitement" which can be reinstated and which intensify feelings of anger and aggression. Hence, violence coupled with sex can trigger aggression.

The last argument would respond directly to the worry that unrestricted censorship would result in costly invasions of liberty and privacy. Insisting on sexual explicitness allows us to draw a line, and it's not a merely arbitrary line. We know that most of this material is garbage, in addition to being harmful to women. If we leave this as a necessary condition for censorship, we are less likely to censor art or expression. In addition, fewer people have an interest in seeing sexually explicit material which endorses the degradation and abuse of women than have an interest in seeing similar material which is not sexually explicit, so censoring it won't have such a profound effect on liberty and privacy, and it won't necessitate the kind of legal machinery that censoring all harmful material would. In spite of its flaws, I think that Longino's definition fares better than the standards appealed to by the Supreme Court. My principle reasons for saying so are that Longino's definition is compatible with a harm principle, and is not a mere appeal to legal moralism, and it protects erotica and moral realism, and it picks out just that material most clearly implicated as a causal ingredient in sexual violence. The Supreme Court's current standards, on the other hand are disturbing because they don't censor the right material for the right reasons and because they are, at bottom, mere appeals to legal moralism.

Still, some questions remain. First, should sexual explicitness be a necessary condition for censorship? Second, should we censor a work which is viewed by many as art if the evidence suggests that it is causally implicated in sexual violence? I'm not sure how to answer these questions, but one of the good consequences of the new discussions of pornography is that these kinds of questions are being raised.

NOTES

1. Helen Longino, "Pornography, Oppression, and Freedom: A Closer Look," in *Take Back the Night,* ed. Laura Lederer (New York: Bantam Books, 1980), p. 31.

2. Ibid., p. 28.

3. Indianapolis and Marion County, Ind. Ordinance 35, sec. 2 #16–3 (15 June 1984). Introduced in Minneapolis 1983.

4. See, for example, Linda Lovelace and Mike McGrady, *Ordeal* (Secaucus, N.J.: Citadel Press, 1980) for a description of Lovelace's coerced involvement in pornography.

5. Susan Brownmiller, *Against Our Will* (New York: Bantam Books, 1975), p. 444.

6. Robin Morgan, "Theory and Practice: Pornography and Rape," in *Take Back the Night*, p. 131.

7. See Pauline B. Bart and Margaret Jozsa, "Dirty Books, Dirty Films, and Dirty Data" for a discussion of studies. In *Take Back the Night*, pp. 201–215.

8. Many of the later studies are summarized in *Pornography and Sexual Aggression*, ed. Neil M. Malamuth and Edward Donnerstein (New York: Academic Press, 1984).

9. Dolf Zillman and Jennings Bryant, "Massive Exposure to Pornography," *Pornography and Sexual Aggression*, pp. 115–138; Edward Donnerstein and D. Ling, "Sexual Violence in the Media: A Warning," *Psychology Today* (January 1984), pp. 14–15.

10. Zillman and Bryant; Neil M. Malamuth and J. V. P. Check, "The Effects of Exposure to Aggressive Pornography: Rape Proclivity, Sexual Arousal and Beliefs in Rape Myths," Paper presented at 89th annual meeting of the American Psychological Association, Los Angeles, CA 1981: Malamuth and Check, "The Effects of Mass Media Exposure on Acceptance of Violence Against Women: A Field Experiment," *Journal of Research in Personality* 15 (1981), pp. 436–446; Malamuth and Check, "Penile Tumescence and Perceptual Responses to Rape as a Function of Victim's Perceived Reactions," *Journal of Applied Social Psychology* 89 (1980), pp. 763–766; Malamud, S. Haber, S. Feschbach, "Testing Hypotheses Regarding Rape: Exposure to Sexual Violence, Sex Differences, and the 'Normality' of Rapists," *Journal of Research in Personality* 14 (1980), pp. 121–137.

11. See Malamud studies cited in 9.

12. Edward Donnerstein, "Aggressive Pornography: The Role of Sexual and Aggressive Content," *Pornography and Sexual Aggression*, pp. 72–80; Edward Donnerstein and L. Berkowitz, "Victim Reactions in Aggressive Erotic Films as a Factor in Violence Against Women," *Journal of Personality and Social Psychology* 41 (1981), pp. 71–724; Mary P. Koss and Kenneth E. Leonard, "Sexually Aggressive Men: Empirical Findings and Theoretical Implications," *Pornography and Sexual Aggression*, pp. 211–232.

13. John H. Court, "Sex and Violence: A Ripple Effect," *Pornography and Sexual Aggression*, pp. 139–172.

14. Zillman and Bryant, Donnerstein and Linz.

15. D. Linz, "Aggressive Erotica and Violence Against Women," *Journal of Personality and Social Psychology* 39 (1980), pp. 269–277; Donnerstein and Berkowitz.

16. Donnerstein, *Pornography and Sexual Aggression*, p. 78.

17. 315 U.S. 568 (1942).

18. See Ronald Dworkin, *Taking Rights Seriously* (Cambridge: Cambridge University Press, 1977), p. 262.

19. See Alexander Meiklejohn, *Free Speech and Its Relation to Self Government* (New York: Harper and Row, 1948), esp. pp. 17–19, 35–40.

20. Joel Fineberg, "Pornography and the Criminal Law," *Pornography and Censorship,* ed. David Copp and Susan Wendell (Buffalo: Prometheus Books, 1983), p. 118.

21. Andrea Dworkin, *Pornography: Men Possessing Women* (New York: Perigee Books, 1981), pp. 31–32.

22. This criticism was pointed out to me by Jill Buroker.

23. 458 U.S. 747 (1983).

24. Exposure to *Swept Away* and *The Getaway,* both films which depicted a rape victim falling in love with her rapist, was found to increase acceptance of interpersonal violence against women. Malamuth and Check, "The effects of mass media exposure on acceptance of violence against women: A field experiment."

25. Robert Baker argues for this in " 'Pricks' and 'Chicks': a Plea for Persons," in Richard Wasserstrom, ed., *Today's Moral Problems* (New York: Macmillan, 1975), pp. 152–171.

26. Robert Solomon is a strong defender of this view. See *The Passions* (New York: Doubleday-Anchor, 1976).

27. Barry S. Sapolsky, "Arousal, Affect, and the Aggression-Moderating Effect of Erotica," *Pornography and Sexual Aggression,* pp. 83–113.

20

Liberty and Pornography

Ronald Dworkin

The following is based on an essay appearing in Isaiah Berlin: A Celebration, *edited by Edna and Avishai Margalit, to be published by the University of Chicago Press.*

When Isaiah Berlin delivered his famous inaugural lecture as Chichele Professor of Social and Political Theory at Oxford, in 1958, he felt it necessary to acknowledge that politics did not attract the professional attention of most serious philosophers in Britain and America. They thought philosophy had no place in politics, and vice versa; that political philosophy could be nothing more than a parade of the theorist's own preferences and allegiances with no supporting arguments of any rigor or respectability. That gloomy picture is unrecognizable now. Political philosophy thrives as a mature industry; it dominates many distinguished philosophy departments and attracts a large share of the best graduate students almost everywhere.

Berlin's lecture, "Two Concepts of Liberty," played an important and distinctive role in this renaissance. It provoked immediate, continuing, heated, and mainly illuminating controversy. It became, almost at once, a staple of graduate and undergraduate reading lists, as it still is. Its scope and erudition, its historical sweep and evident contemporary force, its sheer

Reprinted with permission from *The New York Review of Books* (August 15, 1991): 12–15. Copyright © 1991 Nyrev, Inc.

interest, made political ideas suddenly seem exciting and fun. Its main polemical message—that it is fatally dangerous for philosophers to ignore either the complexity or the power of those ideas—was both compelling and overdue. But chiefly, or so I think, its importance lay in the force of its central argument. For though Berlin began by conceding to the disdaining philosophers that political philosophy could not match logic or the philosophy of language as a theater for "radical discoveries," in which "talent for minute analyses is likely to be rewarded," he continued by analyzing subtle distinctions that, as it happens, are even more important now, in the Western democracies at least, than when he first called our attention to them.

I must try to describe two central features of his argument, though for reasons of space I shall have to leave out much that is important to them. The first is the celebrated distinction described in the lecture's title: between two (closely allied) senses of liberty. Negative liberty (as Berlin came later to restate it) means not being obstructed by others in doing what one might wish to do. We count some negative liberties—like the freedom to speak our minds without censorship—as very important and others—like driving at very fast speeds—as trivial. But they are both instances of negative freedom, and though a state may be justified in imposing speed limits, for example, on grounds of safety and convenience, that is nevertheless an instance of restricting negative liberty.

Positive liberty, on the other hand, is the power to control or participate in public decisions, including the decision how far to curtail negative liberty. In an ideal democracy—whatever that is—the people govern themselves. Each is master to the same degree, and positive liberty is secured for all.

In his inaugural lecture Berlin described the historical corruption of the idea of positive liberty, a corruption that began in the idea that someone's true liberty lies in control by his rational self rather than his empirical self, that is, in control that aims at securing goals other than those the person himself recognizes. Freedom, on that conception, is possible only when people are governed, ruthlessly if necessary, by rulers who know their true, metaphysical, will. Only then are people truly free, albeit against their will. That deeply confused and dangerous, but nevertheless potent, chain of argument had in many parts of the world turned positive liberty into the most terrible tyranny. Of course, by calling attention to this corruption of positive liberty, Berlin did not mean that negative liberty was an unallowed blessing, and should be protected in all its forms in all circumstances at all costs. He said, later, that on the contrary the vices of excessive and indiscriminate negative liberty were so evident, particularly in the form of savage economic inequality, that he had not thought it necessary to describe them in much detail.

The second feature of Berlin's argument that I have in mind is a theme repeated throughout his writing on political topics. He insists on the complexity of political value, and the fallacy of supposing that all the political virtues that are attractive in themselves can be realized in a single political structure. The ancient Platonic ideal of some master accommodation of all attractive virtues and goals, combined in institutions satisfying each in the right proportion and sacrificing none, is in Berlin's view, for all its imaginative power and historical influence, only a seductive myth. He later summed this up:

> One freedom may abort another; one freedom may obstruct or fail to create conditions which make other freedoms, or a larger degree of freedom, or freedom for more persons, possible; positive and negative freedom may collide; the freedom of the individual or the group may not be fully compatible with a full degree of participation in a common life, with its demands for cooperation, solidarity, fraternity. But beyond all these there is an acuter issue: the paramount need to satisfy the claims of other, no less ultimate, values: justice, happiness, love, the realization of capacities to create new things and experiences and ideas, the discovery of the truth. Nothing is gained by identifying freedom proper, in either of its senses, with these values, or with the conditions of freedom, or by compounding types of freedom with one another.[1]

Berlin's warnings about conflating positive and negative liberty, and liberty itself, with other values, seemed, to students of political philosophy in the great Western democracies in the 1950s, to provide important lessons about authoritarian regimes in other times and places. Though cherished liberties were very much under attack in both America and Britain in that decade, the attack was not grounded in or defended through either form of confusion. The enemies of negative liberty were powerful, but they were also crude and undisguised. Joseph McCarthy and his allies did not rely on any Kantian or Hegelian or Marxist concept of metaphysical selves to justify censorship or blacklists. They distinguished liberty not from itself, but from security; they claimed that too much free speech made us vulnerable to spies and intellectual saboteurs and ultimately to conquest.

In both Britain and America, in spite of limited reforms, the state still sought to enforce conventional sexual morality about pornography, contraception, prostitution, and homosexuality. Conservatives who defended these invasions of negative liberty appealed not to some higher or different sense of freedom, however, but to values that were plainly distinct from, and in conflict with, freedom: religion, true morality, and traditional and proper family values. The wars over liberty were fought, or so it seemed, by clearly divided armies. Liberals were for liberty, except, in some circumstances, for the negative liberty of economic entrepreneurs. Conservatives were for that liberty, but against other forms when these collided with security or their view of decency and morality.

But now the political maps have radically changed and some forms of negative liberty have acquired new opponents. Both in America and Britain, though in different ways, conflicts over race and gender have transformed old alliances and divisions. Speech that expresses racial hatred, or a degrading attitude toward women, has come to seem intolerable to many people whose convictions are otherwise traditionally liberal. It is hardly surprising that they should try to reduce the conflict between their old liberal ideals and their new acceptance of censorship by adopting some new definition of what liberty, properly understood, really is. It is hardly surprising, but the result is dangerous confusion, and Berlin's warnings, framed with different problems in mind, are directly in point.

I shall try to illustrate that point with a single example: a lawsuit arising out of the attempt by certain feminist groups in America to outlaw what they consider a particularly objectionable form of pornography. I select this example not because pornography is more important or dangerous or objectionable than racist invective or other highly distasteful kinds of speech, but because the debate over pornography has been the subject of the fullest and most comprehensive scholarly discussion.

Through the efforts of Catharine MacKinnon, a professor of law at the University of Michigan, and other prominent feminists, Indianapolis, Indiana, enacted an antipornography ordinance. The ordinance defined pornography as "the graphic sexually explicit subordination of women, whether in pictures or words . . ." and it specified, as among pornographic materials falling within that definition, those that present women as enjoying pain or humiliation or rape, or as degraded or tortured or filthy, bruised or bleeding, or in postures of servility or submission or display. It included no exception for literary or artistic value, and opponents claimed that applied literally it would outlaw James Joyce's *Ulysses*, John Cleland's *Memoirs of a Woman of Pleasure*, various works of D. H. Lawrence, and even Yeats's "Leda and the Swan." But the groups who sponsored the ordinance were anxious to establish that their objection was not to obscenity or indecency as such, but to the consequences for women of a particular kind of pornography, and they presumably thought that an exception for artistic value would undermine that claim.[2]

The ordinance did not simply regulate the display of pornography so defined, or restrict its sale or distribution to particular areas, or guard against the exhibition of pornography to children. Regulation for those purposes does restrain negative liberty, but if reasonable it does so in a way compatible with free speech. Zoning and display regulations may make pornography more expensive or inconvenient to obtain, but they do not offend the principle that no one must be prevented from publishing or reading what he or she wishes on the ground that its content is immoral or offensive.[3] The Indianapolis ordinance, on the other hand, prohibited any "production, sale, exhibition, or distribution" whatever of the material it defined as pornographic.

Publishers and members of the public who claimed a desire to read the banned material arranged a prompt constitutional challenge. The federal district court held that the ordinance was unconstitutional because it violated the First Amendment to the United States Constitution, which guarantees the negative liberty of free speech.[4] The Circuit Court for the Seventh Circuit upheld the district court's decision,[5] and the Supreme Court of the United States declined to review that holding. The Circuit Court's decision, in an opinion by Judge Easterbrook, noticed that the ordinance did not outlaw obscene or indecent material generally but only material reflecting the opinion that women are submissive, or enjoy being dominated, or should be treated as if they did. Easterbrook said that the central point of the First Amendment was exactly to protect speech from content-based regulation of that sort. Censorship may on some occasions be permitted if it aims to prohibit directly dangerous speech—crying fire in a crowded theater or inciting a crowd to violence, for example—or speech particularly and unnecessarily inconvenient—broadcasting from sound trucks patrolling residential streets at night, for instance. But nothing must be censored, Easterbrook wrote, because the message it seeks to deliver is a bad one, or because it expresses ideas that should not be heard at all.

It is by no means universally agreed that censorship should never be based on content. The British Race Relations Act, for example, forbids speech of racial hatred, not only when it is likely to lead to violence, but generally, on the grounds that members of minority races should be protected from racial insults. In America, however, it is a fixed principle of constitutional law that such regulation is unconstitutional unless some compelling necessity, not just official or majority disapproval of the message, requires it. Pornography is often grotesquely offensive; it is insulting, not only to women but to men as well. But we cannot consider that a sufficient reason for banning it without destroying the principle that the speech we hate is as much entitled to protection as any other. The essence of negative liberty is freedom to offend, and that applies to the tawdry as well as the heroic.

Lawyers who defend the Indianapolis ordinance argue that society does have a further justification for outlawing pornography: that it causes great harm as well as offense to women. But their arguments mix together claims about different types or kinds of harm, and it is necessary to distinguish these. They argue, first, that some forms of pornography significantly increase the danger that women will be raped or physically assaulted. If that were true, and the danger were clear and present, then it would indeed justify censorship of those forms, unless less stringent methods of control, such as restricting pornography's audience, would be feasible, appropriate, and effective. In fact, however, though there is some evidence that exposure to pornography weakens people's critical attitudes toward sexual violence, there is no persuasive evidence that it causes more actual incidents of assault. The Seventh Circuit cited a variety of studies (including that of the Williams Commission in Britain in 1979) all of which concluded, the court said, "that it is not possible to demonstrate a direct link between obscenity and rape. . . ."[6] A recent report based on a year's research in Britain said: "The evidence does not point to pornography as a cause of deviant sexual orientation in offenders. Rather, it seems to be used as part of that deviant sexual orientation."[7]

Some feminist groups argue, however, that pornography causes not just physical violence but a more general and endemic subordination of women. In that way, they say, pornography makes for inequality. But even if it could be shown, as a matter of causal connection, that pornography is in part responsible for the economic structure in which few women attain top jobs or equal pay for the same work, that would not justify censorship under the Constitution. It would plainly be unconstitutional to ban speech directly *advocating* that women occupy inferior roles, or none at all, in commerce and the professions, even if that speech fell on willing male ears and achieved its goals. So it cannot be a reason for banning pornography that it contributes to an unequal economic or social structure, even if we think that it does.

But the most imaginative feminist literature for censorship makes a further and different argument: that negative liberty for pornographers conflicts not just with equality but with positive liberty as well, because pornography leads to women's *political* as well as economic or social subordination. Of course pornography does not take the vote from women, or somehow make their votes count less. But it produces a climate, according to this argument, in which women cannot have genuine political power or authority because they are perceived and understood unauthentically—that is, they are made over by male fantasy into people very different from, and of much less consequence than, the people they really are. Consider, for example, these remarks from the work of the principal owner of the Indianapolis ordinance. "[Pornography] institutionalizes the sexuality of male supremacy, fusing the eroticization of dominance and submission with the social construction of male and female. . . . Men treat women as who they see women as being. Pornography constructs who that is. Men's power over women means that the way men see women defines who women can be."[8]

Pornography, on this view, denies the positive liberty of women; it denies them the right to be their own masters by recreating them, for politics and society, in the shapes of male fantasy. That is a powerful argument, even in constitutional terms, because it asserts a conflict not just between liberty and equality but within liberty itself, that is, a conflict that cannot be resolved simply on the ground that liberty must be sovereign. What shall we make of the argument understood that way? We must notice, first, that it remains a causal argument. It claims not that pornography is a consequence or symptom or symbol of how the identity of women has been reconstructed by men, but an important cause or vehicle of that reconstruction.

That seems strikingly implausible. Sadistic pornography is revolting, but it is not in general circulation, except for its milder, soft-porn manifestations. It seems unlikely that it has remotely the influence over how women's sexuality or character or talents are conceived by men, and indeed by women, that commercial advertising and soap operas have. Television and other parts of popular culture use sexual display and sexual innuendo to sell virtually everything, and they often show women as experts in domestic detail and unreasoned intuition, and nothing else. The images they create are subtle and ubiquitous, and it would not be surprising to learn, through whatever research might establish this, that they indeed do great damage to the way women are understood and allowed to be influential in politics. Sadistic pornography, though much more offensive and disturbing, is greatly overshadowed by these dismal cultural influences as a causal force.

Judge Easterbrook's opinion for the Seventh Circuit assumed, for the sake of argument, however, that pornography did have the consequences the defenders of the ordinance claimed. He said that the argument nevertheless failed because the point of free speech is precisely to allow ideas to have whatever consequences follow from their dissemination, including undesirable consequences for positive liberty. "Under the First Amendment," he said, "the government must leave to the people the evaluation of ideas. Bald or subtle, an idea is as powerful as the audience allows it to be. . . . [The assumed result] simply demonstrates the power of pornography as speech. All of these unhappy effects depend on mental intermediation."

That is right as a matter of American constitutional law. The Ku Klux Klan and the American Nazi Party are allowed to propagate their ideas in America, and the British Race Relations Act, so far as it forbids abstract speech of racial hatred, would be unconstitutional in the United States. But does the American attitude represent the kind of Platonic absolutism Berlin warned against? No, because there is an important difference between the idea he thinks absurd, that all ideals attractive in themselves can be perfectly reconciled within a single utopian political order, and the different idea he thought essential, that we must, as individuals and nations, choose, among possible combinations of ideals, a coherent, even though inevitably and regrettably limited, set of these to define our own individual or national way of life. Freedom of speech, conceived and protected as a fundamental negative liberty, is the core of the choice modern democracies have made, a choice we must now honor in finding our own ways to combat the shaming inequalities women still suffer.

This reply depends, however, on seeing the alleged conflict within liberty as a conflict between the negative and positive senses of that virtue. We must consider yet another argument which, if successful, could not be met in the same way, because it claims that pornography presents a conflict within the negative liberty of speech itself. Berlin said that the character, at least, of negative liberty was reasonably clear, that although excessive claims of negative liberty were dangerous, they could at least always be seen for what they were. But the argument I have in mind, which has been offered by, among others, Frank Michelman of the Harvard Law School, expands the idea of negative liberty in an unanticipated way. He argues that some speech, including pornography, may be itself "silencing," so that its effect is to prevent other people from exercising their negative freedom to speak.

Of course it is fully recognized in First Amendment jurisprudence that some speech has the effect of silencing others. Government must indeed balance negative liberties when it prevents heckling or other demonstrative speech designed to stop others from speaking or being heard. But Michelman has something different in mind. He says that a woman's speech may be silenced not just by noise intended to drown her out but also by argument and images that change her audience's perceptions of her character, needs, desires, and standing, and also, perhaps, change her own sense of who she is and what she wants. Speech with that consequence silences her, Michelman supposes, by making it impossible for her effectively to contribute to the process Judge Easterbrook said the First Amendment protected, the process through which ideas battle for the public's favor. "[It] is a highly plausible claim," Michelman writes, "[that] pornography [is] a cause of women's subordination and silencing. . . . It is a fair and obvious question why our society's openness to challenge does not need protection against repressive private as well as public action."[9]

He argues that if our commitment to negative freedom of speech is consequentialist—if we want free speech in order to have a society in which no idea is barred from entry, then we must censor some ideas in order to make entry possible for other ones. He protests that the distinction that American constitutional law makes between the suppression of ideas by the effect of public criminal law and by the consequences of private speech is arbitrary, and that a sound concern for openness would be equally worried about both forms of control. But the distinction the law makes is not between public and private power as such, but between negative liberty and other virtues, including positive liberty. It would indeed be contradictory for a constitution to prohibit official censorship while also protecting the right of private citizens physically to prevent other citizens from publishing or broadcasting specified ideas. That would allow private citizens to violate the negative liberty of other citizens by preventing them from saying what they wish.

But there is no contradiction in insisting that every idea must be allowed to be heard, even those whose consequence is that other ideas will be misunderstood, or given little consideration, or even not be spoken at all because those who might speak them are not in control of their own public identities and therefore cannot be understood as they wish to be. These are very bad consequences, and they must be resisted by whatever means our Constitution permits. But acts that have these consequences do not, for that reason, deprive others of their negative liberty to speak, and the distinction, as Berlin insisted, is very far from arbitrary or inconsequential.

It is of course understandable why Michelman and others should want to expand the idea of negative liberty in the way they try to do. Only by characterizing certain ideas as themselves "silencing" ideas—only by supposing that censoring pornography is the same thing as stopping people from drowning out other speakers—can they hope to justify censorship within the constitutional scheme that assigns a preeminent place to free speech. But the assimilation is nevertheless a confusion, exactly the kind of confusion Berlin warned against in his original lecture, because it obscures the true political choice that must be made. I return to Berlin's lecture, which put the point with that striking combination of clarity and sweep I have been celebrating:

> I should be guilt-stricken, and rightly so, if I were not, in some circumstances, ready to make [some] sacrifice [of freedom]. But a sacrifice is not an increase in what is being sacrificed, namely freedom, however great the moral need or the compensation for it. Everything is what it is. Liberty is liberty, not equality or fairness or justice or culture, or human happiness or a quiet conscience.

NOTES

1. Isaiah Berlin, *Four Essays on Liberty* (Oxford University Press, 1968), p. lvi.

2. MacKinnon explained that "if a woman is subjected, why should it matter that the work has other value?" See her article "Pornography, Civil Rights, and Speech," in *Harvard Civil Rights-Civil Liberties Law Review*, Vol. 28, p. 21.

3. See my article "Do We Have a Right to Pornography?" reprinted as Chapter 17 in my book *A Matter of Principle* (Harvard University Press, 1985).

4. *American Booksellers Association, Inc. et al. v. William H. Hudnit, III, Mayor, City of Indianapolis, et al.*, 598 F. Supp. 1316 (S.D. Ind. 1984).

5. 771 F. 2d 323 (US Court of Appeals, Seventh Circuit).

6. That court, in a confused passage, said that it nevertheless accepted "the premises of this legislation," which included the claims about a causal connection with sexual violence. But it seemed to mean that it was accepting the rather different causal claim considered in the next paragraph, about subordination. In any case, it said that it accepted those premises only for the sake of argument, since it thought it had authority to reject decisions of Indianapolis based on its interpretation of empirical evidence.

7. See *The Daily Telegraph*, December 23, 1990. Of course further studies might contradict this assumption. But it seems very unlikely that pornography will be found to stimulate physical violence to the overall extent that non-pornographic depictions of violence, which are much more pervasive in our media and culture, do.

8. See MacKinnon's article cited in footnote 2.

9. Frank Michelman, "Conceptions of Democracy in American Constitutional Argument: The Case of Pornography Regulation," *Tennessee Law Review*, 56, No. 291 (1989): 303–304.

Part Four

Religious Perspectives

21

The Mental Poison

Tim LaHaye

Throughout the nation violent rape, child molestation, sexploitation of children, homophilia, sadomasochism, perversion, and even sex murders have been increasing at an alarming rate during the past decade. During the same period of time, pornographic literature has burst into a $5 billion business in America.

"Two hundred seventy magazines deal with sex filth," reported Attorney Charles H. Keating, Jr., head of Citizens for Decency Through Law. These magazines "glorify child molesting, rape and gang orgies. There are films and videotapes which outdo the ancient Greeks and Romans in depicting pagan perversion." Slick periodicals and films contain telephoto scenes of every conceivable pose which the perverted minds of pornographers can conceive. With a two-dollar price tag for smut hustlers like *Playboy* and *Penthouse*, it is twice as profitable to the distributors as *Time*, *Life*, and *Saturday Evening Post*.

Many of the most shocking crimes today are inspired when morally sick words and living-color pictures are transmitted, through the printing press, into an equally sick mind, arousing the individual to horrifying action. We will not halt this sordid, sex-crazed crime rate until we rid our nation of pornography in magazines, X-rated and "adult" movies, and particularly "kiddie porn." As sick as it may seem, over 5,000 child molesters in Los

From *The Battle for the Family* by Tim LaHaye. Copyright © 1982 by Tim LaHaye. Used by permission of Fleming H. Revell Company.

Angeles devotedly read kiddie porn, even though the use of children in such poses is against the law. In a distorted application of "freedom of speech" (which is taken to mean freedom to read and freedom from censorship), who can be certain that his child is protected?

A couple in our church called for counseling. I had performed their marriage ceremony and dedicated their four-year-old girl. The reason for their call: Their daughter had been molested by a neighbor. Investigation showed that he was a porn reader with a fascination for kiddie porn. If proper investigation were made, I am confident that pornographic literature and movies would be declared the prime causes of today's sex crimes.

As I have shown in previous books, the emotions serve as the motor of man. These emotions (or heart) are responsive to the thoughts we maintain in our minds, and the most effective assault on the mind is through the eyes. Consequently we artificially inflame our emotions by reading or seeing sexually inflammatory material.

PORNOGRAPHY IS ANTIFAMILY

It is easy to make a case for the fact that modern pornography in all its sophisticated forms is harmful to the family. My counseling experience suggests that it causes couples to commence a marriage with unnatural expectations. This is even more true when only one is a porn user. How can a chaste, modest wife measure up to the fiendish fantasies in the mind of her porn-reading bridegroom? She may perform 100 percent normally, but return from her honeymoon feeling inadequate, dirty, and used. The scenes in pornographic literature are anything but normal. And the problem is not limited to the young. Some couples have written our Counseling by Mail ministry or have sought counseling, due to sexual strife, after twenty-five years of marriage. We have determined that the unfulfilled expectations cited could not have been conceived in a normal brain, but were passed on by professional perverters called pornographers. I would judge that fully two-thirds of the sexual problems in marriage today can be traced to the use of pornography.

The Bible, which is very clear on this subject, condemns it in no uncertain terms.

> But fornication and all uncleanness or covetousness, let it not even be named among you, as is fitting for saints; neither filthiness, nor foolish talking, nor coarse jesting, which are not fitting. . . . And have no fellowship with

the unfruitful works of darkness, but rather expose them. For it is shameful even to speak of those things which are done by them in secret. (Ephesians 5:3, 4, 11, 12 NKJV-NT)

TEENS ARE EXTREMELY VULNERABLE

No teenager will ever profit from an obsession with sex. Boys particularly need to steer clear of anything visually inflammatory. As their bodies go through the process of development, they are extremely excited by lewd pictures. At a time when they should be channeling their energies into academic and athletic interests or learning to work with their hands, it is very harmful for them to gain easy access to pornography, which captivates their imagination and supersedes all other thoughts. For most young boys it serves to destroy the beauty of sex and reduce it to a base level. Femininity is stripped of its mystique, and in its place girls are fantasized as objects of lust, to be used at will. Instead of placing girls on pedestals of respect that used to incite young men to protect a girl's modesty and virtue, porn users find it easy to spew foul language in the company of the opposite sex and offend girls with dirty jokes or suggestive remarks. Nice girls are repulsed by porn users.

Pornography, of course, is not limited to boys. It also corrupts the morals of girls and sears their sensibilities. But due to a psychological difference between men and women, it is more harmful to boys than girls. Women who use pornography are usually well down the road to depravity. Unless introduced to it through their sex education course in school or through a friend, most girls don't seek it out. Although a few pornographic magazines have appeared for women, the big users are men.

Jack Palmer, a supervisory counselor in Juvenile Hall in San Diego for twenty-five years, is a personal friend and a member of the church I serve. To my question, "What percentage of the young men in Juvenile Hall are pornography users?" he responded, "Over 90 percent." Then I asked, "What about juvenile sex offenders?" He replied, "Virtually all of them!"

Authorities and parents fail to realize that pornography affects a person much like drugs and alcohol. Just as drugs artificially excite the emotions (up or down), making a person feel good or bad, hostile or passive, pornography passing through the eye into the brain can artificially inflame a person to sexual arousal.

On the last day of 1980, a seventy-six-year-old former Hollywood actress was attacked in her home by a seventeen-year-old who had been released from juvenile confinement for a "holiday furlough" to see if he was ready to be paroled into society. According to her testimony, he grabbed her and said, "I don't want to hurt or rob you; all I want is sex!" Had she not been able to pick up a claw hammer and strike him between the eyes, he would have raped her. Whom do you blame for such a tragedy? The humanistically trained psychiatrist who recommended his early release? The liberal-minded (humanist) parole board that seems more interested in "rehabilitating criminals" than in protecting the innocent taxpayers? The pornographers who publish and distribute the smut that so inflamed his mind that he was willing to attack a woman old enough to be his grandmother? The five United States Supreme Court members who voted to make such printed filth easily accessible? The parents who did not teach their son to purify his mind and failed to block his access to lewd or suggestive literature and fellowship with youths with similar values? All share the responsibility for such crime; but the courageous old woman, the pathetic teenager, and society are the victims.

IT CAN HAPPEN TO YOU!

Don't protest that such a nightmare can't happen to you or your family. I know better, and in your heart so do you. Your family is not any more exempt from such tragedy than the Christian couple who came to me heartbroken when their nineteen-year-old daughter admitted that she had left home the year before to become a prostitute. Naturally the couple asked, "Where did we go wrong?" At fifteen their daughter was a sweet, innocent girl who regularly attended church with them. They did note her peculiar associations with the "out of it" group at church, but they prayed she would come around. Investigation revealed that at sixteen she had started having sex with a boyfriend. He invited her and three other couples to the home of a friend whose parents worked during the day. The boy distributed his father's *Playboy* magazines, and they all began reading them until they got so worked up that they stripped off their clothes and performed sexual acts in front of each other. This was followed by sex orgies, until their daughter had run the gamut of sexual experience by the time she was seventeen. Depravity never happens suddenly. It is a progressive process, but nothing speeds a normal person's decency into the maelstrom of indecency faster than pornography.

THE DECENCY-IN-LITERATURE AMENDMENT

This country needs an amendment to our federal Constitution that will permit law-enforcement officials to close down smut peddlers and stop this very profitable and corrupting business. It won't be easy, of course, because $5 billion provides them sufficient incentive and political buying power to hire the best pornographic lawyers in the country. In fact, some who specialize in this field of law may volunteer their services just to keep from losing their high-paying clients. That is why a decency-in-literature amendment is the one way to put teeth into our laws. It should be carefully prepared so as not to violate reasonable rights under the First Amendment, but we need to protect our families from this vile scourge.

The moment we mention decency in literature, guaranteed either by amendment or legislation, hypocritical cries of "Censorship" are raised by pornographers and their humanist friends. That is merely a smoke screen. We have laws that protect our citizens from poisoning each other; we prohibit prostitution; speed limits are legislated; compulsory education, taxation, safety, and pollution standards are mandated; even cigarettes must carry the surgeon general's warning that smoking is dangerous to one's health, and tobacco-industry advertising has been legally dropped from TV. Why not protect the minds of our citizens (and particularly our children) from the corrupting effects of pornography? With all due respect to the importance of clean lungs, it is far more important to have a clean mind, for the brain is the most important organ in the body.

The humanist ACLU lawyer from Texas who has defended more pornography publishers than any other was interviewed on a TV talk show. I found his arguments quite interesting. Like all pornography defenders, he immediately declared that we must protect the First Amendment guarantee of free speech and press. According to his philosophy, anything that limits that is "worse than pornography." He then pointed out that the antipornography movement is dangerous because it would "legalize morality." After further questioning, however, he surprisingly indicated that he opposed kiddie porn as despicable and illegal, claiming he would not defend a kiddie-porn publisher.

This man's testimony simply illustrates that we *must* legalize morality to some degree or be doomed to live in filth. Why would he legislate against kiddie porn, but not adult porn? Why does the former violate the First Amendment, but not the latter? Because he says so! Frankly we have just as much right as the humanists to set the standards of morality, particularly since we represent the overwhelming majority of the population in this country. The real difference between us (though the humanists will not admit it) is not whether a society must legislate morality, but *where* the lines are set. Even humanists know that we have consistently used the legislative process to protect morality, as in our laws against stealing, rape, perjury, and murder. We differ, however, on the issue of sexual practices. Some humanists even want to legalize incest, which is unthinkable to anyone committed to traditional moral values.

Simply stated, the laws of our country prohibit indecent exposure, public nudity, child molesting, intercourse between an adult and minor, and many other activities. Any literature or film that portrays such illegal sex acts should likewise be declared pornographic and outlawed. The fines for such offenses should be multiple. For example, each time a publisher is fined for the same offense, the penalty should be doubled. Currently the fine is so low and pornography is so profitable that many pornography publishers gladly pay the modest penalties out of their profits.

Personally I look for a groundswell of reaction to pornography that will soon demand that our elected leaders protect us from this plague. Women in particular will raise voices of protest, for it is gradually dawning on them that the frightening rise in rape statistics is primarily due to two things: pornography and leniency on rapists.

I am convinced that the elimination of pornography from America would reduce forcible rape by 30 to 40 percent, and stiffer and faster penalties for rapists would cut it another 30 to 40 percent. It is just a matter of time before one of our Moral Majority organizations or our pro-moral senators put together a well-organized campaign to outlaw it. Together with outraged and fearful women throughout the country, we will succeed in putting pornographers out of business. The streets of America should gradually become safe for unescorted women, day or night. That is a right that should be guaranteed by our Constitution. The present lenient laws on pornography discriminate against that natural right of womanhood.

Until such a law or amendment is passed, parents must be vigilant to see that their children are not being secretly polluted by the cesspool of pornography.

22

The Impact of Pornography on Marriage

Thomas Parker

... Human beings are the only part of creation that can be naked; for the rest of creation, nakedness has no meaning. A forest can be dressed in a freshly fallen snow or a river in a cascade of light, but they are only mere metaphors of human clothing. Only man covers himself with that which is foreign to his body. Everything else stands bare, exposed to God without shame.

What is so provocative about it? Why all the embarrassment and secrecy? What is this construct called shame that only humans know? The Canadian Mike Mason writes:

> There is no satisfactory explanation for this mystery of shame, except to say that it is inextricably bound up with those other riddles called "evil" and "sin." The Book of Genesis, in fact, traces the history of both clothing and human wickedness back to a common origin; the discovery of sin and the discovery of nakedness appear to have been one and the same event. Before the Fall, *"the man and his wife were both naked and they felt no shame."* But once having tasted the forbidden fruit, *"then the eyes of them were opened, and they realized that they were naked; so they sewed fig leaves together and made coverings for themselves"* (Genesis 2:25;3:7).

Reprinted by permission of the Southern Baptist Christian Life Commission. Item is an excerpt from the 1989 CLC Annual Seminar Proceedings.

The passage implies that it was not the presence of unpleasant elements for which the man and his wife covered up. There was no blizzard. No, we have sinned, and therefore we dress, and in this our clothing becomes an ever-present symbol that we are refugees, fleeing from the presence of a perfect God.

Whether it is in the church nursery or nudist colony, public nudity is possible only for those unconscious or heedless of their sinfulness. Only the godless and the immature go naked.

The one, single exception to this principle is found in marriage. For it is only within the shelter and boundaries of marriage that the ban of shame can be removed. As husbands and wives share their bodies with each other, they demonstrate a sacred trust of intimacy and commitment. For a husband and a wife to be disrobed with each other is a picture of perfect honesty, trust, giving, and commitment, and if the heart is not exposed along with the body, the whole transaction becomes a lie and a mockery. It is a tragic contradiction, the giving of the body but the withholding of the self.

The sexual relationship between a man and his wife is not a step that establishes and builds deep intimacy, but one that presupposes it. Though banished from Eden, the first couple was not banished from one another's arms, nor from the marriage bed. There is still one garden to which God continues to welcome husbands and wives. When it comes to the beauty of the flesh, husbands and wives are truly artists because, more than anyone else, they are in a position earned through love and sacrifice to see the body as it really is. The relationship is a powerful outward symbol of the inner temper of the marital relationship. Even here, sex is never depended upon to establish love, but can only grow out of it. While some problems in a sexual relationship may be overcome simply through a deeper knowledge of physiology or the introduction of new techniques, these improvements will be short-lived if they are not backed up by profound changes in the heart at the emotional and spiritual level. The Lord is the author of sex; so He is its interpreter, and it is His therapy which is to be most treasured.

There are few dangers to the sanctity of this divinely ordained institution that exceed the threat of pornography. It is here that the holy communion of the sexual relationship between a husband and wife is trivialized. Pornography attacks the concepts of love, affection, commitment, and fidelity. In fact, it despises them, and it literally teaches contempt for the very glue that holds the marriage and the family together. There is no longer any necessary connection between sex and families, between sex and love, between sex and commitment.

When Ronald Reagan signed the Child Protection Act into law in May, 1984, he also announced the formation of an Attorney General's Commission on Pornography. It was the second such effort of the executive branch to examine the growing problem. In 1967, the White House appointed and staffed the Presidential Commission on Obscenity and Pornography. The 1970 report of the commission, in a move that stunned the social science research community and the American public, based its research and report on the following:

- Pornography, first, was harmless, and even had potential therapeutic and cathartic value;

- It had no negative effect on adults or children;

- It was not a social problem;

- Its production and distribution should be free from any regulation or control.

Due to the report of the commission, pornographic materials were seen as ethically neutral and psychologically cathartic. Direct, if not implied, was the message that pornography promised beneficial results to normal persons who would be helped in their sexual expression. It is important to note that the report even advocated the use of pornography as a way to inhibit and help rehabilitate sex offenders who, after viewing this material, would experience an emotional catharsis that would deter them from committing subsequent sexual offenses. Rightly so, the report was soundly rejected by the United States Senate by a vote of 60–5.

Although the Senate rejected the report, the media did not. Led by sympathetic media reports, the public tended to swallow the "no harm" ideal, whole and unexamined. However, while it is true that the 1970 Presidential Commission on Obscenity and Pornography "found no evidence to date that the exposure to explicit sexual materials plays a significant role in the causation of delinquent and criminal behavior," the more recent Meese Commission found that the conclusion reached above was "starkly obsolete." Why? Pornography has changed radically since 1970, and many new techniques bring it directly into homes. The geometric expansion of the parameters of pornography now include sadomasochistic themes, torture, violence, and death. Examination of pornographic media and the testimony of victims available to the most recent commission leave little room for skepticism.

A number of content analyses done in the last twenty years—the majority in the last five—dispel any doubts that pornographic themes and imagery have increased in prevalence over the past three decades. Depictions of sex combined with violence have proliferated as a prominent theme in media.

For example, in June 1983, the Canadian Committee on Sexual Offenses Against Children, chaired by University of Toronto sociologist Robin Badgely, undertook the most exhaustive content analysis ever done of widely distributed pornography magazines in Canada. All of the magazines were of U.S. manufacturers and were the same ones that are best-sellers in the United States. In most of the photographs showing sexual acts, often involving two or more persons, the committee found that "while the portrayal is often vividly graphic, the situations depicted are almost simulations rather than actual sexual acts performed while these photographs were taken." There was, however, no pretense of simulation in the types of sexual acts described in the text of these magazines. Sexual acts were fully and explicitly described.

Shockingly, the study found 24 situations in the text of these 11 nationally distributed pornographic magazines in which children and youths were portrayed in sexually explicit activities. The youngest child described in situations of this kind was eleven years old. The usual range was between thirteen and seventeen years of age. The study also found that characteristic of the sexually explicit descriptions of children and youths is the description of acts of this kind as though they constituted normal sexual behavior in which children become involved. In most of these situations, they found that the children and youths were portrayed as either passive or novices who were being tutored about sexual behavior, and very often they were cast as eager and active participants who willingly had intercourse with adults.

The social scientist who tries to protect the distribution of pornography in America today now has a much more difficult task. For example, interviews with 411 sex offenders, conducted by the most recent Attorney General's Commission, revealed "a staggering number" to be addicting. In one study conducted partly by Commissioner Becker, each criminal "had attempted an average of 581 sex offenses and completed typically 533 offenses each." The commission found that rapists are fifteen times as likely as nonoffenders to have had exposure to hard-core pornography "during childhood, or between 6–10 years old." They also tend to report an age of peak experience with pornography.

Even more germane to this presentation are the effects of pornography on marriage. Recent studies by Indiana University's Dolf Zillmann and the University of Houston colleague Jennings Bryant show that massive exposure to nonviolent, noncoercive, consensual heterosexual (*i.e.*, softcore) pornography, leads to sexual dissatisfaction in both men and women, particularly in men. Both men and women, in comparing their spouse's responses to sexual behavior portrayed in pornographic materials, became dissatisfied with the sexual performance in their marriage and even physical appearance of their intimate partners, coming to see them as less attractive, even less worthy individuals. Moreover, they began to value their intimate partners in the same way as they had the victims of rape in laboratory tests.

These same studies show that massive exposure to these materials leads to a devaluation and a depreciation of the importance of a monogamous, permanent relationship and to a lack of confidence in marriage as either a viable or lasting institution. Diana Russell, Mills College sociologist and author of the book *Rape in Marriage*, reports the results of her long-term study of sexual abuse of females, in particular the relationship between male interest in pornography and deviant sexual behavior and its effect on the subsequent abuse of women. In her study of 930 victims of rape and other forms of sexual abuse, Russell found that the depiction and dissemination of the "rape myth" type pornography was a significant element in reducing the inhibitions to the use of violence in marital relationships, habituating both males and females to the idea of rape and the acceptance of sexual deviance as normal behavior. Repeated exposure to the "rape myth" imagery contributed significantly to her subjects' reports of dissatisfaction in their sexual relationships with their spouses.

While critics charge that the majority of these studies' results cannot be generalized from the laboratory to the general public, and that the interview of victims may be, at best, a biased approach, one might fairly ask, "Have we slipped so far in the values of our society that we need the confidence of social science in elemental decisions?" As Christians, we cannot wait for an undisputed methodology to reassure us of the enormous destructive effects of pornography on the users, the victims, the sanctity of sex, the marriage, and the family.

"How much evidence is needed, or how convinced should we be, before reaching the conclusion that certain sexually explicit material causes harm?" Given the ethics of randomly exposing different segments of population to various exposures of a variety of sexual materials, there will never be conclusive proof that a causal relationship between sexually explicit materials and harm exists. We place at risk the common and reasonable, certainly the sacred, when we look to social science for fundamental values and to seek indisputable evidence. It is one thing to attempt to understand the impact of policy through research. To rely exclusively on the same to develop policy and abandon biblical values on sex and marriage contributes to the rape of the family and the sanctity of marriage. Our children are not in the position of benefiting from an attempt to secure without question the harmful effects of exposure to sexual themes in television programming, literature, or voice media through causal research.

The evidence that linked smoking to cancer has never been proven conclusively; the evidence was overwhelmingly correlational, showing higher death and illness rates among smokers than in nonsmokers. Yet public policy has been profoundly influenced. The spiritual and emotional well-being of our society is no less important.

For myself, few things have engraved the harmful effects of pornography on marriage and the individuals in those marriages as my practice. My days are fairly evenly divided between seminary classes and the locked doors of a community psychiatric unit. I see patients in the unit individually and have contact with most of my patients, since I provide group counseling. In my preparation for this presentation I decided to review those cases I participated in for all of last year and the first two months of this year. Fully four out of every five of the women treated during that time period had been at some point in their lives sexually abused, used for pornography media, or raped. Two out of every five males were either sexual offenders, consumers of "hard-core" pornography, or abused themselves. And those statistics only reflect the patients who reported those issues. I would be hard pressed to believe the rest were without similar experiences.

RECOMMENDATIONS

1. . . . Aggressively report on the failure of enforcement of existing laws against obscenity. The laws presently existing in most communities are sufficient to deter the presence of pornography in our stores and on our screens. The existing laws are rarely enforced, but evidence suggests that present laws can be enforced. No legally obscene material is sold in Cincinnati or Atlanta without great difficulty. The prosecutors there have made aggressive use of the three-pronged definition of obscenity outlined by the Supreme Court in the 1973 case, *Miller* v. *California*. These criteria are:

a. The average person, applying contemporary community standards would find that the work, taken as a whole, appeals to prurient interest.

b. The work depicts or describes, in a patently offensive way, sexual conduct specifically defined by the applicable state (or federal) law.

c. The work, taken as a whole, lacks serious literary, artistic, political, or scientific value.

Obscene material is unprotected by the First Amendment. The Supreme Court in *Paris Theatre* v. *Slaton* (1973) ruled:

> The sum of experience, including that of the past two decades affords an ample basis for legislatures to conclude that a sensitive, key relationship of human existence, central to family life, community welfare, and the development of human personality, can be debased and distorted by crass commercial exploitation of sex.

The court further stated:

> We categorically disapprove the theory that obscene films acquire constitutional immunity from state regulation simply because they are exhibited for consenting adults only. The rights and interests other than those of the advocates are involved. These include the interests of the public in the quality of life, the total community environment, the tone of commerce, and possibly, public safety itself.

It is precisely the guarantees of the First Amendment that provide an avenue for our . . . papers to communicate lack of responsibility in the prosecution of these crimes. If the community or state does not demand that these laws be enforced, chances are they will go without attention.

If a local prosecutor knows he will be interviewed as to why obscene material is distributed to tens of thousands of readers statewide, chances are his or her span of attention will be significantly increased.

2. . . . [C]reate and publish an "Obscenity Enforcement Guideline" to aid in the prosecution of pornographers by state and local prosecutors. . . .

3. . . . .[D]istribute the 1986 *Final Report of the Attorney General's Commission on Pornography*. While it is far from perfect, the report summarizes the enormous effort of the commission and, more importantly, provides guidelines for combating pornography in local communities. The evidence of social science, the testimony of victims, the graphic de-

scriptions of sexual violence are not bedtime reading. But a lack of understanding of the seriousness of this issue at a grassroots level will profoundly affect the efforts of denominational leaders and agencies to be effective.

4. Provide increased levels of victim assistance through counseling services for the individuals involved and the marriages affected. Seminary course work that addresses pastoral counseling must include information and training for counseling victims of sexual abuse, sexual disfunction in marriage, and also information for parents regarding the sexual development of their children. Given the lack of structure provided by increasing absence of intact families, the character development, processes of maturation, and nurturing abilities of children who are moving into adulthood now and in the future grow increasingly questionable. It is exactly these concerns for this generation that will make them all the more attracted to the superficial comfort of sex without love, commitment, or marriage. Some have argued that a generation without the motive to sacrifice self-interests for others cannot parent. With the coming limitations on third-party payments to the professional mental health system, the local church is going to be in a demanding, but remarkable, position to evangelize and nurture true Christian maturity.

5. Produce visual media to address the atrocities of pornography and to strengthen the marriage and the family. Present and future generations will be enormously affected by the visual media. . . .

6. Do not equate denial of the development of human sexuality and the discussion of sexuality in marriage with pornography. . . . In many ways we have failed to actively disseminate a sound biblical view of sexuality. I would choose two principal criticisms: First, in our families and churches we have often communicated sexuality and sex even in marriage as a taboo topic. Second, the administration of discipline for leaders who have participated in sexual sin is pathetic.

My professional affiliation is The American Psychological Association. When a member is found guilty of becoming sexually involved with a client, that person loses the license to practice. His or her name is disseminated among all 65,000 members of the American Psychological Association. They take that travesty and that fracture of trust very seriously, and to date the evangelical church . . . [has] failed to meet even the standards of a very secular society in this regard. . . .

Pornography libels our society and incites it to violent acts against its members and its most treasured institutions. It is a treason against the American family and a treason against our society. Treason has no First Amendment rights.

23

Pornography and the Religious Imagination

Mary Jo Weaver

One of the more perverse images in the current debate about pornography pictures anti-pornography feminists and right-wing evangelicals joining hands to defeat a common enemy. In this scenario Susan Griffin, say, or Andrea Dworkin forms a chorus with Jerry Falwell or Jimmy Swaggart to raise their voices against those entrepreneurs whose fortunes are built on the debasement and dismemberment of women. While this imaginal coalition has been criticized by Beatrice Faust as politically dangerous, because "people who are conservative about porn are usually conservative about lesbianism, abortion, health education and rape crisis centers" (1980, p. 19), it has not been analyzed for its religious incongruities.

An alliance between an anti-pornography feminist like Susan Griffin and a right-wing evangelical Christian like Jimmy Swaggart is unwise on the basis of irreconcilable theological assumptions.[1] A pact between Andrea Dworkin and Jerry Falwell is impossible because of their profound disagreements about the nature of pornography itself. Although I will use Susan Griffin and Jimmy Swaggart to concentrate on some theological issues raised by the pornography debate, I want to note a crucial distinction between militant feminists and fundamentalists that touches upon the vexing question of defining pornography.

Whatever problems one might have with, for example, Dworkin's

---

From *For Adult Users Only,* edited by Susan Gubar and Joan Hoff (Bloomington, Ind.: Indiana University Press). Copyright © 1989. Reprinted by permission of the publisher.

overstatements—as, for example, throughout *Woman Hating* (1974) or *Intercourse* (1987)—or with her legal strategies, it is still possible to praise her contributions to the definition of pornography. Her work has helped to change the terms of the debate so that pornography is now an issue of power rather than an index of purity. And since her arguments are political rather than moral, her work makes some clear definitional distinctions between anti-pornography feminists and anti-pornography religious conservatives. To Jerry Falwell, for example, pornography means dirty movies, whereas to Dworkin (1979) it means representations of sexually explicit violent attacks upon women by men. As Alexander Bloom has said, "trying to define pornography is like peeling an onion . . . [but] what is at issue for the Right is not what is at issue for the feminists. It is, in fact, more likely that their notions of what is and is not pornographic are widely divergent" (1987). In fact, because religious conservatives imagine God as a dominating sovereign who demands human submission, they fail to criticize what antipornography feminists perceive as the root of pornography, power used to render others sexually docile.

Both Griffin and Swaggart make connections between religion (or the lack thereof) and pornography that are predicated on traditional Christianity. On the one hand, according to Susan Griffin (1981), Christianity is the foundation of the pornographic imagination because it legitimizes patterns of domination and submission, patterns that are hyperbolized in pornographic enactments. When she warns that "we cannot choose to have both eros and pornography" (p. 249), she means in part that we must choose between Christianity and eros, between the bondage and discipline of traditional Christianity and the biophilic freedom of erotic nature. Jimmy Swaggart, on the other hand, links pornography with the failure of Americans to follow fundamentalist Christian teachings. For him, a strong religious commitment is the only means of saving American culture from the "demons of pornography." When he warns, as he often does on his televised revivals, that we must choose between pornography and religion, he means that a return to that "old-time religion" is the only defense against the perverse panderings of the pornography industry.[2]

By connecting pornography and traditional Christianity, Griffin appears to be anti-religious. At the same time, by calling people to return to traditional Christian values in order to overcome pornography, Swaggart appears to be deeply religious. But in the context of a contemporary theological movement—indebted to process thought—that is critical of traditional Christianity, it is possible to suggest, paradoxically, that Griffin's viewpoint is more profoundly religious and Swaggart's more deeply pornographic than either appears at first glance.

When writers like Susan Griffin, Steven Marcus (1964), Sara Harris (1969), Milton Rugoff (1971), and Bernard I. Murstein (1964) criticize Christianity, they often focus on Christian sexual ethics in order to show the links between sexual repression and pornography. Furthermore, by attaching sexual repression to Christianity, historians like Barbara Walker (1983, pp. 910–20) assume that other religions are sufficiently free sexually that one need not look to them for the roots of the pornographic imagination. Finally, by basing their anti-religious argument solely on traditional Christianity, anti-pornography feminists like Andrea Dworkin (1974, p. 73) fail to allow for the possibility that new directions in contemporary theology might allow them to argue against pornography and religious conservatives at the same time without dismissing Christianity itself.

I will argue that the elective affinity between Christianity and pornography does not rest with Christian teachings about sex but with traditional Christian teaching about women as inherently inferior. Although such teaching is not peculiar to Christianity—it can be shown that the patterns of domination and submission found in Christianity are based on an ancient male fear of women found in virtually all religions—the Christian tradition appropriated ideas about female inferiority and combined them with a tendency to spiritualize erotic language in its mystical tradition.

TRADITIONAL CHRISTIANITY AND PORNOGRAPHY

To both anti-pornography feminists and anti-pornography religious conservatives,[3] Christianity is an institutionalization of divine/human interaction based on a dualistic system in which the divine is understood to be transcendent, superior, and dominant, whereas humanity is considered immanent, inferior, and submissive. This revealed order of things, as found in the Bible and in the Christian tradition, is presumed to be replicated in human relations so that the male inherits the lordly qualities of God the Father, while the female is enjoined to be submissive to God's rule as it is enacted by the male (father, husband, brother, bishop). But if critics like Griffin and preachers like Swaggart both accept this traditional version of Christianity as normative, they disagree about how to interpet it.

Anti-pornography feminists condemn traditional Christianity because it provides a religious justification for the pornographic imagination. According to them, its teachings about the inferiority of the body and the identification of the body with the female support the humiliation and degradation of women that is the emotional and theoretical foundation for pornography.

Feminist theologians like Rosemary Ruether (1975) and Mary Daly (1968), as well as critics like Susan Griffin (1981), condemn traditional Christianity both for its treatment of women and for its teachings about sex. From the very beginning, they say, Christianity has taught us how to debase women and hate sex. And, indeed, even a casual reading of the "Fathers" of the church (Tavard, 1973) shows that the Christian tradition is full of scorn for women, scorn that overflows into canon law (Henning, 1974) and medieval theology (McLaughlin, 1974). The notion of women as inherently lustful, an opinion of "the Fathers," is reflected in clerical attitudes toward women and in the witchcraft mania (Russell, 1972).

If the Gospel is "good news" about salvation, it is bad news about sex. Ancient warnings against the allurements of "the world, the flesh and the devil" were most easily imagined in terms of the flesh, and although one could easily make a case, as Rosemary Ruether has done (1974),[4] that the explicitness of patriarchal warnings against sexual expression constituted a way for agitated celibates to discharge some of their sexual energy, the fact remains that the teachings of traditional Christianity are built upon a hatred of women and a profound abhorrence of sex. Nietzsche's chilling comment—"Christianity gave Eros poison to drink; he did not die of it, but degenerated into a vice" (cited in Sadock, Kaplan and Freedman, 1976, p. 32)—seems no more than a commonsense interpretation of a flawed tradition. When Christian crimes against women are castigated, especially in the context of the witchcraft mania, Christian teaching about sex is often cited as bearing the burden of those crimes. R. E. L. Masters says simply, "Almost the entire blame for the hideous nightmare that was the witch mania, and the greatest part of the blame for poisoning the sex life of the West, rests squarely on the Roman Catholic church" (1962, xxvi). To overcome pornography, therefore, it appears as if one must reject Christianity, with its dominating God and its double standard of sexual relations as substantiated in Christian sexual ethics.

Anti-pornography religious conservatives, on the other hand, find in traditional Christianity the basis for a well-ordered, divinely inspired plan for human conduct. Gene Getz (1974), a conservative Christian author, uses texts about bishops from the pastoral epistles to show that God intended men to be gentle, temperate, sensible, and in command of their households. In this view, wives are enjoined to support, love, and understand their husbands so that all can grow in Christ. From the very beginning, say religious conservatives, Christianity has taught us how to honor women and to regulate sex so that it can be enjoyed. "Sex was given to us for pure pleasure," according to Jack and Carole Mayhall (1978), and Rusty and Linda Raney Wright (1981) tell their readers that they can get the most out of sex by placing it within a context of communication and commitment. Christianity, therefore, provides believers with those parameters that insure stable family life. Religious conservatives like Tim and Beverly LaHaye have used statistical data to prove that "Christians are considerably more satisfied with their love life than non-Christians" (1976, p. 206), and the Christian philosopher Neil Gallagher argues that "if husbands and wives gave each other the robust sex God intended, there'd be very little market for porno" (1981, p. 207). The "eternal woman" whose vocation was surrender, described by Gertrude von le Fort (1934), a religious writer and convert to Catholicism, has been appropriated and transformed by Marabel Morgan (1973) into "the total woman," whose "surrender" ought to be to seduce her husband every day for a week. "The Creator of sex intended for His creatures to enjoy it," she chirps (p. 131); "sex is as clean and pure as eating cottage cheese" (p. 141).

Conservative Christians find in their tradition a consistent honoring of womanhood and an elevation of female status. Dr. James C. Dobson's *Straight Talk to Men and Their Wives* is clear in its assertion that those ordained by God to be bearers and nurturers of new life have an exalted place within Christianity: they are protected and revered, saved from the hostile interactions of the workaday world and assured of stability and love. The relations between the sexes are based on a divinely ordained complementarity that involves human beings in covenant relationships with one another for the good of all. The divine scheme of the relations between the sexes enhances virtue and leads to happiness. If sex has been disparaged by Catholics, who subordinate the ideal of marriage to the ideal of virginity, Protestants extol marriage as a blessed vocation and fundamentalists have taken pains in the last few years to relate sex to the life of the spirit.[5] Josh McDowell, a traveling evangelist for Campus Crusade for Christ, talks about sex and prayer as two dimensions of the same experience, and Peter Gardella, a scholar who examined conservative Christian sexual ethics in *Innocent Ecstasy* (1985), argues that Christianity gave America an ethic of sexual pleasure. According to religious conservatives, the wholesome sexuality advocated by Christianity is antithetical to the presumably perverse eroticism fostered by the pornographic imagination. In order to overcome pornography, therefore, it appears as if one must accept fundamentalist Christianity.

CHRISTIAN SEXUAL ETHICS AND PORNOGRAPHY

When we examine attitudes toward Christian sexual ethics, we find two distinct lines of thought. The first, relating to the perception that Christianity is detrimental to a happy sex life, tends to indict Christian sexual ethics as hopelessly repressive and to suggest that Christianity, more than any other religion, bears the blame for the linkage between sex and pornography. The second, based on biblical celebrations of marriage and family, praises Christianity for making a healthy sex life possible.

Those who perceive Christian sexual teachings as repressive argue in effect that sex was an acceptable and healthy pastime until Christian sexual ethics made it into a guilt-ridden, barely tolerated duty limited to the begetting of children (Walker, 1983, p. 910–20). By describing sex in purely functional terms, they argue, Christians have separated sex from pleasure and made it into a forbidden, evil, dangerous activity. Growing out of this attitude is the view that pornography is a reaction to such a distorted view of sex or an extension of its images to perverse intensifications. Pornography, therefore, can be laid at the doorstep of Christian sexual ethics, which perpetuates negative teachings about sexual interaction. "The worship of virginity must be posited as a real sexual perversion," says Dworkin; "the dualism of good and evil, virgin and whore . . . inherent in Christianity finds its logical expression in the rituals of sadomasochism" (1974, p. 73).

In opposition to these views, one can find a positive evaluation of Christian sexual ethics by religious conservatives who understand Christianity as enhancing human sexual life by regulating it with the virtue of chastity. Since unbridled sex, according to them, is destructive of virtue, and since virtue helps to integrate sex into a stable and loving pattern of human life, pornography thrives on the denial of Christianity, not on its affirmation. Christianity defeats pornography by drawing men and women into God's plan for human relationships and future happiness in heaven. Erotic sexuality is healthy within marriage and, for Catholics, perfectly acceptable within its procreative and unitive context.

Ambiguities in Christian Sexual Ethics

Christianity contains statements about sex that have had a deleterious effect on sexual pleasure. As Ruether has shown, the "lack of any development of the sex relationship as a personal love relationship . . . committed patristic thought to a puritan-prurient ambivalence toward sex as either 'dirty' or objectively instrumental" (1974, p. 166). The hagiographical tradition, as Donald Weinstein and Rudolph Bell have shown, exalted virginity in such a way that it made "women's place in society [something] that can only be described as dismal" (1982, p. 97). Stories of female saints who debased or punished themselves to prove their love for God reveal, claims Marina Warner, "the psychological obsession of the religion with sexual sin, and the tortures that pile up one upon another with pornographic repetitiousness underline the identification of the female with the perils of sexual contact" (1976, p. 71).

At the same time, however, Christian teachings about sex reflect an inherited tradition that in some ways, celebrated sex. The biblical injunction to "increase and multiply" gives divine sanction to sexual activity within marriage. In addition, the blessings of children and the joys and special pleasure attached to sexual intercourse on the Sabbath testify to the inherent goodness of sexual activity. And, of course, one of the most erotic poems in ancient literature is found in the Bible. The Song of Solomon celebrates the joys of sexual love: the lovers in the poem long for one another's touches and smells as they anticipate the pleasures of sexual intercourse. The uninhibited celebration of the body as the male rapturously describes his beloved's lips, breasts, and belly is a canonical endorsement of sexual pleasure. Contemporary fundamentalists, who look to scriptural texts as a warrant for their behavior, have taken a verse from this book—"Oh that his left hand were under my head and his right hand embraced me"—as a divine approval for clitoral stimulation (Ehrenreich, Hess, and Jacobs, 1986, p. 50). New translations of this biblical text, notably the one by S. Craig Glickman (1976), are meant to show Christians what God intended romantic love to be.

Finally, it is not altogether clear that Roman Catholic teaching about sex is universally repressive or, as Boswell has shown (1980), that it has been universally consistent. While it is true that Catholic teaching about marriage is based on natural law theory, which makes procreation the primary end of marriage with sexual pleasure clearly secondary, Peter Gardella perceives in Catholic sexual ethics a fundamental sensuality. According to him, the first American writer to prescribe orgasm for women was the Catholic bishop of Philadelphia, Francis Patrick Kenrick, who said, among other things, that women have the right to experience orgasm by touches after intercourse if they have not achieved orgasm during intercourse (p. 9). Orgasm is also a growing concern for conservative fundamentalists. Jack and Carole Mayhall (1978) tell their readers that sex is good and that God's command to increase and multiply means "do not cheat each other of normal sexual intercourse . . . a wife who never has an orgasm is being cheated." (p. 216).

Excursus: World Religions and Women's Place

When critics blame Christianity for teaching us how to hate women, they indict Christianity for not overcoming an ancient male fear of women that predates the birth of Christ (Lederer, 1968). Even granting the negative impact Christianity has had on women, however, one must be careful to examine other religious traditions as well so that Christianity does not assume more blame for its treatment of women than other groups.[6] Christians are sometimes perceived as bringing a cold shower of repression to a relatively uninhibited sexual world, a perception that must be tested against the roles and opportunities for women afforded by other traditions. Phyllis Bird has shown (1974), for example, that women in Judaism were treated as chattel, as son-makers, and as legal nonpersons whose chief glory lay in making time and space for men to study Torah.[7]

Similarly, in recalling Plato's fond relationship with Eros, it must be remembered that he was talking not about his sex life but about his ability to perceive contemplation as a lusty experience. As Susan Moller Okin (1979) has shown, women in ancient Greece were defined and treated functionally, made to serve men's needs and those of the state. If the Hindu pantheon has a representation of goddesses, there is no reason to believe that women's social, economic, or political status in India was enhanced by their religious system. The Buddhist canon contains several revealing stories about the Buddha's abhorrence of women: once when someone offered him a woman, the Buddha replied, "Why try to tempt me with that thing? It is a bag full of shit and piss. I wouldn't touch it with my foot" (*Sutanipata: The Group of Discourses* IV. 9, Magandiya #835). Scanty sources make it hard to evaluate pagan religions. Judith Ochshorn (1981) has argued that ancient polytheistic religions were good for women until monotheistic Yahwism, led by misogynist priests, destroyed women's possibilities in the ancient Near Eastern world. But her argument has been criticized by scholars like Carol P. Christ (1984) and Sarah Pomeroy (1982). Indeed, Joan O'Brien (1982) has concluded that Ochshorn's work is "flawed by her failure to see the pervasive effects of patriarchy, whether in a polytheistic or a monotheistic setting" (p. 744).

Some feminists want us to believe that societies dominated by goddesses were matriarchal (Stone, 1976, 1979), but it is not clear that such was the case (Binford, 1982). Carol P. Christ argues persuasively that women need to reclaim the power of Goddess religion (1985), but that does not necessarily mean that life was any better in societies that honored the Goddess. If Christianity is bad for women, therefore, it is one part of a complex pattern of male fear of women that has pervaded virtually every religion. As Jill Raitt (1980) has shown, stories about vaginas with teeth—found in almost every society we know about—symbolize male fear of castrating females and make the *vagina dentata* a particularly useful symbol to interrogate the neutralization of the female threat by religious authorities. Raitt's collection of examples shows the universality of male fear of women and leads us to expect a male need to tame women in virtually every canon of folklore and religion in the world.

Christian Sexual Ethics Not Totally at Fault

Ironically, I would suggest that Christian sexual ethics are bad for women not because of Christian teachings about the life of the body, but because of religious beliefs about the life of the soul. The Christian roots of the pornographic imagination, as described by Griffin and others, are to be found not in moral handbooks about sexual conduct, but in the textbooks of theology and the spiritual life, both ancient and modern. Theology, the study of God's nature and of the relationships between the divine and human realities, is based on a dualistic understanding of the spiritual and material worlds, a distinction upheld by the belief that God is a radically transcendent and dominating being. In Western Christian spirituality, especially in Roman Catholicism, virginity, as "an ideal that derived ultimately from pre-Christian sources in Hellenistic dualism, pervaded every segment of medieval society" (Weinstein and Bell, 1982, p. 99).

Blaming Christian sexual teachings, themselves, for the pornographic imagination, therefore, is untenable; it will be more productive to look for the foundations of the pornographic imagination in the patterns of domination and submission that are found primarily in Christian beliefs about women as inferior creatures, and in the tendency of the Christian tradition to separate procreative sex from erotic pleasure, or in the teachings that place eroticism within a context of female submission.

SPIRITUAL LIFE AND THE INFERIORITY OF WOMEN

Traditional Christian theology is based on a belief in the radical transcendence of God and a consequent division of all reality into higher and lower realms. In this system, everything is divided according to a pattern of heavenly (spiritual) existence and earthly (bodily) life. In the creation story in the Bible, for example, the maker is divided from the thing made in such a way that the creator is inherently superior to the created order and stands in a relationship of mastery over it. According to traditional

Christology, the redeemer, though "truly man," has a divine nature and so is divided from those redeemed by virtue of his status as the preexistent son of God. In human relations, the "degrading idea that 'man is the beginning and end of woman' is reinforced by the parallel man: woman; God: creature," as Mary Daly reminded us (1968, p. 51). In religious life, the spiritual realm is divided from earthly life on the assumption that bodily life is inherently inferior to the life of the soul.

Christian sexual teaching and Christian spirituality both follow these divisions. Using Aristotelian biological categories, medieval Catholics were able to define sex in purely functional terms and argue that women were passive vessels of the male life force. Pleasure was subordinated to procreation in such a way that sexual intercourse could be assessed solely in terms of its childbearing functions, and since those functions were considered to be the result of the divine curse placed on Eve, women who were wives and mothers were not considered worthy of spiritual advancement. The spiritual life, as Ruether (1986) has shown, was based on the misogynist belief that only males were made in the image of God. Since sex was designed for procreation, and women made to be used for the propagation of the species, both sex and women were assigned to the lower realms of existence, believed to be necessary evils, and perceived as highly dangerous to the life of the spirit.

The mystical life was the heroically attainable goal of those who could abstain from the allurements of the body and channel their energies into spiritual pursuits. Abstinence from sex was part of a program that enjoined devotees to fast from food and sleep, mortify their flesh, ward off demons of self-involvement and self-abuse, and spend long hours in prayer and contemplation. This system is not peculiar to Christianity: mystics with an ascetic agenda can be found in most of the world's religions. In the Christian tradition, only virgins (those who had never had sex, or who had renounced it) could attempt to pursue the higher calling of mystical life, because virginity allowed devotees to transcend the body in order to ascend, spiritually, into heaven. Women who hoped for mystical union with God could do so only by denying their sexuality in vows of perpetual virginity, a heroic renunciation that, according to Weinstein and Bell "was virtually assured of failure not only because the flesh was weak, but because the world demanded marriage and motherhood" (1982, p. 98). Furthermore, whereas "men could be sanctimonious about their ability to resist sexual assaults, women, considered the lustful and morally weak sex, had great difficulty in establishing their credibility in the face of gossip and male ridicule" (p. 88).

Paradoxically, therefore, it is in the spiritual tradition, where, rhetorically at least, all souls are equal before God, that some of the most virulent misogynist language can be found. The theological understanding of a radically transcendent God whose qualities were appropriated by males to the disparagement of women and bodily life is the basis for the double standard identified by anti-pornography feminists as the foundation of the pornographic imagination. Stories of medieval sanctity, as Weinstein and Bell have shown, were full of tales of heroic men beset by the devilish power of women: "heroic resistance to blatant, sexual seduction could never be repeated often enough" (p. 81). In the lives of male saints, women were portrayed as sexual predators and allies of the devil, but female saints "who described their own sexual problems did not often allow themselves the luxury of blaming them on the devil, perhaps being too deeply instilled with the prevalent notion that women were the lustful sex to think of shifting their responsibility to outside forces" (p. 87). This tendency to associate women with sex and its powers, and the belief that mystical experience was most properly reserved for men constitute common religious themes, giving further substance to the view that male hatred for and "fear of women lies deep in the mythic consciousness of men" (Russell, 1972, p. 283).

In traditional Roman Catholicism and conservative fundamentalism, women must be ruled by a father and then by a husband (or, in the case of nuns, by a bishop). The medieval adage—*aut maritus, aut murus,* either a husband or an enclosure wall (Suenens, 1963, p. 46)—presented women with their only options. Furthermore, the doctrine of complementarity—a form of sex-role discrimination that relegates men and women to specific roles on the basis of their supposed divinely assigned natures— continues to tell Christian women that God designed them for subservient roles. Since this traditional vision operates on a model in which women are necessarily subservient, anti-pornography feminists rightly suggest that it must be rejected, and anti-pornography religious conservatives wrongly link the defeat of pornography to the Christian vision. It is not far-fetched to say that pornography is an intensification of the gender differences in traditional Christianity. "Good Christian businessmen" who spend their lunch hours in "adult" bookstores live not in two worlds but in one, single universe in which men dominate women. Pornography, therefore, does not grow at the expense of traditional Christianity but as a further distortion of the already distorted social roles embodied in its own religious vision.

Jimmy Swaggart's recent fall from grace, resulting from his kinky sexual practices with a prostitute, underscores my point. It is revealing that Swaggart did not have sexual intercourse with the "fallen woman" he accompanied to motel rooms but "used her" for autoerotic stimulation and fellatio. In his tearful public confession he admitted to weakness and "shameful conduct" but was able to assure his congregation that he had not "committed adultery" with her, thereby ensuring that his own personal pillar of a good Christian society—the sanctity of his marriage and family—remained solid. Religious traditions that tend to be overly agitated about sexual misconduct often define legitimate sexual activity in narrow ways so that "proper" sexual expression is limited to "the missionary position." As long as a man does not assume this position, he has not had "sexual intercourse." Swaggart's conduct may not be typical, but his theological beliefs are shared by a majority of religious conservatives who inhabit a world where God dominates men and men dominate women.

SPIRITUALIZATION OF EROTIC LANGUAGE

Although the functional definition of women and sex supported the Neo-platonic desire for a disembodied spiritual life, spiritual communion was often articulated in highly erotic language. Those women who had taken vows of virginity in order to seek spiritual union with God gave up sex but did not necessarily forego erotic pleasure. In fact, when looking for highly erotic passages in the Christian tradition, I find it instructive to read the mystics. Teresa of Avila's sixteenth-century experience of God as a lover marks the apex of her spiritual quest and, at the same time, is astonishingly erotic:

> The Lord wanted me while in this state to see sometimes the following vision: I saw close to me toward my left side an angel in bodily form. . . . I saw in his hands a large golden dart and at the end of the iron tip there appeared to be a little fire. It seemed to me this angel plunged the dart several times into my heart and that it reached deep within me. When he drew it out, I thought he was carrying off with him the deepest part of me; and he left me all on fire with great love of God. The pain was so great that it made me moan, and the sweetness this greatest pain caused me was so superabundant that there is no desire capable of taking it away. (1976, p. 193).

Such erotic descriptions of spiritual union were not confined to women. Indeed, John of the Cross, probably the most consistently erotic spiritual writer in the Christian tradition, describes his own spiritual experience with passion. Addressing God, he says, "You dwell alone, not only as in Your house, nor only as in Your bed, but also as in my own heart, intimately and closely united to it. And how delicately You captivate me and arouse my affections toward you" (1979, 644). The theme of spiritual betrothal to God was a mainstay of religious life. The "Office of St. Agnes," recited before a woman took her vows of perpetual virginity, makes a romantic connection between the candidate for religious life and God: "For Him alone I keep my troth; to Him I surrender . . . with His ring my Lord Jesus Christ has betrothed me" (*The Hours of the Divine Office in English and Latin,* 1963, vol. I, pp. 1702, 1708).

The use of erotic language to describe relations with an asexual deity upheld a dangerous separation between sexuality and eroticism in the Christian tradition. By pairing sex exclusively with procreation, the Roman Catholic church's teachings never allowed for sex as a pastime, a pleasure, or a means of intimate communication between spouses. This limited understanding of sex may account for the fact that one finds little on eroticism, sexual perversion, or pornography in Catholic moral theology textbooks. Because any extramarital activity was mortally sinful, celibate moralists were not as interested in proscribing perverse sex as they were in speculating about the various kinds of questions that arose within the confines of procreational, married sex. Moral theology textbooks usually have significant sections on married sexual activity: when to have intercourse, in what position, after what kinds of foreplay, with what kinds of intentions, with what kinds of fantasies, under what conditions (Ford and Kelly, 1963, vol. 2, pp. 208-34). Perversions of erotic pleasure are relatively absent in moral texts—with, perhaps, the exception of Alfonso de Liguori (1821, pp. 298-337), who discusses various "unnatural sexual practices"—because the erotic impulse had been effectively removed from sexual life. Erotic language was kept alive in celibate longing for God.

This tendency to spiritualize erotic feelings, embedded deeply in the Christian tradition, is not confined to Catholics. Nineteenth-century American Methodists regularly produced ecstatic testimonies (Merritt and King, 1843); Pentecostal Aimee Semple McPherson "taught that fulfillment came through ecstatic experience and showed how such experience looked and felt" (Gardella, p. 83); and the pious Phoebe Palmer, who waited for God in "thrilling anticipation," assured her readers that her own "insatiable desires" had been filled by God, and that her Savior was even now "wooing [her six-year-old daughter] to the embrace of his love" (1871, pp. 36, 258).

Nor was erotic spirituality a one-sided affair. Bernard of Clairvaux, a twelfth-century spiritual writer, puzzled over the annunciation story in the New Testament. Since the angel says to Mary, "Hail, the Lord is with you," it appeared to Bernard that the Lord was already there (with Mary) before asking her permission. Little wonder, exclaimed Bernard, since "the virgin's ointment yielded its sweet odour; its fragrance came up to His glorious presence and found favor in His sight." God, "borne upon the wings of His exceeding longing, . . . reached the Virgin whom he loved, whom He had chosen for Himself, whose beauty He desired" (1954, p. 128). John of the Cross repeatedly praised virginity for its power to attract the divine lover.

Eroticism, therefore, is a central part of the Christian tradition, but in a spiritualized form. When Griffin bids her readers to choose eroticism, she opposes it to traditional Christianity without making the distinction between Christian literature about female inferiority and spiritual treatises about erotic relationships between the soul and God. Christianity contains a possibility for the erotic that can be appreciated even though the traditional teachings about women as inferior and subservient, in need of male mastery, must be rejected. On the other hand, when conservative fundamentalists link the erotic impulses of sex to traditional Christianity without questioning its sexual double standards, they fail to see that the vision they endorse is inherently pornographic because it is based on patterns of domination and submission.

Virtually all of the books by conservative Christian writers about marriage assume that proper sexual pleasure can be found only in marital relationships where the man is clearly the head of the family. Writing collaboratively, Jack and Carole Mayhall, in *Marriage Takes More than Love* (1978), describe marital "Responsibilities." Interestingly, Jack wrote the chapters "Choosing to Lead," "Choosing to Solve Problems," "Choosing Headship," "Choosing to Encourage," and "Choosing Responsibility," whereas Carole wrote the chapter entitled "Choosing to Submit." She did not want to submit to her husband, she says, but was finally led to the profound truth that "to obey God meant obeying Jack" (p. 189). She was rewarded for her decision by Jack's behavior: "when I chose to obey," she assures her readers, "Jack became less demanding and . . . we grew closer" (p. 189).

The conservative Christian vision, therefore, is predicated on a pattern of dominance and submission, and the erotic possibilities of Christian spirituality are linked with a reading of the tradition that upholds male mastery. If an alternative theological vision were explored, however, it might be possible to argue against pornography and traditional Christianity without relinquishing the spiritually satisfying parts of the religion.

AN ALTERNATIVE CHRISTIAN VISION AND EROTIC LIFE

With its double standard of sexual relations, Christian dualism postulates a theological system in which God is utterly transcendent, totally Other, the Lord and Master of the universe. Since that system has been criticized by feminist theologians of many different theological persuasions, it is not surprising that alternatives to it are diverse and often controversial. Some feminist interpreters reject religion altogether, whereas others abandon Judaism or Christianity in favor of Goddess religion (Christ, 1987; Starhawk, 1979). Many of those who reject Christianity to embrace some form of neo-paganism claim to be searching for a religion of immanence that cannot be found within the Christian tradition (Spretnak, 1982).

Although I understand the attraction of an immanent deity as found in Goddess religion, I do not agree that it is totally absent from the Christian tradition. Undoubtedly divine transcendence has been the predominant theme in Christianity, but not the only one, and it is worth examining an alternative offered by process thought to see whether it, too, upholds the pornographic imagination. In *Beyond God the Father* (1973), Mary Daly flirted with a process alternative but was so repulsed by official Christianity that she did not pursue "God the Verb" beyond that book either as an argument or as a spiritual possibility for women.

Classical Western spirituality has been based on a system of mastery believed to replicate God's relationship with the world: the Creator masters the primal chaos to create the world, and men master the flesh to attain the life of the spirit. In poetic terms, mystics look at the material universe and say, "This, neither, is Thou": nothing that can be seen, felt, experienced, or touched is genuinely divine, and those attempting spiritual union with the deity are enjoined to put a "cloud of unknowing" between themselves and everything else in order to make room for God. Known as the *via negativa,* or the way of negation, this form of spiritual life is based on a denial of human experience, a denial of what Griffin refers to as eros, that is to say, the child in us, the experience of falling in love, the exquisite joys of bodily life, and the experience of vulnerability and suffering. Given a God who is uninvolved in changing patterns of existence, whose relationship to humanity is one of omnipotent mastery, a spirituality attempting union with God encourages qualities that replicate the divine personality. Traditional Catholic spirituality and contemporary fundamentalist spirituality both follow this pattern. Although neither group continues to argue that women are naturally *inferior,* both continue to believe that women have a divinely ordained place within the universe that requires the direction and control of men.

Yet a minor and radically different theme in the Christian tradition is that of the divine immanence. One modern expression can be found in process theology, a system based on the work of Alfred North Whitehead (1929). Process thought has adumbrations in biblical stories of divine immanence, in the Christian doctrine of the Incarnation, and in those poets of the spiritual life who look at the created order and say, "This also is Thou." Dante's cosmic drama of salvation is upheld by his experience of having fallen in love with Beatrice,[8] and Meister Eckhart's creation-centered spirituality is based on the belief that what can be experienced, felt, touched, and known in this world is, very often, of the divine order.[9] Known, if at all, as the "way of affirmation," this kind of spirituality celebrates those experiences Griffin identifies with eros and conceptualizes the relationship with God as one of partnership and mutual vulnerability.

Process thought is a modern appropriation of these spiritual insights coupled with a sense of the dynamism of nature, the reality of time, and the possibility of novelty. Process theology has been nurtured by the revolution in the scientific worldview—Darwin's evolutionary work and Einstein's theory of relativity—and the scientific respect for mystery as found in the work of subatomic physicists like Fritjof Capra (1975, 1982).

Because process theology develops the partnership and communicative elements of the divine/human interaction, it can break the tradition of religious tyranny and make way for a theology that can displace the dominance of men over women with genuinely mutual patterns of relationship. In the classical theology of traditional Christianity, although the creative center of the universe, God is the supreme exception to human experience and has no necessary relationship with the world. God, in other words, appears not to need the world at all and is said to sustain its life as an act of supreme goodness and generosity. For process theologians, however, God does need the world and the bustle of choices that make up human and subhuman existence. For Whitehead, God is the supreme exemplification of all metaphysical and human categories, not their exception. Far from being unrelated to this world, the process God is that being who is conditioned and affected by everything that happens here and understandable only in terms of relationships. God is absolute not in the traditional sense of being final, total, unlimited, and unchangeable, but by being encompassing in influence, related to and suffering with all entities, and being the ultimate and highest destiny of each.[10]

In process philosophy, God's power lies in the lure of beauty, in the tenderness of compassionate persuasion, not in force or domination or mastery. If experience has claimed that human beings relate to God in strength, love, vulnerability, and weakness, process thought has made the same claims for God. God relates to humanity in strength because of the visions present in what Whitehead calls the divine primordial nature; in love because of a desire for more extensive and intensive relationships; in vulnerability because the divine destiny is tied to human destiny; and in weakness because God needs what human beings can give. Since the divine concrete experience depends on what human beings are able to give, God lures humanity on so that human beings—all life, really—will experience more and so have more to give to the process. Process thought assumes that God is related, persuasive, and involved with the world and that religion is a relationship with the deity that enriches both partners beyond their ability to achieve alone.

According to process theologians, human beings emulating this God are open to possibility, involved with the whole created order, aware of their choices and their own development, and unwilling to define the universe or themselves in dualistic terms. In process theology there is no double standard for males and females, or for animate and inanimate life; there are no gender differences to exploit, no mastery images to uphold, no need to control the passions, the body, or, by extension, women. For Whitehead, what used to be perceived as oppositions are now merely contrast: "It is as true to say that God is one and the World many, as that the World is one and God many . . . as true to say that God creates the World, as that the World creates God" (1929, p. 530). For Charles Hartshorne, Whitehead's chief interpreter, God is like a teacher who is enriched by his or her sympathetic involvement in the pupil's learning experience (1967).

Although it may be hard to imagine that such a theology could be born out of a sexist culture, or, more to the point, that it could change centuries of traditional belief and behavior that encourage mastery, domination, and submission, the utopian possibilities offered by process thought have been articulated by a growing number of philosophers and theologians and have found some resonance in feminist theology (Davaney, 1981). If the hierarchical model of Christianity found in traditional Catholicism and contemporary fundamentalism upholds the pornographic imagination by encouraging believers to emulate a dominant God who requires submission from believers, then the very possibility for an alternative theological vision holds some promise for another order of divine-human interaction that can alter patterns of human interaction. In the process model, mutuality does not depend upon a hierarchical arrangement but encourages vulnerability and mutual openness.

CONCLUSION

Process theology opens a new dimension of the religious imagination. As Marjorie Suchocki says, "the process concept of God provides a metaphysical grounding to the values of openness and mutuality so essential to the feminist program" (1981, p. 65). Process theology enables one to imagine a Christianity that is not a source of and foundation for the pornographic imagination and makes it possible for anti-pornography feminists to retrieve those parts of the Christian vision which some of them may find life enhancing. What Griffin associates with eros—celebration of life, falling in love, poetry, mutuality, change, vulnerability, and beauty—are the very elements that a process system recognizes as most clearly embodying the divine reality. In this system, the God of mastery is replaced by a God whose only power over humanity is in the lure of beauty. While one must choose between eros and pornography, therefore, one does not necessarily have to choose between Christianity and eros.

For religious conservatives, however, whatever joy they may find in sex, the choice remains fixed between religion and eros precisely because religion is conceptualized in the traditional terms of domination and submission. There can be no real relationship between Christianity and eros in a religious system that insists on subservience from women and is built upon the double standards derived from the God of mastery. Religion as defined by conservatives is not antithetical to pornography but supportive of it, and an appropriation of the "old-time religion" is an affirmation of the very framework upon which perverse extensions of dominating masculinity are constructed. The anti-pornographic views of religious conservatives that purport to be deeply religious, are, therefore, profoundly pornographic, whereas the anti-pornographic views of feminist critics that appear to be anti-religious are open to the designs of a new theological vision. Because the theological assumptions of conservative religionists and feminists are so clearly antithetical to one another, there can be no fruitful alliance between them. It is not possible to imagine traditional religion and eros, nor is it possible to argue that conservative religion can save the world from pornography. It is possible, however, to have a newly imagined religion that welcomes eros, a religion based on process thought, which not only undermines pornography but also undermines the old, tyrannizing tradition of conservative Christianity.

NOTES

1. I realize that my coalition is more imaginary than real, and that Susan Griffin, herself, is not part of any such group. Because her writings are so lucid about the incompatibility of eros and Christianity, however, she makes a perfect foil for religious conservatives and allows me to raise some intriguing theological questions. The possibility of a real coalition between conservative Christians and some antipornography feminists has frightened more than one interpreter (see Bloom, 1987, and Faust, 1980).

2. Readers may be frustrated by the lack of *textual* support for the opinions of Swaggart and Falwell. I find it maddening, myself, since their predilection for preaching over writing has forced me to watch more hours of television evangelism than is healthy. Falwell's book, *Listen, America!* (1980) is only vaguely useful and Swaggart's *Rape of a Nation* (1985) is, like his preaching, a series of condemnations against the evils of the modern world. Both men are powerful preachers and hold common cause against illicit sex, drugs, pornography, the women's movement, homosexuality, welfare, and other American "vices." Swaggart has recently been caught in a sexual scandal, and it is not yet clear what the facts are in the case. According to Debbie Murphree (*Penthouse,* 1988), the television evangelist engaged her in a series of perverse sexual practices.

3. I am using "religious conservatives" as a catch-all phrase including right-wing Roman Catholics. Evangelical Christians, and mainline Protestants. I have chosen Swaggart as a representative of that view because he preaches it so forcefully and because he has an enormous televison outreach. His current moral disgrace does not change my point that the theological presuppositions of conservative Christians make any alliance between them and antipornography feminists impossible.

4. Indeed, Ruether continues to criticize traditional Christianity and to refine her arguments. This particular contention is not only an early example of her thinking, but one of the most explicit on this particular issue.

5. Some of the conservative Christian impetus toward a more sensual Christianity can be found in Gardella, 1985. A review of some of the literature and ideas of fundamentalists about sex can be found in Ehrenreich et al., 1986.

6. Indeed, not all people who study pre-Christian periods are as hard on Christianity as feminist interpreters. Michel Foucault (1980), for example, sees some positive aspects to early Christian views on women in terms of the erotic aspects of heterosexual relations.

7. Since I am trying to demonstrate that there are multiple intellectual strands in Christianity, I do not want to reduce other religious traditions to one, dispiriting theme. I recognize that women in Judaism were also revered as mothers, sometimes praised for bravery, and celebrated for insight. On the whole, however, Bird's interpretation gives me a way to say that Christianity is not the only religion where women's lives were dismal in a religiously sanctioned way.

8. Although it is anachronistic to make a clear connection between Dante

and process thought, the fact that Dante's work is an exercise in the "way of affirmation of the images" makes him a historical forerunner. Dorothy L. Sayers has been most explicit on Dante's connections with the way of affirmation. See her *Introductory Papers on Dante* (1954) and her introduction to her translation of *The Divine Comedy* (1949, 1955). In some ways Sayers popularized the interpretation of Dante made by her friend Charles Williams. See his posthumously published *The Figure of Beatrice* (1961).

9. Eckhart, a German Dominican (1260–1337), was a famous preacher and spiritual director who taught at the University of Paris but is primarily remembered for his sermons, which are replete with references to feminine dimensions of the divine and which were preached primarily to the Beguines, a late medieval independent sisterhood persecuted and suppressed for their refusal to capitulate to the cloister model of religious life. For a modern reading of Eckhart, see Matthew Fox, *Breakthrough: Meister Eckhart's Creation Spirituality in a New Translation* (1980).

10. Process thought has its own vocabulary and cannot be easily reduced to simple explanations as I have tried to do here. My intention, however, was not to provide a full-blown explanation of process thought—for that, see Cobb, 1976; Cousins, 1971; Suchocki, 1986; and Williams, 1981—but simply to suggest that the Christian tradition may not be as bankrupt as some antipornography feminists claim it is, and that Christianity cannot be reduced to the "traditional" dualistic interpretations that bolster the conservative viewpoint.

REFERENCES

Bernard of Clairvaux (1954). *Super Missus Est,* Homily III. In *Saint Bernard On the Christian Year: Selections from his Sermons.* London: A. R. Mobray. Original work written in twelfth century and can be found in *Sancti Bernardi Opera Omnia,* vol. I, Part 1, p. 1686. Paris: Apud Gaume Fratres, 1839.

Binford, Sally R. (1982). "Are Goddesses and Matriarchies Merely Figments of Feminist Imagination?" *The Politics of Women's Spirituality,* ed. Charlene Spretnak. New York: Doubleday, pp. 541–49.

Bird, Phyllis (1974). "Images of Women in the Old Testament." In *Religion and Sexism,* ed. Rosemary Ruether. New York: Simon and Schuster, pp. 41–89.

Bloom, Alexander (1987). "Peeling the Pornographic Onion." *The World and I 2* (February 1987): 424–31.

Boswell, John (1980). *Christianity, Social Tolerance and Homosexuality.* Chicago: University of Chicago Press.

Capra, Fritjof (1975). *The Tao of Physics.* New York: Bantam Books.

——— (1982). *The Turning Point.* New York: Simon and Schuster.

Christ, Carol P. (1984). "The Female Experience and the Nature of the Divine [Review]." *Journal of the American Academy of Religion* 52:786–88.

Christ, Carol P. (1985). "Symbols of Goddess and God in Feminist Theology." *The Book of the Goddess Past and Present,* ed. Carl Olson. New York: Crossroad, pp. 231–51.

—— (1987). *The Laughter of Aphrodite: Reflections on a Journey to the Goddess.* San Francisco: Harper and Row.

Cobb, John B. (1976). *Process Theology: An Introductory Exposition.* Philadelphia: Westminster Press.

Cousins, Ewert H., ed. (1971). *Process Theology: Basic Writings by the Key Thinkers of a Major Modern Movement.* New York: Newman Press.

Daly, Mary (1968). *The Church and the Second Sex.* New York: Harper and Row.

—— (1973). *Beyond God the Father.* Boston: Beacon Press.

Davaney, Sheila Greeve, ed. (1981). *Feminism and Process Thought.* Lewiston, N.Y.: Edward Mellen Press.

De Beauvoir, Simone (1952). *The Second Sex.* New York: Alfred A. Knopf.

Dobson, James C. (1980). *Straight Talk to Men and their Wives.* Waco, Tex.: Proven Word.

Dworkin, Andrea (1974). *Woman Hating.* New York: E. P. Dutton & Co.

—— (1979). *Pornography: Men Possessing Women.* New York: Putnam Perigree.

—— (1987). *Intercourse.* New York: The Free Press.

Ehrenreich, Barbara; Hess, Elizabeth; & Jacobs, Gloria (1986). "Unbuckling the Bible Belt," *Mother Jones,* July/August 1986, pp. 46–51, 78–85.

Falwell, Jerry (1980). *Listen, America!* New York: Doubleday.

Faust, Beatrice (1980). *Women, Sex and Pornography.* New York: Macmillan.

Ford, John C., and Kelly, Gerald (1963). *Contemporary Moral Theology.* Westminster Md.: The Newman Press.

Foucault, Michel (1980). *History of Sexuality,* vol. I. New York: Vintage Books.

Fox, Matthew (1980). *Breakthrough: Meister Eckhart's Creation Spirituality in a New Translation.* New York: Doubleday.

Gallagher, Neil (1981). *The Porno Plague.* Minneapolis: Bethany House Publishers.

Gardella, Peter (1985). *Innocent Ecstasy: How Christianity Gave America an Ethic of Sexual Pleasure.* New York: Oxford University Press.

Getz, Gene A. (1974). *The Measure of a Man.* Ventura, Cal: Regal Books.

Glickman, S. Craig (1976). *A Song for Lovers.* Downers Grove, Ill.: Varsity Press.

Griffin, Susan (1981). *Pornography and Silence.* New York: Harper Colophon.

Harris, Art, and Berry, Jason (1988). "Jimmy Swaggart's Secret Sex Life." *Penthouse,* July 1988, p. 104.

Harris, Sara (1969). *The Puritan Jungle.* New York: G. P. Putnam's Sons.

Hartshorne, Charles (1967). *A Natural Theology for Our Time.* Lasalle, Ill.: Open Court.

Henning, Clara (1974). "Canon Law and the Battle of the Sexes." In *Religion and Sexism,* ed. Rosemary Ruether. New York: Simon and Schuster, pp. 267–91.

The Hours of the Divine Office in English and Latin (1963). Translated by the Staff of Liturgical Press. Collegeville, Minn.: Liturgical Press.

John of the Cross (1979). "The Spiritual Canticle." In *The Collected Works of St. John of the Cross.* Trans. Kieran Kavanaugh. Washington, D.C.: Institute of Carmelite Studies, pp. 394–565. (Original work written c. 1582.)

LaHaye, Tim and Beverly (1976). *The Act of Marriage.* New York: Bantam Books.

Lederer, Wolfgang (1968). *The Fear of Women.* New York: Harcourt Brace Jovanovich.

Liguori, Alfonso Maria de (1821). *Theologia Moralis.* Tomus Secundus, pp. 316–37. Antwerp: Janssens and van Merlen. (Originally written 1763.)

McLaughlin, Eleanor (1974). "Equality of Souls, Inequality of Sexes: Woman in Medieval Theology." In *Religion and Sexism,* ed. Rosemary Ruether. New York: Simon and Schuster, pp. 213–66.

Marcus, Steven (1964). *The Other Victorians.* New York: Basic Books.

Masters, R. E. L. (1962). *Eros and Evil.* New York: Julian Press.

Mayhall, Jack and Carole (1978). *Marriage Takes More Than Love.* Colorado Springs, Colo.: NavPress.

Merritt, Timothy, & King, D. S. (1843). *The Guide to Christian Perfection.* Boston: Merritt and King.

Morgan, Marabel (1973). *The Total Woman.* Old Tappan, N.J.: Fleming H. Revell Company.

Murstein, Bernard I. (1974). *Love, Sex and Marriage through the Ages.* New York: Springer.

O'Brien, Joan (1982). "The Female Experience and the Nature of the Divine [Review]." *Theological Studies* 43:742–44.

Ochshorn, Judith (1981). *The Female Experience and the Nature of the Divine.* Bloomington: Indiana University Press.

Okin, Susan Moller (1979). *Women in Western Political Thought.* Princeton: Princeton University Press.

Palmer, Phoebe (1871). *The Way of Holiness, with Notes By the Way.* 51st ed. New York: W. C. Palmer, Jr. (Originally written in 1854).

Penthouse (1988). "Debbie Does Swaggart." *Penthouse,* July 1988, pp. 107–22.

Pomeroy, Sarah B. (1982). "The Female Experience and the Nature of the Divine [Review]." *American Historical Review* 87:1367–68.

Raitt, Jill (1980). "The *Vagina Dentata* and the *Immaculatus Uterus Divini Fontis.*" *Journal of the American Academy of Religion* 48:415–31.

Ruether, Rosemary (1974). "Misogynism and Virginal Feminism in the Fathers of the Church." In *Religion and Sexism,* ed. Rosemary Ruether. New York: Simon and Schuster, pp. 150–84.

——— (1975). *New Woman, New Earth.* New York: Seabury Press.

——— (1986). *Sexism and God-Talk.* Boston: Beacon Press.

Rugoff, Milton (1971). *Prudery and Passion.* New York: G. P. Putnam's Sons.

Russell, Jeffrey Burton (1972). *Witchcraft in the Middle Ages.* Ithaca: Cornell University Press.

Sadock, B. J.; Kaplan, H. I.; & Freedman, A. M. (1976). *The Sexual Experience.* Baltimore: Williams and Wilkins.

Sayers, Dorothy L. (1954). *Introductory Papers on Dante.* London: Methuen.

—— (1949, 1955). *The Divine Comedy.* London: Penguin Books.

Spretnak, Charlene, ed. (1982). *The Politics of Women's Spirituality: Essays on the Rise of Spiritual Power within the Feminist Movement.* New York: Doubleday.

Starhawk (1979). *The Spiral Dance.* San Francisco: Harper and Row.

Stone, Merlin (1976). *When God Was a Woman.* New York: Harcourt Brace Jovanovich.

—— (1979). *Ancient Mirrors of Womanhood.* Boston: Beacon Press.

Suchocki, Marjorie (1981). "Openness and Mutuality in Process Thought and Feminist Action." In *Feminism and Process Thought,* ed. Sheila Greeve Davaney. Lewiston, N.Y.: Edward Mellen Press, pp. 62–82.

—— (1986). *God, Christ, Church.* New York: Crossroad.

Suenens, Leon Josef Cardinal (1963). *The Nun in the World.* Westminster, Md.: Newman Press.

Swaggart, Jimmy (1985). *Rape of a Nation.* Baton Rouge: Jimmy Swaggart Ministries.

Tavard, George (1973). *Woman in Christian Tradition.* Notre Dame: University of Notre Dame Press.

Teresa of Avila (1976). *The Book of Her Life.* In *The Collected Works of St. Teresa of Avila,* vol. I, pp. 1–308. Trans. Kieran Kavanaugh. Washington, D.C.: Institute of Carmelite Studies. (Original Work written c. 1568).

Von le Fort, Gertrude (1934). *The Eternal Woman.* (English trans. 1962.) Milwaukee: Bruce Publishing Co.

Walker, Barbara G. (1983). *The Woman's Encyclopedia of Myths and Secrets.* San Francisco: Harper and Row.

Warner, Marina (1976). *Alone of All Her Sex.* New York: Alfred A. Knopf.

Weinstein, Donald, & Bell, Rudolph M. (1982). *Saints and Society.* Chicago: University of Chicago Press.

Whitehead, Alfred North (1929). *Process and Reality: An Essay of Cosmology.* New York: Macmillan.

Williams, Charles (1961). *The Figure of Beatrice.* London: Noonday Press.

Williams, Daniel Day (1981). *The Spirit and the Forms of Love.* Lanham, Md.: University Press of America reprint. (Original work published 1968).

Wright, Rusty and Linda Raney (1981). *Love, Sex, and Marriage.* Westwood, N.J.: Barbour Books.

Part Five
The Causal Issue

24

America's Slide into the Sewer

George F. Will

I regret the offensiveness of what follows. However, it is high time adult readers sample the words that millions of young Americans are hearing.

Which words are lyrics, which are testimony?

In a Manhattan courtroom testimony continues in the trial of young men accused of gang rape and other sadistic violence against the Central Park jogger in last April's "wilding" episode. "We charged her and we got her on the ground. Everybody started hitting her and stuff, and she's on the ground and everybody's stomping and everything . . . I grabbed one arm, and this other kid grabbed one arm and we grabbed her legs and stuff. And then we took turns getting on her." They did it for fun, for entertainment.

"After she was hit on the head with the pipe, did someone take her clothes off?"

"Yeah."

"OK, who took her clothes off?"

"All of us."

"Did somebody have sex with her?"

"Yeah."

"Did a lot of people have sex with her?"

"Yeah."

When arrested a defendant said, "It was something to do. It was fun." Where can you get the idea that sexual violence against women is fun? From a music store, through Walkman earphones, from boom boxes blaring forth the rap lyrics of 2 Live Crew:

> To have her walkin' funny we try to abuse it
> A big stinking p—y can't do it all
> So we try real hard just to bust the walls

That is, bust the walls of women's vaginas. 2 Live Crew's lyrics exult in busting women—almost always called bitches—in various ways, forcing anal sex, forcing women to lick feces. "He'll tear the p—y open 'cause it's satisfaction." "Suck my d—k, bitch, it makes you puke." That's entertainment.

This is medicine. The jogger lost most of her blood, her temperature plunged to 85. Doctors struggling to keep her alive had to tie down her arms and legs because, even hours after the attack, while in a coma that would last weeks, she was flailing and kicking as if "in a fighting stance." Her face was so disfigured a friend took 15 minutes to identify her. "I recognized her ring."

Do you recognize the relevance of 2 Live Crew?

> I'll break ya down and d—k ya long
> Bust your p—y then break your backbone

The furor (if anything so evanescent can be called that) about 2 Live Crew has subsided, for two reasons. Saturation journalism, print and broadcast, around the clock, quickly wrings the novelty out of subjects, leaving them dry husks. Then, if someone raises the subject again, the answer is a journalistic shrug: "Not again. We've already done that." But for 2 Live Crew the tour rolls on and the money rolls in.

Anyway, the "fury" over the lyrics was feigned. It had to be because everyone dependent on journalism did not learn what the offending words were. Media coverage was characterized by coy abstractness, an obscuring mist of mincing, supercilious descriptions of the lyrics as "explicit" or "outrageous" or "challenging" or "controversial" or "provocative." Well, now. Provoking what, precisely?

From the jogger trial: "Steve was holding her with his leg and someone was ripping off her clothes and pulling her down. She screamed and

Steve held her while Kevin pulled down his pants and had sex with her. Steve hit her with a brick twice."

Fact: Some members of a particular age and social cohort—the one making 2 Live Crew rich—stomped and raped the jogger to the razor edge of death, for the fun of it. Certainty: the coarsening of a community, the desensitizing of a society will have behavioral consequences.

Juan Williams of *The Washington Post* is black and disgusted. The issue, he writes, is the abuse of women, especially black women, and the corruption of young blacks' sensibilities, twisting their conceptions "of good sex, good relationships and good times." Half of all black children live in single-parent households headed by women. The black family is falling apart, teen pregnancy regularly ruins lives, the rate of poverty is steadily rising and 2 Live Crew "is selling corruption—self-hate—to vulnerable young minds in a weak black America."

NO MORALS

In such selling, liberals are tools of entertainment corporations. The liberals and the corporations have the morals of the marketplace. Corporations sell civil pollution for profit; liberals rationalize it as virtuous tolerance in "the marketplace of ideas." Not to worry, yawn the *New York Times* editorialists, "The history of music is the story of innovative, even outrageous styles that interacted, adapted and became mainstream." Oh, I see: First Stravinsky's "Rite of Spring," now 2 Live Crew's "Me So Horny." ("I won't tell your momma if you don't tell your dad/I know he'll be disgusted when he sees your p—y busted." Innovative. When that is "mainstream," this will be an interesting country.)

2 Live Crew, who are black, resemble the cretinous Andrew Dice Clay, the white "comedian." There is nothing new about selling the talentless to the tasteless. What is new is the combination of extreme infantilism and menace in the profit-driven degeneration of popular entertainment. This slide into the sewer is greased by praise. Yes, praise. When journalism flinches from presenting the raw reality, and instead says only that 2 Live Crew's lyrics are "explicit" and "controversial" and "provocative," there is an undertone of approval. Antonyms of these adjectives are "vague" and "bland" and "unchallenging." Somehow we never reach the subject of busting vaginal walls.

America today is capable of terrific intolerance about smoking, or toxic waste that threatens trout. But only a deeply confused society is more concerned about protecting lungs than minds, trout than black women.

We legislate against smoking in restaurants; singing "Me So Horny" is a constitutional right. Secondary smoke is carcinogenic; celebration of torn vaginas is "mere words."

Words, said Aristotle, are what set human beings, the language-using animals, above lower animals. Not necessarily.

25

Elicitation of Violence: The Evidence

F. M. Christensen

Roughly speaking, three types of evidence could be appealed to in regard to the causes of behavior: stories about individual cases, statistical analyses of groups in the population, and experimental studies. Each has its strengths and weaknesses, and we must consider all three.

ANECDOTAL CLAIMS

The anecdotal variety of evidence is perhaps the most commonly abused in everyday thinking. . . . To put it schematically, merely finding instances of A accompanied by B—for example, women who leave school with health problems—is not legitimate evidence that A causes B. Such thinking has been especially common in regard to the charge that pornography elicits violence. We constantly hear claims about sex criminals found to own pornography—ignoring all those who do not, and all the non-criminals who do. Similar stories of rapists and murderers who were Bible readers can equally well be found, from Albert Fish to Leonard Lake.

Some of the most manipulative uses of this sort of reasoning are to be heard at those perennial governmental hearings on obscenity. Indi-

Reprinted by permission of Greenwood Publishing Group, Inc., Westport, CT, from *Pornography: The Other Side* by F. M. Christensen (New York: Praeger Publisher Division). Copyright © 1990 by F. M. Christensen.

viduals presented as "victims of pornography" tell horror stories about physical and emotional violence they have suffered. It is even sometimes stated that if one does not believe pornography is to blame for the plight of these people, one does not have any compassion for them. Though their experiences are tragic, however, in most of the cases it is plain the sexual materials were present in only an incidental way in lives already disordered and violent for obvious sociological reasons. (In fact, sometimes those testifying merely assume pornography must have been present.) The same may be said of those cases where erotic materials were employed in the commission of an assault, say, where someone was forced to look at them or to participate in making them. They no more support the claim that pornography causes coercive tendencies than the existence of slavery and forced labor argues that labor in itself tends to produce coercive behavior. The fact that some are willing to use force to get what they want does not argue that what they want is itself evil or evil-inducing, be it sex or love or a baby or money or anything else. Yet that is the insane inference that is constantly being drawn.

Some of these stories turn out on closer inspection to involve serious distortions of fact, or even to be wholly fictional.[1] From media reporters pandering to public fears to lawyers attempting to prove a client was not responsible for what he did, people are always susceptible to dishonesty. One must maintain an attitude of critical judgment in such matters. All the same, it is certain there have been instances of pornography triggering violent behavior. The reason is that virtually anything can incite such a response on the part of a psychotic or sociopathic personality. To mention just two infamous cases, the British murderer John George Haigh reported that he had been impelled to his acts of vampirism by an emotionally charging Anglican high mass. Then there was Nannie Doss, who poisoned four husbands in succession; when finally caught, she explained that none of them had measured up to the romantic males she read about in *True Romances*. Nevertheless, if we are to say meaningfully that some type of thing causes violence, singling it out from the multitudes of other elements in life that can incite the unstable, it must be involved in a more systematic way than is suggested by such incidents as these.[2]

One crude type of more systematic evidence are the reports of police and FBI agents who say they regularly find pornography in the possession of rapists. However, these tend to be subjective, nonquantitative impressions, and they are not shared by other police and agents. In fact, some of them are reminiscent of claims, made by certain officials in earlier years, that most civil rights workers were Communists; ideology exerts a powerful influence on what some people will report having found out.

A few researchers have attempted to gather data on pornography and violent sex crimes in a more rigorous way by studying cases of rape reported to authorities. In general, these efforts have discovered no good reason to suspect a causal connection between the two. For example, the Williams Committee, which studied the pornography issue for the British government, reported it was unable to uncover any cases of a probable link between pornography and violent sex crime. Instead, the committee remarked, "One can study case after case of sex crimes and murder without finding any hint at all that pornography was present in the background." A similar conclusion was drawn earlier by researchers who surveyed juvenile criminal cases in the United States.[3]

Interviews with violent sex criminals themselves have provided another type of evidence on this matter. One recent survey of a group of convicted rapists elicited reports from a larger number of them that they had used sexual materials just before seeking out a victim.[4] That certainly indicates a connection of some type, but the nature of the link is problematic. By itself, this information may be no more significant than the fact that rapists *think* about sex before raping. It is too obvious that a strong desire for sex could constitute a motive both for using pornography and for committing a sex crime; there is no reason to suppose it was the former that produced the latter. In fact, the researcher described many of the rapists as employing the materials to excite themselves in preparation for the act, so the intention was evidently there in advance. Without the pornography, they could just have stoked themselves up on their own fantasies, as rapists so often report doing.

As for the possibility that these rapists would have committed their crimes less often without the added stimulation, that encounters another question, . . . namely, how many would-be rapists have been deterred by the use of a sexual substitute. For all we know, they more often lose their cravings as a result of masturbating with sexual portrayals. To speak schematically again, the important question is not whether A ever causes B but whether it does so "on balance," that is, more frequently than it prevents it. In this same vein, stories are often told of rapists who were carrying sexual materials when caught. Doesn't *that* show a causal link? But by the account some rapists have given, pornography is used as a backup; they masturbate with it if they cannot easily find a victim. What they might do if they did not have a substitute to relieve their urges is a serious question. All these facts leave too many questions unanswered.

What about criminals' own perception of what causes their behavior, then? In one questionnaire survey of convicted rapists, eleven out of sixty responded yes to the question of whether pornography had had "anything to do" with their being in prison or psychiatric hospital.[5] An even higher proportion, 39 percent, felt pornography had led them at some time to commit a "sexual crime." (Note that that vague phrase, given the laws in the area at the time, could have included noncoercive acts of oral and anal intercourse.) This is a worrisome result; but as various researchers have pointed out, it cannot be accepted at face value. For one thing, the indeterminateness of a questionnaire answer raises issues we have considered before. For example, perhaps the prisoners would have said pornography had something "to do" with their situation only in the same sense that any source of sexual knowledge of arousal might have done, such as seeing women in provocative dress. Questions concerning the latter sort of stimulus are conspicuously absent when rapists are asked about pornography these days.

A much more serious doubt hinges on the fact that violent criminals as a group tend to be very unaware of their own motivations (which may have a lot to do with their being violent in the first place) and highly prone to rationalization. They could simply have been falling back on an "explanation" they have often heard, one that would tend to relieve their own blame, at that. Statements of this type that we occasionally hear from rapists sound very like the politically correct "confessions" that turn up in other ideologically charged contexts (e.g., those old Chinese Communist "self-examination" sessions). Other excuses the rapists commonly give, such as "she led me on," are rightly regarded with skepticism and often clearly false. The notorious Ted Bundy case obviously could have involved such motives, including the desire for a last-minute stay of execution. (Sources close to Bundy have pointed to a broken home and other childhood factors to explain his murderous rage.) If we buy our psychological theories from a certified psychopath, he will be conning us even from the grave.

Quite apart from such doubts, however, there is positive evidence on the other side. For one thing, this survey result conflicts with those of others who have interviewed sex criminals extensively. From their questioning of convicted rapists and pedophiles, for example, Goldstein and Kant concluded that "few if any" had been appreciably influenced by pornography. Instead, they decided, real persons in the environment "are far more potent sexual stimul" for the sex criminal. In fact, many psychiatrists who have worked with sexually disturbed patients believe that pornography often has the effect of preventing sexual violence. Many sex offenders themselves report that this is the case, moreover.[6] According to Dr. Money, persons requesting help in a sex-offender clinic "commonly disclose in the course of counseling therapy that pornography helps them contain their abnormal sexuality within imagination only, as a fantasy." In fact, in the questionnaire just discussed, 39 percent of the convicts also agreed that pornography "provides a safety valve for antisocial impulses." Overall, this type of evidence provides at least as much reason to believe sexually explicit materials prevent violence as that they incite it.

STATISTICAL ANALYSES

The attempt to solve the problems facing the foregoing kind of data has led researchers to statistical methods. Now, it would not help us to learn that a high percentage of rapists use pornography; after all, a very great proportion of them drink coffee! What is needed instead is a correlation: that more pornography users than others commit rape (or, equivalently, that more rapists than nonrapists use pornography). Schematically, it is not whether or not the most As are Bs that counts; it is whether a higher percentage of As than of non-As are Bs, even if both percentages are low. In such a case, provided the statistics are collected carefully enough to rule out biased data and coincidence, we have good evidence for a causal relationship of some sort between A and B. This relationship, how-ever, could be different things, notably that A causes B, that B causes A, or that A and B are collateral effects of some common cause, C. As an illustration of the latter, consider the operation of a barometer. The falling of its fluid level does not cause a storm to come; instead, a de-crease in air pressure tends to produce both a storm and a drop in the barometer level.

So merely finding a correlation does not reveal a cause. . . .

One important type of statistical survey brought to bear on this ques-tion attempts to compare the backgrounds of those who have and those who have not committed violent sex crimes, in order to see if they dif-fer, on average, in their prior exposure to sexually explicit materials. For we would expect a correlation between such acts and some aspect of such exposure if the one tends to cause the other. Five studies of this type were performed at the request of the U.S. Commission on Obscenity and Pornography at the end of the 1960s.[7] To the surprise of many, only one of them found a larger amount of exposure to pornography in the backgrounds of those who had committed serious sex crimes than among those who had not. In fact, three of them, like an earlier study by the Kinsey Institute, found a *smaller* amount of prior exposure among violent sex criminals than in a "control group" of persons not known to have committed sex crimes. (The remaining study was not able to employ a quantitative analysis.) This seems to suggest that sexually explicit materials tend to prevent violence; at least it argues that they do not cause it. But there are various possible sources of error in studies of this kind. For just one thing, they had to depend on memory reports of what had been seen in previous years, which are certainly fallible, and on the answers being honest. Though such results are of some value, then, they are far from conclusive.

Another way to get evidence regarding the influence of pornography would be to compare the frequency of sex crimes committed by offenders who use pornography with the number committed by sex offenders who use none, in order to see if there is any difference. One clinical study of this type, involving rapists and child molesters, has been conducted in recent years, and it found no such difference.[8] (Even if it had, however, that might have been the result of some other common factor, such as a higher sex drive among those who committed more offenses—more on this point below.) Any new result requires corroboration, but this is evidence against the correlation needed by the hypothesis that pornography promotes sexual crimes. Although concerned that violent or paraphilic portrayals might reinforce deviant desires, the authors of this study felt there was no good reason to suspect ordinary sexual materials caused harm. Quite the reverse is generally believed by clinicians who treat sex criminals, in fact; ordinary pornography is standardly used by therapists in an attempt to replace the offenders' perverted desires and fantasies with normal ones.

The evidence on this matter is mixed, however. Two recent studies have found a correlation in their sample between the current use of pornography and coercive sexual acts by the offenders.[9] Though these surveys also face doubts over such things as the reliability of self-disclosure, their results are actually quite plausible. There are a number of reasons for suspecting that sex offenders would use erotic materials more, some of which have already been hinted at. For example, these individuals often have an obsessive preoccupation with sex; this would tend to express itself *both* in acts of sexual coercion and in more frequent use of sex substitutes. A study of men who admitted having raped but had not been prosecuted found they had an appreciably greater felt need for sex than other men, which suggests the same causal influence.[10] Secondly, rapists as a group are known to feel alienated from women; this could also be a partial cause of a greater use of such substitutes as well as of a greater likelihood of hostile interaction with women.

For another such reason, rapists are known in general to come from social and family backgrounds that are less sheltered and stable, less constrained by the prevailing standards of society (e.g., the families are more violent. This was reconfirmed by one of the studies just cited.) Such persons might well be less inhibited about seeking out socially disapproved things like pornography, as well as in regard to the use of anti-social violence. Conversely, those who receive stronger training against harming others are often, in this culture, taught that pornography is degrading to women; they would be less apt either to commit violent crimes, especially against women, *or* to use pornography a great deal. (By way of analogy, in a culture teaching that both theft and eating pork are evil, a correlation between those two things would not be surprising.) This might be especially true for religious groups, which were disproportionately represented in the one study of the five mentioned earlier that did find a correlation between sex crimes and prior exposure to pornography. A society in which sexual openness is considered offensive to women may well display an association between rape and consumption of sexual materials, even if the latter has no tendency whatever to cause the former.

This last comment is the main point of the foregoing discussion. In circumstances where a common cause for two phenomena is not only possible but known to exist, a correlation between them is by itself useless as evidence that the one causes the other. To appeal to another simile, there is a very strong correlation between lying down and dying, but this is hardly evidence that the former produces the latter. Indeed, one who supposed that it did so and tried to avoid death by always standing up would probably hasten his or her own demise considerably. As this example reveals, a correlation between two factors is quite compatible with the one *preventing* the other. Even should it ultimately become clear that rapists and other sex offenders do use more pornography, we would have no grounds to believe that such use in any way causes their behavior unless all the other plausible explanations for the correlation could be ruled unlikely by the evidence.

A different kind of statistical approach looks at the rates of sex crime and of consumption of sexual materials for the population as a whole. One recent study of this type in the United States did find a correlation between rape and sales of big-selling "soft-core" magazines; it did so by comparing the rates of each in the different states.[11] Although many sources of error and nonuniformity exist in the reporting and gathering of crime statistics, the large size of the population involved makes the results look significant. On the other hand, as the authors of the study stress, there are various possible explanations for its outcome. For example, most of the "common causes" just considered could apply here. So might such things as a higher percentage of young men in certain states, which would tend to increase both the rate of rape and the consumption of sexual materials, independently. In fact, the researchers later tested a hypothesis of the general-social-disinhibition type, and it seemed to account for the correlation entirely.

The situation is extremely complex, however. Trying to measure causal influences across the whole country requires highly indirect indicators, and it is such a difficult task overall that it is unlikely to produce firm conclusions any time soon. Consider just two complications. A study of the numbers of "adult" bookstores and theaters across the country showed *no* correlation with the reported rates of violent sex crimes.[12] However, a correlation has been found between those rates and sales of the feminist magazine *Ms*, and further, there is an even stronger association between progress in women's rights and sales of sex magazines.[13] The latter fact runs directly counter to feminist claims about *how* pornography leads to rape. Indeed, the other correlation argues that sexual materials incite rape no more than this one argues they promote respect for women's rights. The fact that many states with high rates of lethal violence and Klan membership have the highest levels of religious fundamentalism should also give pause to some who wish to see evidence against pornography in these data.

One way of trying to decide among alternative explanations is to look for correlations through time rather than across space; some of the possible common causes noted here could be effectively ruled out in this manner. In fact, those opposed to pornography frequently claim such evidence, though usually in a very crude form. "There have been large increases in both the amount of pornography available and the number of sex crimes against women and children in recent years," the claim runs, "so the former must be the cause of the latter." This reasoning is so bad it is difficult to know how to respond. One could with equal justification—that is, none—pick out as the cause of increased sex crime any of the multitude of other social phenomena that have changed during the same period, from the cost of living to sales of pantyhose to the rise of feminism to the resurgence of evangelical and fundamentalist Christianity. Part of what is wrong with this thinking is that the data are terribly imprecise. Those who employ it usually have no idea how much the amount of pornography available or of sex crimes committed has changed. In fact, it is notoriously difficult to get reliable statistical data of this type at all. For example, U.S. government surveys that ask people whether they have been the victims of various crimes indicate a large decrease in the rate of rape since 1973, whereas the rate of rape reports recorded by police has increased greatly during that time.

It is instructive to contrast this argument with others that do supply some evidence. The Danish experience with legalizing pornography is particularly noteworthy in this regard.[14] Denmark's homogeneous population, together with the careful gathering of data by the social scientists involved, make one reasonably confident of the statistics. That the increase in availability of erotic materials was so large and so sudden, occurring under fairly stable social conditions, eliminates from consideration a lot of other variables that might conceivably have had a causal role. As is widely known, the rate of reported sex crimes of various types dropped greatly while that increase was taking place. By questioning people about their feelings, the researchers determined that the decline in reports of milder offenses (e.g., exhibitionism) could plausibly be accounted for by a general softening of attitudes regarding their seriousness, rather than by a change in the frequency of the offenses themselves. That is, the milder offenses were simply not reported to the police as often as they had been.

Yet they found no comparable change in feelings about "peeping" (still regarded as a frightening invasion of privacy) or adult-child sex, even though reports of both had declined drastically—by 80 percent and 69 percent respectively—thus indicating a genuine decrease in their occurrence. Lacking any other plausible explanation for such a result, the researchers found it reasonable to conclude that it was brought about by the sudden high availability of sexually explicit performances and materials. In fact, it is known that both of these offenses are often committed by socially inadequate individuals as substitutes for socially acceptable sex; so it is quite plausible that the new availability of erotic materials simply provided a legally safe substitute. Whatever the explanation, given that so much of today's concern over pornography stems from fear for children's safety and women's peace of mind, these statistics are highly significant.

The safety-valve hypothesis thus gained support in the case of certain sex crimes, but this was not so for rape. Through the period of vastly increasing amounts of pornography in Denmark, the rate at which this crime was reported remained at roughly the same level. From this it would appear that the psychology of rapists does not allow for substitution, on the aggregate, of coercive acts by use of sexual materials. But the claim we are considering here is that pornography causes sexual violence, and in that regard, this is a very important result. That under such conditions there should have been no increase in reports of these crimes (and again, seemingly no change in attitude as regards their seriousness) argues against that allegation. In fact, Denmark's continuing low rate of coercive sex crime, in spite of its liberal attitude toward pornography, is itself worth remarking here. To date, this study is the only really careful investigation of the availability of pornography and rape trends over time.[15]

One researcher has claimed that such trends in various countries show a positive correlation. As the Williams Report revealed, however, the researcher's data were incredibly weak and his manipulation of statistics dishonest. His more recent claims of the same type are no better.[16] In fact, data from various nations reveal no acceleration in the existing trend of occurrences of rape when big increases in the availability of pornography took place. This is the case, for example, for Germany and the United States. In the latter and in England, violent sex crime was increasing at the time, but it had been doing so before the proliferation of sexual materials occurred; there was no apparent change in the rate of increase. (See Berl Kutchinsky's article in *Comparative Social Research*, Vol. 8, 1985.) In England, according to the Williams Committee, there was a five-year period during which the availability and explicitness of sexual materials increased but reports of sexual assault decreased; then a crackdown on hard-core pornography that greatly reduced the supply was followed by an increase in such reports. During the first half of the 1980s (before the latest rash of local and federal crackdowns) the availability of pornography in the United States, in the form of home videotapes, expanded rapidly; but the rate of rape remained level or even decreased.

It must be stressed again, however, that we are facing a great deal of uncertainty in all this. There may always be unrecognized social forces at work in producing the net results the statistics reveal, masking the effects or lack of effects of any given factor. At the time of the big increase in sexual entertainment in Denmark, for instance, the more general "sexual revolution" was occurring; the United States was also then experiencing the social upheaval associated with the "baby boomers" coming of age, the Vietnam War, and the civil rights movement. To mention another problem, the rise in awareness of and concern about rape that has taken place in recent years may well have increased the percentage of rapes that are reported to and recorded by police; if so, a climb in the police statistics would not mean any actual increase had occurred after all. Since the latter rate in the United States is only up to half of that reported to the victimization surveys, this is a plausible reason for the discrepancy between the changes in the two rates.[17]

As a final point, changes in the rate of rape tend to occur in parallel with those in the occurrence of other violent crimes. This suggests that the social influences producing violent behavior in general, for example, those that make people more willing to use force to achieve their ends, are more to blame than anything else. Given the often erratic variation in crime rates from year to year, from a multitude of jurisdictions, it is bound to be possible to find at least short periods in at least some places where changes in the statistics for pornography sales and for various crimes either match each other or fail to, as one chooses. Nevertheless, the best evidence we currently have from crime trends over time, such as it is, weighs against the claim that pornography induces sexual violence to any discoverable degree.

EXPERIMENTAL EVIDENCE

The main weakness of statistical studies in society, their lack of control over possible causal variables, leads naturally to a consideration of experimental approaches. They cannot eliminate, but can greatly reduce, the influence of extraneous factors. The most common type of experiment, repeated in a large variety of ways by different researchers, involves getting the subjects to perform acts they believe are physically punishing another person (e.g., with supposed electric shocks). If those who have first been exposed to a certain stimulus—say, sexually explicit presentations— are on average likely to give more severe or less severe "punishments" than those who have not, it is concluded that something about the stimulus has been a factor in causing this result. What has the verdict been? The researchers have almost uniformly gotten the same result: subjects simply exposed to pornography beforehand are not inclined to administer harsher treatment than those not so exposed.

A variation on these tests was also devised in order to discover whether sexual explicitness would have any effect on persons who already have a predisposition to aggress. This has usually been done by having the target of the intended punishment anger the subject in some way beforehand. In the many experiments of this latter type, the results have been inconsistent. In some, those who had viewed erotic scenes have been more aggressive in giving punishment, on average; but in others, they have been distinctly less punitive than angered subjects who had not been exposed to sexual stimuli. Though there originally was some dispute over how to interpret such mixed results, the explanation is now agreed to be this: those who observed less sexually arousing scenes (still photos rather than movies, notably) were the ones who tended to exhibit reduced aggression. Indications are that it is the pleasurable feelings induced by mild pornography that result in reduced tendencies toward aggression. But what of the other results? May we conclude from them that erotic movies probably do tend to induce violent behavior in real life?

Some have been anxious to do so. (They have not been equally willing to embrace the result that nude pinups reduce violent tendencies, or the corollary that we should therefore spread lots of them around.) But for various reasons, we may not draw that conclusion. For one thing, there is the fact that the laboratory setting, with its authority-given permission to aggress, is highly artificial. It is not at all clear that the same results would occur in "real life." For another, there is the question of whether and to what extent the mild "pain" administered in these tests can be extrapolated to the serious harm done in a real physical attack. Beyond this, we must notice again that what sort of portrayal is found arousing is very elastic, being dependent on what one is commonly exposed to. As if to confirm this, it has been found that experimental subjects who are more sexually experienced, or who have already viewed large amounts of pornography in the past, are not induced to aggressiveness by highly erotic presentations in the lab—a fact that could argue for greater exposure to sexuality in general, if these results seem worrisome.

The most important response to these laboratory data, however, is the one that emerges from discovering the underlying reason for them. Various experiments have made it now seem very clear that the source of the greater aggessiveness induced by sexual presentations is nothing more than the excitement they produce. It is not a feeling of contempt for women, or a special moral nastiness, or anything of the sort; it is just a general state of heightened physiological activity.[18] Similar results of enhanced aggression have been obtained from such excitement-arousing things as exericse and comical films, even without angering the subject first. And the greater aggressiveness lasts only as long as the state of excitement persists: a few minutes.

These facts heavily underscore the question of extrapolation beyond the laboratory. Would anyone seriously suppose that, say, the recent explosion of interest in exercise has increased the level of violence in our society? In any case, the lab results provide no more reason to oppose pornography than they do to oppose jogging. Moreover, it has been discovered that aggression is not the only activity that can be enhanced by a state of excitement. Experiments in which the subject is supposed to reward another person have generally found that excitement, including sexual arousal, also leads to the giving of higher rewards.[19] It would seem that the effect of being excited is to mildly exaggerate *all* of a person's responses—hardly a novel idea. In sum, sexually produced emotional arousal by itself has not been found to be any more dangerous than that induced by countless other experiences in daily life. Yet another type of evidence concerning the effects of pornography has failed to provide any adequate reasons for considering it objectionable. . . .

Up to now, we have focused exclusively on the effects of sexual explicitness per se. Whether it might have importantly different effects when in combination with other special features is an independent issue. In particular, the issue of pornography that is violent is one that must be addressed.

NONSEXUAL AGGRESSION

The first matter to be explored is whether violent media presentations in general, with or without sex, have any appreciable and systematic tendency to elicit violent behavior. In this case—unlike that of sexual explicitness in itself—there are good grounds for believing it might. To be sure, they are far from conclusive, and the issue continues to be hotly debated among behavioral scientists. Nevertheless, it seems to many that such evidence as we presently have points more in that direction than in the other. We cannot begin to survey the data here, but we will look at a few salient points.

To start with—and again, this is quite unlike the case of sexual explicitness—there are some clear explanations of why portrayals of violence might evoke real violence, explanations that are already reasonably well established in other contexts. For example, there is modeling and imitation. These involve the tendency to do what others in one's environment do and to regard it as normal, acceptable behavior. This is a significant feature of human psychology, one that is extremely important in the case of children. In particular, then, observing violence, especially if it is perceived as natural and ordinary, can lead to acceptance of it. The *type* of aggression seen might be especially apt to be imitated: in the same circumstances, with the same sort of victim, and so on. A second such explanation is desensitization: even if certain behavior is initially considered repugnant, repeated exposure to it can make it come to seem less serious, lowering the barriers to doing it oneself. Of course, that is a good thing if the behavior is good (e.g., the media have in recent years used positive portrayals of minority races and of integration to desensitize racist feelings). To habituate the acceptance of violence is another matter, however. Other psychological mechanisms that might have a tendency to elicit aggression will emerge as we continue.

The evidence that violence is actually caused in these ways comes in several forms. To begin with anecdotal evidence, most of us have heard of such cases. After each highly successful violent movie, stories appear in the press about "copycat" crimes: *A Clockwork Orange, Deer Hunter, The Burning Bed,* and very many others have reportedly triggered such actions. There have been a whole rash of reports of Rambo imitators killing and terrorizing people in the past few years. As warned before, we must not just accept these accounts at face value. In some instances the connection seems clear, however, especially when the details of the act closely match those of the portrayal. Yet even there, the question remains whether the film affected only the form the aggression took, not its occurrence. Moreover, these cases often involve pathological mental states; hence it may be argued that if the movie had not triggered these individuals, something else would sooner or later have done so. Once again, just about anything can set off an unstable personality.

On the other hand, experiments in the laboratory and in real-life situations have given indications that ordinary persons are also influenced by portrayals of aggression. A huge number of such tests have observed depicted violence to elicit or facilitate minor aggressive actions.[20] This has been found even without producing anger or that trivializing excitement effect in the experimental subjects. One type of test has discovered that salient aspects of the original viewed violence have a special influence in this regard. For example, when the experimental "victim" has had the same name or been of the same sex (female) as the portrayed victim, higher levels of aggression have occurred in the laboratory.[21] Of course, the strong doubts raised earlier apply to these experiments as well, notably, whether the permission-bred minor aggression involved in most of them can be extrapolated beyond the laboratory to real life.

Evidence for societal statistics suggests it can, though it faces doubts of its own. In one remarkable study, for example, it was concluded that the homicide rate in the United States jumps appreciably for a few days after each widely broadcast major prizefight. More specifically, the additional victims tend to be of the same race (and sex—male) as the loser in the fight. It would seem from this that observing violence inflicted on someone can indeed trigger hostile acts, at least on the part of individuals already prone to violence. On the other hand, this result has been seriously challenged by other researchers.[22] As has been warned here repeatedly, getting firm knowledge about anything as complex as human behavior is often extremely difficult.

Something that may be much more serious than the immediate triggering of aggression is the subtle effect of long-term, large-scale exposure to presentations of violence on the population in general. It is certain that the level of aggression in a given society is largely determined by socialization; though violence is a human universal, some groups have far less of it than others. Given that fact, and given that the media are such a pervasive force in our own society, it is difficult to believe all the violence they portray does not have a significant impact. This suspicion has been reinforced by a number of long-term studies of children and adolescents. Correlations between exposure to media violence and real aggression by them have indeed been found: those who watch the most TV violence tend to be the most aggressive. Unfortunately, getting reliable data of this type is much more difficult, and the results of different investigators have been mutually inconsistent.[23] In particular, as usual, it is difficult to tell whether the viewing of aggression caused the real aggression or some common cause—notably, a previous liking for violence—produced both.

So the debate goes on. For whatever it is worth, the majority of investigators evidently believe that exposure to media aggression produces long-term and short-term tendencies toward the real thing.

SEXUALLY VIOLENT DEPICTIONS

If portrayals of violence in general are able to elicit violent behavior, one would expect that the same holds for depictions of sexual violence. In fact, the same sorts of anecdotes and experimental evidence are reported in this special case as in the general one.[24] In addition, two factors that might make portrayed violence particularly dangerous have come to light in connection with sexual explicitness. One of these is stimulus-response conditioning: if something a person finds highly desirable, such as sex, is associated unconsciously with something else, the latter will tend to be seen in the same positive light as the former. The use of honor by association to sell products, we should all be aware, has been very successful in modern advertising. In particular, then, associating the desirable thing with violence can result in the one triggering thoughts of the other, and could possibly even result in real violence. Some evidence for this sort of response, over and above the effects of disinhibition expected from exposure to violence per se, has been found in certain experiments in the form of higher aggression levels.[25] As usual, to what extent this laboratory reaction represents an increased danger in real life is not at all clear. Even so, one might suspect that a steady diet of such associations could make the connection seem very strong to susceptible persons; perhaps young people would be particularly vulnerable.

A related type of influence might be of even greater concern, that involved in the case where violence is represented as bringing about some good end. This not only associates it with something desirable but makes it appear that the violence—something which in itself is an evil—is justified by the end it achieves. The particular scenario that has been experimentally investigated in connection with sex is that of a rape in which the victim is shown as becoming sexually aroused and enjoying it. Since this type of scene is found sexually exciting by many of both sexes, it is sometimes found in pornography and romances. It is also symbolically played out in many a Hollywood and TV movie. A kiss is forced on the woman; at first she resists but then becomes aroused and passionately returns it. Once again, such portrayals are not meant to send any general message about what women or men really want. But the question here is, might that message not be received by some individuals? Or might the use of force be seen as less serious, if not completely justified, by the positive outcome?

There is some evidence, acquired from experiments on college students, for a small effect of this type.[26] After being exposed to the kind of scene just described, male subjects have been found to aggress more strongly against females in the laboratory. The effect is very short-lived, however, and it has been found to occur only immediately after exposure to violent sex films, not later on. Moreover, the seeming triviality of other laboratory results we have looked at that involve aggression counsels against putting much weight on these. The increased "aggression" is of the same kind as that occurring after exercise or watching comedy.

Nevertheless, another type of experimental result does warrant concern, one that has to do with attitudes. After viewing rape scenes with a "positive" ending, certain males are a little more apt to report a belief that women may enjoy being raped. They also show a somewhat reduced perception of the amount of trauma involved or similar attitude changes. Such results have been obtained repeatedly, in fact. Even these tests have yielded mixed results, however; some of them have been unable to replicate the others. In one of the latter, male subjects assigned *longer* prison terms to rapists after viewing rape scenes of the type in question. Furthermore, whether the seeming attitude changes go very deep, or would last very long, is still not at all clear. It seems unlikely that a few books or movies could have much effect on a person's thinking compared to all the other influences of a lifetime of socialization.

On the other hand, there are disturbed individuals who might expose themselves to large amounts of this type of thing, and there are persons whose tendencies already have them on the borderline of employing coercive behavior. We also know that a certain type of rapist has a difficult time distinguishing reality from fantasy in regard to sex.[27] He imagines either that the woman already wants to be forced or else that he will make her want him through his masterful manner or lovemaking skill. So complete is the self-deception in some cases that such rapists have not infrequently been caught as a result of arranging a future date with the woman: they find the police waiting instead. It would certainly be important to know whether any of these rapists have been appreciably influenced by movies or stories depicting rape (or by those forced-kiss scenes, for that matter). Anecdotal evidence of such an effect from pornography depicting "enjoyed" rape and sadomasochistic acts has recently been uncovered, in fact, in the form of statements reportedly made by sadistic rapists while in the act.[28] Given that individuals willing to use violence will grasp at any pretext they can find, whether the effect is real is uncertain, but this serious matter must continue to be studied.

So there is evidence of particular dangers posed by certain kinds of violent pornography. As usual, however, both the evidence and the effects seem to be mixed. For one thing, psychiatrists have told of cases of disturbed individuals using violent materials in order to ward off their desires for real sexual violence.[29] For another, laboratory studies indicate that repeated exposure to portrayals of sexual aggression make them less sexually arousing to the viewer, not more so. Nor are there any good correlational data from real life on this matter. In fact, at the time when large amounts of violent pornography became available in Germany, the United States, and other countries, there was no increase in the rate of reports of violent sex crimes.[30] Nevertheless, the bulk of the evidence involving violence in general and certain types of sexual violence in particular indicates that such depictions may carry a serious risk.

ARE SEXUALLY VIOLENT PORTRAYALS MORE DANGEROUS?

Should one conclude from the foregoing that portrayals of violent sex are especially dangerous—more so, that is, than violent presentations in general? . . . No such conclusion may be drawn. For once again, sex is only one of many factors that powerfully influence people's emotions. It is only one of many strongly desired things that can be associated with violence in the imagination, or that can be portrayed as ultimately justifying aggression. To name a few others that commonly are so portrayed, there is ambition for money or power, honor, loyalty, love, ideology—even the desire for justice and right. Moreover, it seems quite clear that the association of these things with violence has long been, and continues to be, instrumental in promoting coercive and violent actions in the world. Let us look at each of them briefly.

The last one on the list is often mentioned with concern by social scientists because the portrayal of aggression by "good guys" to achieve their ends is so common in the entertainment media. But nearly everyone sees himself or herself as a "good guy," sees her or his own ends as legitimate. Hence the effect of such portrayals could well be to elicit a lot of real (and not at all genuinely justified) physical and nonphysical aggression. That this is the case has again been suggested by the results of several laboratory experiments. As a closely related matter, the association of ideology with violence has a long history of producing violent behavior. Take religious ideology, for instance, and in particular the Bible: it carries many messages, not only of love and peace but also of hostility toward outsiders and unbelievers. Its commandments to kill witches and homosexuals and its endorsements of slavery have quite clearly been a factor in some gross evils of the past. Even today, we constantly hear stories about individuals and sects who murder, calling it God's vengeance on evil ones, and about parents who beat their children unmercifully, quoting a certain biblical passage as requiring the beating to save their children form the devil.[31] The human proclivity for blind allegiance to a grand system of beliefs makes it a very serious matter what such systems contain.

As for honor and self-esteem, we certainly know how often they are behind acts of violence. Moreover, the possibility of borderline personalities being triggered by media presentations of the violent defense of honor seems clear. To mention just one example, a man who was reportedly obsessed by the violent movie *First Blood* killed a policeman who stopped his car on the street. ("Persecuted little guy fights back against the corrupt system.") The matter of ambition seems too obvious to need comment. To end with the case of romantic love, let us merely note that it, not sexual desire, is the most plausible reason for the results of a much publicized experiment.[32] Questionnaires given to male students after they had viewed certain films indicated a slightly increased acceptance of violence against women. The two movies were not sexually explicit—hence would not generally be regarded as pornographic—but they did involve rape and/or brutality toward women. And the acts were portrayed in each case as winning the love of the woman involved.

So there are many kinds of portrayed violence that present dangers. Nor can it even be claimed that those involving sex are *more* apt to provoke anti-social acts.[33] That might or might not be true; we have no good evidence one way or the other, and such would be very difficult to get.

In fact, there is a little laboratory evidence that violence without sexual explicitness has a more negative effect on attitudes than sexually explicit violence does.[34] To be concrete, the latter may well be less likely to promote rape myths than children's movies and cartoons are to promote the belief in them that violence does not really hurt anyone. It is worth noting in this same regard that many rapists are sexually aroused by *non*sexual as well as sexual violence.[35] In general, in fact, there is every reason to suppose that some of the violence stimulated by nonsexual portrayals of aggression would itself be of a sexual nature. Add to all this the fact that people are exposed to vastly greater amounts of nonerotic violence, and it is very clear where the real problem lies.

Another possible defense of special concern over sexual violence is that the welfare of women is particularly at stake in that case, and that they are more vulnerable to assault. But, for reasons such as the proportion of aggression against each sex in the media in general, it is not at all clear that the dangers to them from violent portrayals are greater. Furthermore, some of the things typically associated with violence toward males are especially powerful motivators, things like glory, comradeship, and social approval. The best-documented anecdotal case to date for violence incited by a movie involves the many self-inflicted deaths of young men imitating the Russian roulette scenes in *Deer Hunter*.[36] Most powerful of all, perhaps, even more so than the desire for sex, is the basic need to be regarded as a man. Yet what media image is constantly associated with manhood? Being brave and tough, being able to face harm and danger "like a man." The feminists and traditionalists who complain only about portrayals of violence against women plainly do not care as much about the welfare of men. Yet even these sexists ought to realize their tactics may be counterproductive. After all, empathy toward others requires being able to acknowledge one's own pain; thus men conditioned to accept violence against themselves are also apt to see it as more acceptable against women. Furthermore, there is no guarantee that condoning violence against one class of human beings will not generalize, in the minds of the violent, to include the others as well.

It would be a serious mistake, however, to become so concerned about portrayed violence that we lose sight of the really important sources of social violence. The correlations found to exist between the latter and exposure to the former are always small at best, indicating that other causes of aggression are much more significant. Those other causes are already well known: unstable or disturbed family life, physical and emotional abuse by parents (modeling, again), chronic unemployment, drug and alcohol abuse, mental illness, and so on. It would be tragic if these were ignored in favor of efforts to clean up the media, especially since the latter's influence on behavior is still uncertain. . . .

NOTES

1. The Williams Report cites cases in which an alleged stimulus to violence, seeing a particular movie, has not really occurred.

2. Among other places, the Haigh story is told in an article by Earl Finbar Murphy in the *Wayne Law Review*, Vol. 10. For the Doss account, read Richard Deming's *Women: The New Criminals.*

3. From the paper by Thornberry and Silverman, in Vol. 9 of the *Technical Report, USCOP.*

4. William Marshall, in an unpublished report to the Federal Department of Justice (Canada), 1983. An expanded account was later published in the *Journal of Sex Research*, 252.

5. C. Eugene Walker, Vol. 8, *USCOP Technical Report.*

6. For instance, this is discussed in the Williams Report. Another example of many such claims is in Carter et al., *Report to NIMH* (1985), cited in the *AGCP Final Report*, p. 961. Money's remarks are from testimony at a U.S. government hearing, cited in Lynn, p. 34. Goldstein and Kant's work is reported in their *Pornography and Sexual Deviance.*

7. In Vol. 8 of the *Technical Report, USCOP.* The studies by Goldstein et al., Cook and Fosen, and Walker all found greater prior exposure to sexual materials in at least one major control group than among their sex offenders; the one by Johnson et al. was not suitable for a quantitative conclusion; and the one by Davis and Braucht found more such exposure among sex criminals.

8. Abel et al., "The Effects of Erotica on Paraphiliacs' Behavior." The paper was criticized in the Meese Report, but this writer has been unable to obtain a rebuttal from its authors.

9. See the summaries of the studies by William Marshall and Mary Koss in the *Final Report* of *AGCP*, pp. 950, 961. The recent study by Condron and Nutter again found no greater exposure to pornography among sex offenders and deviants than among other men.

10. From Eugene Kanin in *Psychological Reports*, 52:1.

11. Larry Baron and Murray Straus, in Malamuth and Donnerstein's *Pornography and Sexual Aggression.* Their later work is cited in the *AGCP's Final Report* and is reported in "Four Theories of Rape: A Macrosociological Analysis." Though measuring several related variables, they did not directly test the possibility that the proportion of all young men in the total population of each state was the reason for the rape-pornography correlation.

12. The adult bookstore result is from Joseph Scott's paper.

13. Baron and Straus, "Four Theories of Rape."

14. Reported by Richard Ben-Veniste, and by Berl Kutchinsky, in Vol. 8

of the *Technical Report, USCOP*. See also the latter's article in *Diseases of the Nervous System*, March 1976, Vol. 37.

15. There is so much misinformation on these studies among nonprofessionals, and so much shallow treatment of them even by some professionals, that the concerned reader is urged to consult Kutchinsky's own writings to get a clear picture of the data. For instance, it is often claimed that the rate of sex crimes dropped only because certain acts were decriminalized at the same time. This does *not* apply to the statistics presented here. For his own reply to Bachy's claim that his statistics were wrong, see Kutchinsky's 1985 article. See also the discussion in the Williams Report.

16. John Court, in the *International Journal of Criminology and Penology*, Vol. 5; also in Malamuth and Donnerstein. The following information concerns his three more recent claims in the latter. The Australian data conflict with others from the same country, as he himself notes, though I have been unable to get more information on either set. His remarks about New Zealand are vague, and the ones regarding the availability of sexual materials are entirely speculative. The only precise claim involves a large drop in the rate of reported rape following 1974. "It is possible," he writes, "that the decline arose due to the introduction of the Auckland Task Force, established to take a tough line with crime." It is indeed possible, but not for the reason Court insinuates. He clearly wants the reader to believe the task force cracked down on pornography; but from his own cited source, it is equally clear it did nothing of the sort. It was a kind of SWAT team to deal with nighttime violence on the streets: "The concept was one of highly-trained men using superior skills and mobility to quell—rapidly and firmly—any uprisings before they erupted into full-scale brawls" (Gideon Tait, *Never Back Down*, p. 174). As for the Hawaiian case, it is the figment of someone's imagination. There was a drop in the rate of rape in the two years in question, but a review of local newspaper articles for the same period reveals, there was no crackdown on pornography; in fact, there was a glut of it, as well as live sex acts on stage. (See, for example, the *Honolulu Star-Bulletin*, Nov. 6, 1975, p. E1.) It was in earlier and later years, when rape rates were higher, that there was some legal action against sexual materials.

17. Both sets of data can be found in the *Sourcebook of Criminal Justice Statistics—1986* (edited by Jamieson and Flanagan), pp. 180 and 243.

18. See Zillmann for an excellent discussion.

19. For example, consult Donnerstein et al. Their book is the best easily accessible source of information on all the experiments discussed in the preceding paragraphs.

20. For a survey of this data, see *Television and Behavior*, edited by David Pearl et al. for the National Institute of Mental Health, 1982.

21. See Donnerstein in Malamuth and Donnerstein.

22. See the article by Phillips and Hensley in the *Journal of Communication*, Summer 1984, and that by Baron and Reiss, together with Phillips and Bollen's reply, in the *American Sociological Review*, June 1985.

23. Compare the study by Milavsky et al. with the review by Huesman in Pearl et al.

24. A famous court case involving a bottle rape is described, among other places, in the Donnerstein et al. book.

25. Reported in many places; for example, Donnerstein's article in Malamuth and Donnerstein.

26. In the essay by Malamuth in Malamuth and Donnerstein. See also the account in Donnerstein et al.

27. For example, Gebhard et al.

28. Mimi Silbert and Ayala Pines in *Sex Roles*, 10:11/12.

29. The article by Robert Soller in Frank Beach's *Human Sexuality in Four Perspectives* contains an interesting case study.

30. From Kutchinsky in *Comparative Social Research*.

31. The passage about beating children is Proverbs 23:13–14. The statements on homosexual acts and witches are found in Leviticus 20:13 and Exodus 22:18. (During the Inquisition, hundreds of thousands of women were put to death as witches, convicted of things like having sex with devils.) Those about slavery include Deuteronomy 20:10ff. and Leviticus 25:44–46.

32. Described by Malamuth, though he ignores the possibility that the *love*-violence link in *Getaway* and *Swept Away* was to blame for the results. The latter, by the way, is a woman's fantasy of domination, produced by moviemaker Lina Wertmuller.

33. This was admitted by the Attorney General's Commission on Pornography; see p. 328 in their *Final Report*.

34. The evidence for greater ill effects from portrayed violence that is not sexually explicit is reported on p. 111 of Donnerstein et al.

35. For example, see Quinsey et al. in the *Journal of Consulting and Clinical Psychology*, Vol. 52, pp. 651–657.

36. Wayne Wilson and Randy Hunter in *Psychological Reports*, 53:1.

SOURCES

Abel, Gene, Mittelman, M. S., and Becker, Judith. 1985. "The Effects of Erotica on Paraphiliacs' Behavior." Unpublished paper cited in AGCP [Attorney General's Commission on Pornography] *Final Report*, pp. 969–970.

Baron, James N., and Reiss, Peter C. "Same Time, Next Year: Aggregate Analysis of the Mass Media and Violent Behavior," *American Sociological Review* 50 (1985): 347–363.

———. "Four Theories of Rape: A Macrosociological Analysis." *Social Problems* 34, No. 5 (1986): 467–489.

Ben-Veniste, Richard. "Pornography and Sex Crime—the Danish Experience." In Vol. 8, USCOP [U.S. Commission on Obscenity and Pornography] *Technical Report*, 1970.

Carter, D. L., et al. "Use of Pornography in the Criminal and Developmental Histories of Sexual Offenders." Report to the National Institute of Mental Health. Cited in AGCP *Final Report*, 1985, p. 961.

Check, James V. P. "The Effects of Violent and Non-Violent Pornography." Unpublished submission to the Department of Justice for Canada, 1985.

Condron, Mary Kearns, and Nutter, David E. "A Preliminary Examination of the Pornography Experience of Sex Offenders, Paraphiliacs, Sexual Dysfunction Patients, and Controls Based on Meese Commission Recommendations." *Journal of Sex and Marital Therapy*, 14, No. 4 (Winter 1988): 285–298.

Cook, Robert F., and Fosen, Robert H. "Pornography and the Sex Offender: Patterns of Exposure." USCOP *Technical Report*, Vol. 8, 1970.

Court, John. 1977. "Pornography and Sex-Crimes: A Re-evaluation in Light of Recent Trends Around the World." *International Journal of Criminology and Penology*, 5 (1977): 129–157.

Davis, Keith E., and Braucht, George N. "Exposure to Pornography, Character, and Sexual Deviance: A Retrospective Survey." In USCOP *Technical Report*, Vol. 8, 1970.

Deming, Richard. *Women: The New Criminals*. New York: Thomas Nelson, 1977.

Donnerstein, Edward, Linz, Daniel, and Penrod, Steven. *The Question of Pornography*. New York: The Free Press, 1987.

Gebhard, Paul, et al. *Sex Offenders: An Analysis of Types*. New York: Harper and Row, 1965.

Goldstein, Michael J., et al. "Exposure to Pornography and Sexual Behavior in Deviant and Normal Groups." USCOP *Technical Report*, Vol. 8, 1970.

Goldstein, Michael J., and Kant, Harold S. *Pornography and Sexual Deviance*. Berkeley: University of California Press, 1973.

Jamieson, Katherine M., and Flanagan, Timothy J. (eds.). *Sourcebook of Criminal Justice Statistics—1986*. U.S. Department of Justice, Bureau of Justice Statistics, Washington, D.C., 1987.

Johnson, Weldon T., Kupperstein, Lenore R., and Peters, Joseph J. "Sex Offenders' Experience with Erotica." USCOP *Technical Report*, Vol. 8, 1970.

Kanin, Eugene. 1983. "Rape as a Function of Relative Sexual Frustration." *Psychological Reports* 52, No. 1 (February 1983): 133–134.

Kutchinsky, Berl. "Towards an Explanation of the Decrease in Registered Sex Crimes in Copenhagen." In USCOP *Technical Review*, Vol. 8, 1970.

———. "Deviance and Criminality: The Case of a Voyeur in a Peeper's Paradise." *Diseases of the Nervous System*, 37 (March 1976): 145–151.

———. "Pornography and Its Effects in Denmark and the United States: A Rejoinder and Beyond." *Comparative Social Research: An Annual*. Vol. 8. Greenwich, Conn.: JAI Press, 1985.

Lynn, Barry. *Polluting the Censorship Debate*. Washington, D.C.: American Civil Liberties Union, 1986.

Malamuth, Neil, and Ceniti, Joseph. "Repeated Exposure to Violent and Non-Violent Pornography." *Aggressive Behavior* 12 (1986): 129–37.

Malamuth, Neil, and Donnerstein, Edward (eds.). *Pornography and Sexual Aggression.* New York: Academic Press, 1984.

Marshall, William. "The Use of Pornography by Rapists and Child Molesters." Unpublished report to the Department of Justice for Canada, 1984.

———. 1985. "Use of Pornography by Sexual Offenders." Unpublished paper cited in AGCP *Final Report,* p. 961. Revised version, "The Use of Sexually Explicit Stimuli by Rapists, Child Molesters and Non-Offenders," published in *Journal of Sex Research* 25, No. 2 (May 1988).

Milavsky, J. R., et al. *Television and Aggression: The Results of a Panel Study.* In Pearl et al., 1982.

Murphy, Earl Finbar. "The Value of Pornography." *Wayne Law Review* 10 (1963–64): 655–680.

Pearl, David, Bouthilet, L., and Lazar, J. (eds.). *Television and Behavior: Ten Years of Scientific Progress and Implications for the 80's.* Rockville, Maryland: National Institute of Mental Health, 1982.

Phillips, David P., and Bollen, Kenneth A. "Same Time, Last Year: Selective Data Dredging for Negative Findings." *American Sociological Review* 50 (1985); 369–371.

Phillips, David P., and Hensley, John E. "When Violence Is Rewarded or Punished: The Impact of Mass Media Stories on Homicide." *Journal of Communication* 34, No. 3 (Summer 1984): 101–116.

Quinsey, V. L., Chaplin, T. C., and Upfold, D. "Sexual Arousal to Nonsexual Violence and Sadomasochistic Themes among Rapists and Non-Sexual Offenders." *Journal of Consulting and Clinical Psychology* 52 (1984): 651–657.

Scott, Joseph E. "Violence and Erotic Material—The Relationship between Adult Entertainment and Rape?" Paper presented to the annual meeting of the American Association for the Advancement of Science, May, 1985, Los Angeles.

Silbert, Mimi, and Pines, Ayala. "Pornography and Sexual Abuse of Women." *Sex Roles* 10, Nos. 11/12 (1984): 857–868.

Stoller, Robert J. *Perversion: The Erotic Form of Hatred.* Pantheon Books: New York, 1975.

Tait, Gideon (with John Berry). *Never Back Down.* Christchurch, N.Z.: Whitecoulls, 1978.

Thornberry, Terrence P., and Silverman, Robert A. "Exposure to Pornography and Juvenile Delinquency." In USCOP *Technical Report,* Vol. 9, 1970.

Walker, C. Eugene. "Erotic Sitmuli and the Aggressive Sexual Offender." USCOP *Technical Report,* Vol. 8, 1970.

Williams, Bernard, et al. *Obscenity and Film Censorship.* Cambridge: Cambridge University Press, 1979.

Wilson, Wayne, and Hunter, Randy. "Movie-Inspired Violence." *Psychological Report* 53, No. 1 (1983): 435–441.

Zillmann, Dolf. *Connections between Sex and Aggression.* Hillsdale, N.J.: Lawrence Erlbaum, 1984.

Selected Bibliography

Attorney General's Commission on Pornography: Final Report, 1986. U.S. Department of Justice, Washington, D.C.

Brownmiller, Susan. *Against Our Will: Men, Women and Rape.* New York: Simon and Schuster, 1975.

Christensen, F. M. *Pornography: The Other Side.* New York: Praeger, 1990.

Donnerstein, Edward, Daniel Linz, and Steven Penrod. *The Question of Pornography: Research Findings and Policy Implications.* New York: The Free Press, 1987.

Dworkin, Andrea. *Intercourse.* New York: The Free Press, 1987.

———. *Pornography: Men Possessing Women.* New York: Perigee, 1981.

Gubar, Susan, and Joan Hoff. *For Adult Users Only: The Dilemma of Violent Pornography.* Bloomington and Indianapolis: Indiana University Press, 1989.

Lederer, Laura, ed. *Take Back the Night: Women on Pornography.* William Morrow and Company, Inc., 1980.

Lynn, Barry. *Polluting the Censorship Debate.* Washington, D.C.: The American Civil Liberties Union, 1986.

Malamuth, Neil, and Edward Donnerstein, eds. *Pornography and Sexual Aggression.* New York: Academic Press, 1984.

Soble, Alan. *Pornography: Marxism, Feminism and the Future of Sexuality.* New Haven: Yale University Press, 1986.

U.S. Commission on Obscenity and Pornography: The Report, 1970. U.S. Government Printing Office, Washington, D.C.

Zillmann, Dolf. *Connections between Sex and Aggression.* Hillsdale, N.J.: Lawrence Erlbaum Associates, Publishers, 1984.

Zillmann, Dolf, and Jennings Bryant. *Pornography: Research Advances and Policy Considerations.* Hillsdale, N.J.: Lawrence Erlbaum Associates, Publishers, 1989.

Contributors

ROBERT H. BORK, John H. Olin Scholar in Legal Studies, American Enterprise Institute.

HARRY BROD, Assistant Professor of Philosophy, University of Delaware.

WILLIAM F. BUCKLEY JR., author, syndicated columnist, and host of the weekly television show *Firing Line.*

ROBERT CANNON, attorney, Wireless Telecommunications Bureau of the Federal Communications Commission.

F. M. CHRISTENSEN, Professor of Philosophy, University of Alberta.

MICHAEL CROMARTIE, Senior Fellow, the Ethics and Public Policy Center, Washington, D.C.

BARBARA DORITY, Executive Director of the Washington Coalition Against Censorship.

ANDREA DWORKIN, feminist writer and author of *Pornography: Men Possessing Women.*

RONALD DWORKIN, Professor of Jurisprudence at Oxford University and Professor of Law at New York University.

JAMES EXON, senior senator from Nebraska and cosponsor of the Communications Decency Act.

THEODORE A. GRACYK, Professor of Philosophy, Moorhead State University.

JUDITH M. HILL, Professor of Philosophy, Saginaw Valley State College.

PETER C. JOHNSON, associate, Debevoise & Plimpton, New York, N.Y.

TIM LaHAYE, minister, author, and president of Family Life Seminars.

PATRICK LEAHY, senior senator from Vermont.

WILLIAM A. LINSLEY, retired from the School of Communications, University of Houston.

HELEN LONGINO, Professor of Women's Studies, University of Minnesota.

RITA C. MANNING, Professor of Philosophy, San Jose State University.

THOMAS PARKER, Director of Psychology, The Family Workshop, Austin, Texas.

JEFFREY ROSEN, senior editorial staff, *The New Republic.*

ALAN SOBLE, Professor of Philosophy, University of New Orleans.

GLORIA STEINEM, founding editor of *Ms.* magazine.

MARY JO WEAVER, Professor of Religious Studies, Indiana University.

GEORGE F. WILL, author, syndicated columnist, *Newsweek* columnist.